STUDIEN
ZUR ENGLISCHEN PHILOLOGIE
NEUE FOLGE

Herausgegeben von
Lothar Fietz, Gerhard Müller-Schwefe und Friedrich Schubel
in Verbindung mit Jörg Fichte

Band 28

MARTIN CAMARGO

The Middle English
Verse Love Epistle

MAX NIEMEYER VERLAG TÜBINGEN
1991

Gedruckt mit Unterstützung der Alexander von Humboldt-Stiftung

CIP-Titelaufnahme der Deutschen Bibliothek

Camargo, Martin:
The middle English verse love epistle / Martin Camargo. - Tübingen : Niemeyer, 1991
(Studien zur englischen Philologie ; N.F., Bd. 28)
NE: GT

ISBN 3-484-45028-2   ISSN 0081-7244

Contents

Preface

This book began as the second part of my doctoral dissertation, which I completed in 1978. After an interval of nearly ten years, during which I pursued other research projects, I have written what amounts to a new book on the same subject, albeit one that incorporates portions of the earlier study. Most of the new material was written at the University of Tübingen, during the 1987–1988 academic year.

Financial support for the project came in the form of a Dissertation Fellowship from the University of Illinois, a generous Research Fellowship and a subvention to cover part of the publishing costs from the Alexander von Humboldt-Stiftung, and partial salary and additional travel funds from the Provost and the Research Council of the University of Missouri. To these organizations; to Mrs. Birgitta Zeller, my editor at the Max Niemeyer Verlag; and to the staffs of the many research libraries that I visited in England, Germany, and the United States, I extend my heartfelt thanks.

My initial work on the verse love epistle benefitted from the guidance of my teachers at the University of Illinois, in particular Professors Jackson J. Campbell, John Block Friedman, and James W. Marchand. During the second phase of my research, Professor Jörg O. Fichte was not only a warm and solicitous host but also a constructive critic. Professor Mary-Jo Arn and Dr. Julia Boffey read a late draft of the entire manuscript, and Professor James I. Wimsatt read the same draft of the first three chapters. I am grateful to all three of them for bringing additional bibliography to my attention, for correcting several errors of detail, and for saving me from more than one stylistic infelicity. Mrs. Rosemarie Fischer helped in many small ways but especially in translating the *Zusammenfassung*.

Most of all I wish to thank my wife, Sandy, who gave so generously of her time as editor, typist, and computer consultant, and whose good sense and constant affection kept me going. This book is dedicated to her.

Tübingen, June 1990   Martin Camargo

Abbreviations

BL	British Library
CA	*Confessio Amantis* (Gower)
CB	*Cinkante Balades* (Gower)
CUL	Cambridge University Library
EETS	Early English Text Society
e.s.	extra series
Fil.	*Il Filostrato* (Boccaccio)
Her.	*Heroides* (Ovid)
Index	*The Index of Middle English Verse* (Brown and Robbins)
KA	*Kyng Alisaunder*
LGW	*The Legend of Good Women* (Chaucer)
n.s.	new series
o.s.	original series
PMLA	*Publications of the Modern Language Association*
RTC	*Roman de toute chevalerie*
SATF	Société des anciens textes français
SL	*Secular Lyrics of the Fourteenth and Fifteenth Centuries* (Robbins)
Supplement	*Supplement* to *Index* (Robbins and Cutler)
T&C	*Troilus and Criseyde* (Chaucer)
TCC	Trinity College Cambridge

CHAPTER 1:
Medieval Letters and the Verse Love Epistle

Medieval lovers, no less than ancient or modern ones, often found it necessary to send each other messages. Those fortunate enough to be literate composed their own or copied them from suitable models; those who were not either had someone else compose one for them or found some other way to communicate their feelings or desires – for example, through a go-between. Given the personal and ephemeral nature of such messages – even the written ones would generally have been inscribed on wax tablets, the normal medium for private letters, rather than on parchment – it is no wonder that very few have survived. Moreover, with rare exceptions, the few "genuine" medieval love letters that have survived were preserved precisely because they were not ordinary and often only after undergoing editorial revision. To cite only the most famous example, the correspondence of Abelard and Heloise is a carefully constructed treatise on monastic life, in which the "love letters" at the beginning, dramatizing both the allure and the danger of the secular world, underscore the reasons for disciplined renunciation of that world. Heloise doubtless still felt passion for Abelard after their long separation, but, in the form in which they have come down to us, the expression of desire is no longer the primary function of her words. It is also difficult to judge the authenticity of medieval love letters because the education of medieval clerks predisposed them toward particular methods for treating particular themes: conventionality and even the absence of circumstantial detail in a letter do not of themselves rule out the possibility that it is genuine. Nor should this seem strange even today. Real lovers presumably continue to use those collections of model letters, with blanks left for the names, still found in most bookstores and greeting-card shops, though perhaps less often now in the age of the telephone.

The difficulty in distinguishing between "genuine" and "artificial" medieval love letters is thus due in part to the scarcity of indisputably genuine examples, thanks to the vagaries of survival of texts that were never intended for publication, but just as much to the fluid boundary between what we would call "literary" and "non-literary" texts in the

Middle Ages. Insofar as they were written and hence fell within the province of clerks, medieval letters were always being drawn toward the "literary." Since love was one of the great themes of medieval secular literature, this attraction was especially strong in the case of love letters. The phenomenon is seen at its clearest in the collections of model letters compiled by the teachers of the *ars dictaminis,* the medieval art of letter writing. When love letters began to appear in these collections, they clearly embodied stereotypical attitudes, situations, and language familiar from the poetry of the age. Because students of *dictamen,* especially in central France, also studied the *auctores*, the ironic, sensualist view of Ovid and the Goliards predominates, although the idealistic, courtly sensibility is occasionally represented.[1] Such letters consistently occur at the end of the collection, probably indicating some awareness of their marginality in so fundamentally pragmatic a context. But they are present nonetheless, and in some cases in surprisingly large numbers.[2] From as early as the eleventh century, scattered instances of Latin love epistles in verse exchanged by educated men and women, especially between clerics and their female pupils, are preserved. In many cases these must have been no more than elegant compliments or pleasant opportunities to practice classical versifying, but it is not always easy to rule out a genuinely erotic relationship behind such letters.[3] In such cases, what could easily be mistaken for purely literary texts may have had as practical a purpose as "hende" Nicholas's famous gesture in Chaucer's "The Miller's Tale" (3276).

One of the chief lessons of contemporary genre theory, particularly the variety of "Reception Theory" developed in Germany and associated in medieval studies with Hans Robert Jauss, is that one must consider both social function and form in studying an historical genre. But it is important to recognize that a given form may have a range of functions, just as a given function may be fulfilled by a variety of forms.[4] A verse love epistle may entertain, instruct, or persuade a reluctant lady, while a lover may declare his affection by means of a letter (in verse or prose), a speech

---

[1] See Ernstpeter Ruhe, *De Amasio*, especially pp. 78–81.

[2] The collections associated with Bernard de Meung are especially rich in examples. Boncompagno da Signa is the only *dictator* to devote an entire work to love letters, the *Rota Veneris*. See E. Ruhe, *De Amasio*, pp. 75–81, 127–50.

[3] On this question, see especially Dieter Schaller, "Überlieferung und Verfasserschaft," pp. 25–36, and his review of E. Ruhe's *De Amasio,* in *Arcadia*. A good case in point is the group of letters edited and analyzed by Ewald Könsgen, in *Epistolae duorum amantium*.

[4] See K. W. Hempfer, *Gattungstheorie*, pp. 113, 188–89.

2

by a go-between, or a gift (including a non-epistolary love poem). Because the medieval letter was both a form, whose shape was fixed by centuries of practice and made explicit in the treatises of the *dictatores,* and a function, the communication in writing between persons who are physically separated, it offers special challenges and opportunities to the student of genre. Though the term "letter" is applied by a broad range of authors to a large number of love poems composed during the restricted period of time (about 150 years) covered by the present study, the body of texts so designated is far more heterogeneous than the rather precise label "verse love epistle" would lead one to expect.

Thanks to the careful record-keeping of the Paston family and the kindness of fate, a pair of letters has been preserved, which, through their differences, have much to reveal about the way the verse love epistle existed as a genre in late medieval England. The situation is identical in both letters: Margery Brews writes to her betrothed, John Paston III, at a point when the financial negotiations regarding their marriage seem hopelessly deadlocked. In the first letter, Margery visualizes herself, no doubt in all sincerity, as the conventional courtly lover.[5]

Vn-to my ryght welbelouyd Voluntyn John Paston, squyer, be þis bill delyuered, &c.

Ryght reuerent and wurschypfull and my ryght welebeloued Voluntyne, I recommande me vn-to yowe full hertely, desyring to here of yowr welefare, whech I beseche Almyghty God long for to preserve vn-to hys plesure and ȝowr hertys desyre. And yf it please ȝowe to here of my welefare, I am not in good heele of body ner of herte, nor schall be tyll I here from yowe:

> For þer wottys no creature what peyn þat I endure,
> And for to be deede I dare it not dyscure.

And my lady my moder hath labored þe mater to my fadure full delygently, but sche can no more gete þen ȝe knowe of, for þe whech God knowyth I am full sory.

But yf that ȝe loffe me, as I tryste verely that ȝe do, ȝe will not leffe me þerfor; for if þat ȝe hade not halfe þe lyvelode þat ȝe hafe, for to do þe grettyst labure þat any woman on lyve myght, I wold not forsake ȝowe.

> And yf ȝe commande me to kepe me true where-euer I go
> Iwyse I will do all my myght ȝowe to love and neuer no mo.
> And yf my freendys say þat I do amys, þei schal not me let so for to do,
> Myn herte me byddys euer more to love ȝowe
> Truly ouer all errthely thing.
> And yf þei be neuer so wroth, I tryst it schall be bettur in tyme commyng.

---

[5] Ed. Norman Davis, *Paston Letters,* pt. 1, pp. 662–63.

No more to yowe at this tyme, but the Holy Trinité hafe ȝowe in kepyng.
And I besech ȝowe þat this bill be not seyn of non errthely creature safe only
ȝour-selfe, &c. And thys lettur was jndyte at Topcroft wyth full heuy herte,
&c.

Be ȝour own M. B.

The few circumstantial references, which evoke the pathos of her real-life
situation, only partially conceal the thorough conventionality of the
language and sentiments. Her father does in fact prevent her from choosing a mate and so from celebrating the rites of Saint Valentine's Day in the
natural way; but her response to the situation (complaint; protestation of
steadfast devotion) does not differ essentially from that of the noble
suitors for the formel eagle in Chaucer's *Parliament of Foules*. That this
was a conditioned response, one modeled on an essentially artistic and
ideal conception of love,[6] is shown not only by Margery's later, soberly
pragmatic behavior as wife and mother but also by the letter that she sent
John Paston shortly after the first Saint Valentine's Day greeting.[7]

> To my ryght welebelouyd cosyn John Paston, swyere, be this lettur
> delyueryd, &c.

Ryght wurschypffull and welebelouyd Volentyne, in my moste vmble wyse
I recommande me vn-to youw, &c. And hertely I thanke yowe for þe letture
whech that ȝe send [me] be John Bekurton, wherby I vndyrstonde and
knowe þat ȝe be purposyd to com to Topcroft in schorte tyme, and wyth-
owte any erand or mater but only to hafe a conclusyon of þe mater betwyx
my fadur and ȝowe. I wolde be most glad of any creature on lyve so þat the
mater myght growe to effect. And ther as ȝe say, and ȝe com and fynde þe
mater no more toward þen ȝe dyd afortyme ȝe wold no more put my fadur
and my lady my moder to no cost ner besenesse for þat cause a good wyle
afture, weche causyth myn herte to be full hevy; and yf þat ȝe com and the
mater take to non effect, þen schuld I be meche more sory and full of
heuynesse.

And as for my-selfe, I hafe don and vndyrstond in the mater þat I can or
may, as Good knowyth. And I lete yowe pleynly vndyrstond þat my fader
wyll no more money parte wyth-all in that behalfe but an c li. [and I marke],
whech is ryght far fro the acomplyshment of ȝowr desyre. Wherfor, yf þat ȝe
cowde be congtent wyth þat good and my por persone, I wold be þe meryest
mayden on grounde. And yf ȝe thynke not ȝowr-selfe so satysfyed, or þat ȝe
myght hafe mech more good, as I hafe vndyrstonde be ȝowe [afor], good,
trewe, and lovyng Volentyne, þat ȝe take no such labure vppon ȝowe as to
com more for þat mater; but let it passe, and neuer more to be spokyn of, as
I may be ȝowr trewe louer and bedewoman duryng my lyfe.

---

[6] A seminal treatment of this notion is Johan Huizinga, *Waning*, chapters 8 and 9.
[7] Ed. N. Davis, *Paston Letters*, pt. 1, p. 663.

4

No more vn-to yowe at thys time, but Almyghty Iesus preserve ȝowe bothe body and sowle, &c.

Be ȝour Voluntyne Mergery Brews

Here the proportion between circumstantial detail and "courtly" sentiment is reversed in comparison with the previous letter. It is not that Margery's feelings have changed with the passage of a few days: she still calls John her "Valentine," and the letter is sprinkled with affectionate phrases. The second letter simply belongs to a different genre.

Besides the sentiments expressed, an obvious sign of the generic contrast is the fact that a considerable part of the first letter is in verse. Now it is certainly not unusual to quote love poetry in a Saint Valentine's Day letter, but Margery's citations are especially interesting. Close analogues to both passages are found in poems that have been preserved in MS Rawlinson C.813, a collection assembled between 1527 and 1535 but containing many fifteenth-century poems.[8] What is interesting is that both poems containing analogues to Margery's excerpts are clearly identified as letters. This fact, together with formal features to be discussed later, suggest that Margery's Saint Valentine's Day letter is an important testimony to the widespread consciousness of the letter as a special form

---

[8] Ed. Frederick M. Padelford and Allen R. Benham, "Songs in Rawlinson C.813," pp. 312–97. Compare Margery's couplet with poem #14 (*Supplement* 2532.5), lines 11–12:

> But yn my mynde yet durst no-thyng discure
> how for your sake I dyd suche woo endure.

or with poem #48 (*Supplement* 3917.8), lines 254 and 257:

> my mynde durst I no-thyng discure;
> ...
> how þat for your sake I doo much woo endure

(In quoting Padelford and Benham's edition, I incorporate the corrections of Wilhelm Bolle, "Zur Lyrik," pp. 301, 307.) Lines 239–43 of the latter poem, a love epistle from a man to a woman (#48), also bear some resemblance to the second verse passage in Margery's letter:

> Yet better itt were your frendes were wrothe
> then ageynst your mynde ye shulde obbey,
> for then hereafter ye wylbe sorrye & lothe
> that euer they bare the lokke & þe kaye
> of your mynde ...

The relationship between the Rawlinson poems and Margery's letter is complicated by the fact that the lines from poem #14 and the second passage from poem #48 are borrowed from Stephen Hawes's *The Pastime of Pleasure* (lines 2251–52, 2213–17), first printed in 1509. On the reading habits of the Paston women, see N. Davis, "Style and Stereotype," p. 12.

of the love lyric and even of its special connection with occasions such as Saint Valentine's Day. The popularity of the verse love epistle probably did not reach its peak until around 1500; thus, in 1477, when Margery wrote, it was still on the rise. Scores of love poems from the fifteenth and early sixteenth centuries are called "lettre" or "bill" by their authors or by the scribes who copied them down. By the second half of the fifteenth century the form has even been parodied, a sure sign that the genre's "horizon of expectation" was capable of objectification.

When and why did the verse love epistle's vogue begin? Was it a case of "canonizing the junior branch," to use the Russian Formalists' phrase, of turning a pragmatic prose form into a "literary" verse form? Or did it grow out of preexisting verse forms, perhaps replacing an outmoded genre? What were the stages in its development, its major varieties, its functions? Who wrote verse love epistles, and who read them? Why did the genre die out abruptly only a generation after it achieved its greatest popularity? These questions will be addressed in detail in chapters 2–5. The remainder of this chapter will be concerned with how a fifteenth-century reader would have recognized a verse love epistle and distinguished it from other types of love poems, especially when the poet or scribe neglected to put a label on it. Were there obligatory features? What were the permissible variations? What, to use Jauss's phrase, was the audience's "horizon of expectation"?[9] Did the genre exist finally as a function rather than as a form?

The task of defining an historical genre such as the Middle English verse love epistle entails several complementary operations.[10] In the first place, as has already been stressed, it is essential to consider both the morphology of the genre (form) and its position within a social as well as a literary context (function). Historical genres, as distinct from the "Naturformen der Literatur" (epic, drama, lyric) and other "literary universals," exist as a continuity of form and function embodied in a group of related texts composed within a specific time period. On both the morphological and the functional levels, a problem arises the moment one sets out to write the history of a genre: one has no choice but to identify the formal and functional characteristics of an historical genre inductively from the corpus of texts that comprise the genre; but how is

---

[9] H. R. Jauss, "Theory of Genres," pp. 79, 88, 94.

[10] The best single survey of the theory and methodology of genre study is K. W. Hempfer, *Gattungstheorie*. Alastair Fowler, *Kinds of Literature*, is also excellent, but covers only the Anglo-American tradition. Also helpful on the historical approach to genre study is Uri Margolin, "Concept of Genre."

one to assemble that corpus without knowing in advance the constitutive forms and functions of the genre?[11] In practice, this "hermeneutic circle" is escaped through the use of both deductive and inductive procedures, the one correcting and supplementing the other. If the resulting "definition" is never airtight, this has more to do with the nature of literary genres than with the inadequacies of the method. Genres behave more like "historical families" than like categories of formal logic, and to draw their boundaries with absolute precision is usually to misrepresent the reality of their historical existence.[12]

Though all literary genres, even such formally distinct ones as the sonnet, turn out to have fuzzy boundaries, medieval genres present special problems of definition. To some extent, of course, their obscurity is due to the passage of time and the resulting loss of texts and of information about how surviving texts might have been received. More significant, however, is the scarcity of reflections on genre in the Middle Ages: we know far more about the genres of classical literature, even though far more of those texts have been lost. Nothing like Aristotle's *Poetics* or Horace's *Ars poetica* was produced during the Middle Ages. Medieval reflections on the poet's craft, with few exceptions, occur in the context of grammar studies and are chiefly concerned with finding subject matter for the poem (*inventio*), usually in the form of a preexisting text, and shaping that *materia* into something new by changing the order of its parts and by adding or removing embellishment (*dispositio, elocutio*). The medieval arts of poetry focus on details – how to begin a poem, how to expand or abbreviate a borrowed passage, how to vary an expression – rather than on the principles that give coherence to the entire work and that distinguish one type of work from another. This "tendency toward the small unit," as Franz Quadlbauer calls it, even characterizes the *accessus ad auctores* and the commentaries, where we usually search in vain for systematic statements regarding genre.[13] When the organizing principle of an entire work is offered, it is either a verse form, as in the *formes fixes* of the *arts de seconde rhétorique,* or a very broad plot dis-

---

[11] See Günther Müller, "Gattungspoetik," pp. 129–47, and Karl Viëtor, "Geschichte literarischer Gattungen," pp. 292–309, 365–67.

[12] H. R. Jauss, "Theory of Genres," pp. 79–81. Also see A. Fowler, *Kinds of Literature,* p. 41.

[13] For some exceptions to this general rule of silence, see Rossella D'Alfonso, "Sistema dei generi letterari," pp. 269–93; A. J. Minnis, *Theory of Authorship,* pp. 124–27, 134–36; and A. J. Minnis, A. B. Scott, and David Wallace, *Medieval Literary Theory,* pp. 217–20, 235–36 (and Index, s.v. *modi*). On the "Tendenz zur kleinen Einheit," see Franz Quadlbauer, Genera dicendi *im Mittelalter,* pp. 71–73.

tinction, such as that between comedy (begins badly but ends well) and tragedy (begins well but ends badly).[14]

Moreover, with many, if not most, medieval genres, social function rather than form seems to have been the key determiner of what we would regard as genre.[15] In this regard, the verse love epistle is typical. Though one encounters many texts in which the term "lettre" and its synonyms seem to function generically, it is difficult, if not impossible, to specify a set of formal features that will account for all of them without broadening the definition of verse love epistle to the point where it is coterminous with love poem. But this morphological inconsistency becomes more understandable and less significant once sufficient attention is paid to the reception of the verse love epistles, what the biblical Form Critics would call their "position in life" ("Sitz im Leben"). While the social function of a medieval text is generally far more difficult to identify than its themes, sources, structure, and stylistic techniques, without knowing it one will fail to recognize generic determiners that do not reside in the more directly observable elements of a text but were nonetheless demonstrably important for the medieval poet and his audience.

The verse love epistle differs from most medieval lyric genres in that its generic label automatically associates it with a variety of text that has both a well-defined "Sitz im Leben" and an extensive body of formal commentary. If our goal is to map the area of overlap between medieval letters, on the one hand, and Middle English love poetry, on the other, we begin with the advantage that half of the terrain is already clearly marked.[16] The theoretical treatises and the collections of model letters prepared by teachers of the *ars dictaminis* from the twelfth through the fifteenth centuries provide an abundant source of background information that is especially valuable because it is so explicit regarding the structure and the language of letters. Though the *ars dictaminis* was an attempt to fix existing epistolary conventions, many of them already observable in Carolingian times,[17] by aligning them with the authorita-

---

[14] On the implications of this lack of genre consciousness for the study of the Middle English lyrics, see J. A. Burrow, *Medieval Writers*, p. 61; Heinz Bergner, "Frage der Gattungen," pp. 54–55; and Julia Boffey, *Manuscripts of Lyrics*. Cf. also E. Ruhe, *De Amasio*, pp. 8–9, and A. Fowler, *Kinds of Literature*, pp. 98–99, 142–47.

[15] See especially Matthias Waltz, "Problem der Gattungsgeschichte," pp. 22–39.

[16] On medieval letters in general, see especially Giles Constable, *Letters and Letter-Collections*; on *ars dictaminis*, see James J. Murphy, *Rhetoric in the Middle Ages*, pp. 194–268, and the additional bibliography in J. J. Murphy, *Select Bibliography*, pp. 76–103.

[17] See especially William D. Patt, "Early *Ars dictaminis*," pp. 133–55.

tive model of Ciceronian rhetoric, medieval practice did not always conform strictly to its precepts. The increasingly formalized and standardized tenets of the *ars dictaminis* are adhered to most closely in the official and public letters and documents written by the notaries, secretaries, and clerks trained in the subject, while deviation from those tenets was particularly likely in truly "private" letters, most of which, however, have been lost to posterity.[18] By the same token, most medieval lovers did not behave in reality like Guillaume de Lorris's paradigmatic dreamer. But as the "official models" for how to write a letter and how to conduct a love affair, respectively, the precepts of the *ars dictaminis,* like those of the *Roman de la Rose,* had a determining influence at the level of literary culture, which is what concerns us here.

Much of the *dictator*'s lore – for example, the techniques for varying and embellishing the text – was the common property of all medieval writers and teachers of writing. Other elements, such as the system of rhythmical clause endings called the *cursus,* were too specific to Latin composition to influence significantly the non-Romance vernaculars. The distinctive features of the *dictatores'* teaching correspond most closely to the practices of vernacular letter writers in imposing an inorganic, articulated structure on letters and in employing a limited number of epistolary formulas, especially those of greeting and farewell. Adapted from the six-part Ciceronian oration, the structural scheme developed by the *dictatores* comprised five parts: the formal greeting (*salutatio*); the securing of good will (*captatio benevolentiae; also exordium, proverbium*); the statement of facts (*narratio*); the request for action (*petitio*); and the formal leave-taking (*conclusio*).[19] The treatises typically spend far more time analyzing and illustrating the first two parts than the last three. This is in part because the opening of the letter was so formulaic, and the proper formulas could best be taught by long lists that the would-be letter writer could memorize or save for future reference. The equally formulaic *conclusio* presented fewer options and so received less attention. However, the fact that so many sample *salutationes* and *exordia* were collected, carefully classified, and often analyzed, accurately reflects the relative importance of these parts and discloses an important fact about the social context of medieval letters.

---

[18] On the non-private nature of most medieval letters, see G. Constable, *Letters and Letter-Collections,* pp. 11, 13–14, 53–55; Hans Martin Schaller, "Dichtungslehren und Briefsteller," pp. 256, 265; and Ronald Witt, "Defense of Rhetoric," p. 4.

[19] J. J. Murphy, *Rhetoric in the Middle Ages,* pp. 224–25.

A letter might not succeed solely by virtue of a proper beginning, but an improper beginning would assure its failure. The *salutatio* and the *captatio benevolentiae* served above all to situate the letter within two crucial, hierarchically structured domains, one social, the other intellectual. In the *salutatio* one acknowledged in very precise terms and in fairly complex ways a relationship of superiority, inferiority, or equality with the absent person addressed. In order to decide whose name came first in the salutation, sender or recipient, one had to have a detailed knowledge of the stratifications of contemporary society, from pope to deacon and from emperor to swineherd.[20] The dignities of each party had to be mentioned, in the proper order and measure, and the proper phrases and epithets chosen: bishops are called "venerabiles fratres" by the pope, but abbots are not; the pope never uses "Dei gratia" of himself or others; the kings of France and of Jerusalem are called "viros catholicos" because of their special service to the Church. Conflicts between dignities must be resolved: though a bishop outranks a layman, when a bishop writes to his layman father he must put his father's name first, out of respect. More than simply polite formalities, the language and structure of the *salutatio* announce whether the letter is to be taken as command, as entreaty, or as something in between.

At a different level, the *captatio benevolentiae* or *exordium* performs a similar orienting function by placing the message of the letter within an established cultural-intellectual framework. Rhetorically speaking, the second part of a letter specifies the status of the case to be resolved by selecting the basis of argument. Since the whole point of this part is persuasion, it is generally regarded as dispensable in letters from superiors to inferiors, where the salutation has already established the reason why the desired action should be performed. As some *dictatores* recognized, the *captatio benevolentiae* served as an all-important first premise in an epistolary syllogism: for it one chose a proverb, *exemplum*, or *auctoritas* (scriptural or secular) that compelled widespread assent to a given course of action in given circumstances. If one chose well, it was then possible to show, in the *narratio,* that the present case belonged to the class of circumstances so specified and to conclude, in the *petitio,* that the desired course of action was both reasonable and sanctioned by authority. In short, the function of the second part was to convert the individual and the contingent as nearly as possible into the universal and the categorical.

---

[20] See G. Constable, "Structure of Society," pp. 253–67, and F. Quadlbauer, Genera dicendi *im Mittelalter*, pp. 272–78.

Though the *dictatores* for the most part perpetuated the five-part schema, even among them there is occasional recognition of a more basic, three-part structure. The importance of the *salutatio* and *captatio benevolentiae,* the similarity of their functions, and the tendency to think of them as a fixed series of slots to be filled from a limited set of options always threatened to blur the boundaries between them. A similar blurring of the boundaries between *conclusio* and *petitio* can be observed, probably because the concluding formulas were often so brief and had little practical function in isolation. The fact that so many letters lacked what could be called a distinct *narratio* or *petitio,* either because they alternated elements of both or because they concentrated exclusively on one of the two, also confirmed the perception of an underlying three-part structure, superficially resembling that of the modern letter but differing from it in the proportions and significance of the parts. Thus, the form of many late medieval letters, particularly those not composed by traditional teachers of the *ars dictaminis,* can best be seen as comprising relatively fixed sets of formulas at beginning and end, surrounding a middle of varying size, content, and structure.

Awareness of this underlying structure shows up in some late *dictatores,* but in a paradoxical way. The fourteenth-century English *dictator* Thomas Sampson, for example, names neither five nor three, but no less than twelve parts of a letter: "commendacio, salutacio, status affectus, clausula regraciatoria generalis vel specialis, interclusio, confutacio, confirmacio, conclusio negatiua vel affirmatiua, promissio, superaddicio, <sub>salutacio, subscripcio" (BL, MS Royal 17B.xlvii, fol. 42r).[21] Others produce similarly extended lists, sometimes including "parts," such as the "superscripcio," not found in Sampson's. The examples supplied by such teachers make it clear that these are neither parts in the same sense as the traditional five nor in the same sense with respect to one another. Some, for example, are obligatory, while others are either optional or alternatives for one another. Plotted against the traditional schema, *commendacio* through *clausula regraciatoria generalis* correspond to the *salutatio* and *captatio benevolentiae; clausula regraciatoria specialis* through *promissio* correspond to *narratio* and *petitio; superaddicio* straddles *petitio* and *conclusio;* and *subsalutacio* and *subscripcio* correspond to *conclusio.* What Sampson seeks is to describe more precisely both the *elements* of the opening

---

[21] I have completed an edition of this treatise, which survives in a version compiled in 1396.

and closing formulas and the most common *varieties* of the less fixed middle.[22]

The rationale of Sampson's schema becomes clearer if we use his terms to describe an actual letter, such as the Valentine that Margery Brews sent to John Paston III in 1477. The first sentence ("Vn-to … &c."), called a *"superscripcio"* by some of Sampson's contemporaries, would have been written on the outside of the letter, as an address of sorts. The letter proper begins with a *commendacio* ("Ryght … Voluntyne") and a *salutacio* ("I … hertely"), followed immediately by an enquiry about John's health or a *status affectus* ("desyring … desyre"). As will become evident in chapter 4, the move from the conventional *status affectus* to complaint about one's own bad health due to the lover's absence was standard in fifteenth-century verse love epistles.[23] The body of Margery's letter can be divided in several ways, among them the traditional ones: the section from "And yf" through "full sory" can be treated as a *narratio,* which is then followed by a *petitio* ("But … ʒowe") or, as Sampson might prefer to call it, a *promissio.* The longer section of verse fits Sampson's usage of the term *superaddicio* quite well, and the letter ends in as conventional a fashion as it began: a *subsalutacio,* augmented with a request for secrecy – highly appropriate in a courtly love poem ("No more … ʒour-selfe, &c.") – precedes a perfectly regular *subscripcio.* The conventionality of the opening and closing formulas is further indicated by Margery's practice of supplying only enough of the relevant formula to enable John to recognize it and abbreviating the rest with an "&c." So familiar are the conventions that she can confidently assume his knowledge of them.[24]

Because the structure of the core message was susceptible to such variation, the only consistently reliable markers of epistolary form in

---

[22] Later in his treatise, Sampson also uses more familiar terms such as *narracio* and *peticio,* as well as *arenga* and *prohemium* (by which he means the *captatio benevolentiae,* as described above).

[23] Ed. N. Davis, *Paston Letters,* pt. 1, pp. 662–63. Even in the prose portions of her letter, she employs many of the most popular conventions of the verse love epistle. Compare the opening of her letter, for example, with *Troilus and Criseyde,* V, 1359–72 ("Litera Troili") and with lines 8–11 of the poem attributed to William de la Pole, and printed by Henry N. MacCracken, "English Friend," p. 165; by Rossell H. Robbins, in *SL,* pp. 189–90; and most recently by Johannes Petrus Maria Jansen, *'Suffolk' Poems,* p. 92. The convention in question originates in a pun on the Latin *salus* (i.e., "greeting" [cf. *salutatio*] and/or "health," "well-being"). See Martin Camargo, "Middle English Love Letter," pp. 80–81.

[24] The formulas may well have been written out in the copy actually sent and abbreviated only to save space in the register. Even so, the "&c" implies that the abbreviated portions would be familiar to users of the register.

actual medieval practice turn out to be the formal techniques of introduction and closure. Giles Constable, drawing on the full range of medieval epistolography, concludes as much:

> The only indubitable signs of epistolary form throughout the Middle Ages are in the salutation and subscription, which contain respectively the greetings and the farewell of the writer(s).

He goes on to say that "the presence of a salutation and subscription on any work shows that it was intended to be in epistolary form."[25] We may now go a step farther and say that within this basic structure, the "dominant," the element to which the other elements are hierarchically subordinated, is what can be most conveniently called the "greeting." The overriding importance of the opening formulas and strategies should already be evident from the foregoing brief analysis of the *ars dictaminis*. Letters, whatever their other formal features or functions, are seen as documents that *address* the recipient directly, *speaking for* the writer who cannot be physically present. It is the formal greeting that both establishes and characterizes this relationship of direct address.

Writers of verse letters were of course freer to modify the standard form than were those who composed practical letters in prose. Poetic conventions naturally compete with epistolary conventions in such compositions, often causing the greeting to be deemphasized or shifted from its normal position because another element is given greater prominence. For example, a love letter whose surface structure is that of a ballade will almost inevitably either highlight the formal leave-taking or combine or replace it with a postposed greeting, because that part of the letter conforms so neatly to the ballade's envoy. Even though the range of permissible deviation from the norm is so great in vernacular love epistles that the formal greeting is sometimes attenuated to nothing more than the use of direct address, the greeting remains the dominant, defining element at a deeper level. And it always leaps back into surface prominence, significantly, when a poet wants to foreground the epistolary character of the poem. Consciousness of this dominant is evident in the generic terms that twelfth- and thirteenth-century poets developed for the precursors of the Middle English verse love epistle, the Provençal *salutz* and the Old French *salut d'amour*.[26] The formal dominant may simply be an address, whether at beginning or end, that serves to materialize the

---

[25] G. Constable, *Letters and Letter-Collections,* pp. 17, 18.
[26] On the genre terminology, see E. Ruhe, *De Amasio,* pp. 99–103, 216–18, 232–33.

functional dominant of greeting. But whereas the formal dominant is occasionally, if rarely, suppressed, the functional dominant is always present. Where the form does not disclose it, something else will. But when that "something else" is solely the fact that the poem was sent, we have reached a point where the concept of genre breaks down. The evidence needed to identify specific medieval poems as love letters in this *purely* functional sense has almost totally been lost, especially for poems that are not embedded in larger works.

To this point, two sources of information on which to draw in constructing a corpus of Middle English verse love epistles have been discussed. First, and doubtless most important, is direct testimony by authors, scribes, and members of the genre's audience. The frequent occurrence of the term "lettre" or one of its common synonyms within the texts themselves, as well as in scribal rubrics, colophons, or glosses to similar texts was indeed the first indication that the verse love letter existed as a distinct, recognized, and popular form of late Middle English poetry. Such references are also valuable because they identify poems that *functioned* as love epistles, even though their form is not particularly epistolary (or is even non-epistolary). Less direct but closely related is the codicological evidence: the fact that an unlabeled text has been copied in the same manuscript with other texts clearly identified as letters and that it clearly resembles should count among the reasons for admitting that text into the corpus. Finally, references to the practice of writing and receiving love letters, in literary and (more rarely) non-literary sources, provide important insights into function and, sometimes, into form as well.

A second criterion of selection is of course the formal one. Whether written in the official five-part structure or in the more fundamental three-part structure, medieval letters have a distinctive form that can help in identifying unlabeled examples of the genre. The formulaic language of letters, a third source of generic information, is closely tied to the second, since the characteristic formulas tend to cluster in the most distinct parts of a letter, the formal greeting and farewell. Variations of phrases such as "I recommande me vn-to yowe full hertely" and "No more to yowe at this tyme" will turn out to be among the most constant components of Middle English verse love epistles from the late fourteenth through the early sixteenth centuries.

Theme provides a fourth source of evidence, though one that is seldom conclusive in itself. Arthur K. Moore is correct in observing that when approached thematically, the love epistle is prone to dissolve into the

14

conventional complaint,[27] and it is very difficult to distinguish the secular love epistle from the thematically very similar epistolary poem in praise of the Blessed Virgin. Nonetheless, certain themes tend to occur often enough in the verse love epistles to be called characteristic of the form, if not exclusive to it. Since letters are seen as speaking for an absent person, it is not surprising that the theme of separation and its attendant hardships is proportionally more common in verse love epistles than in amatory complaints as a class. Many verse love epistles also thematize the physicality of the text through apologies for the tearstains that blot it, expressions of envy at the letter's good fortune in being held by the beloved, and simple references to the act of writing. Even concern about the health of one or both of the lovers becomes a characteristic theme of the genre, doubtless due to the conventionality of the *status affectus* and to the long tradition of playing on the derivation of *salutatio* from *salus* ("health," "well being").[28]

Both the explicit references to letters and the implicit evidence of structure, diction, and theme need finally to be supplemented by contrastive analysis: that is, one recognizes a genre not only from what it is but also from what it is not. Comparing a genre to the most closely related contemporary genres is especially valuable in locating areas of overlap (and so avoiding excessively restrictive "definitions") and in isolating the function(s) of the focal genre. It is not always possible to (re)construct a "system of genres" of the sort envisaged by the Russian Formalists. In fact, the Middle English lyric is especially resistant to this sort of classification, especially by comparison with the Provençal or even the Old French lyric.[29] It is therefore difficult to situate the Middle English verse love epistle within a clearly structured hierarchy of genres and to identify the single most closely related genre that by juxtaposition will throw the distinctive features of the love epistle into high relief, as Ernstpeter Ruhe was able to do with the Provençal *salutz* (*canso*) and the Old French *salut*

---

[27] Arthur K. Moore, *Secular Lyric*, p. 146. The relationship between the love letter and the complaint is also examined by E. Ruhe, *De Amasio*, pp. 222–31 (see also p. 274); Heinrich Dörrie, *Der heroische Brief*, pp. 154, 434–35; and Christine M. Scollen, *Birth of Elegy*. Similarly, letters expressing *amor spiritualis* are often difficult to distinguish from those which express *amor carnalis*. See M. Camargo, "Middle English Love Letter," pp. 58, 267, and, for letters of spiritual friendship, Jean Leclercq, "L'Amitié," pp. 391–410, and F. C. Gardiner, *Pilgrimage of Desire*, pp. 53–85.

[28] Cf. n. 23, above.

[29] Cf. n. 14, above. George Kane also notes the special obstacles to the historical study of Middle English lyrics, in "Short Essay," pp. 110–21. For the well-defined system of Provençal lyric genres, see Dietmar Rieger, "Trobadoreske Gattungssystem," pp. 15–28.

d'amour (*complainte d'amour*).[30] On the other hand, one can distinguish several varieties of verse epistle besides the love epistle – the moral treatise in epistolary form, the legalistic "documents" in the allegories and dream visions – all of which include at least a few examples dealing with love; and one cannot avoid the task of mapping the areas of overlap between the verse love epistle and certain classes of contemporary love poetry defined by theme (poems of praise, poems of complaint) or form (ballade).

Both the relationship between the verse love epistle and other contemporary genres and that among the various elements and functions that constitute the verse love epistle must have undergone changes in the course of the genre's 150-year history. We must therefore speak of the genre's identity not as something fixed or static but rather as an evolving set of relationships at the formal, literary, and social levels. However, the effort to chart those shifting relationships is seriously hindered by the impossibility of precisely dating, localizing, or ascribing a great many, if not the majority, of the surviving verse love epistles. Often the only clue to a poem's date is the handwriting in which it was copied down. But such evidence yields at best an approximate date and often no more than a *terminus ante quem* that may be decades removed from the actual date of composition. For example, the manuscript that contains the largest number of Middle English verse love epistles (Rawlinson C.813) was written between 1527 and 1535, but many of the poems that it contains must have been composed much earlier. Because most of the poems are anonymous, it is also difficult to identify particular poets who might have introduced innovations in the form or even to be sure about the locale where a particular poem was composed and the audience for which it was intended. The temptation is great to use those cases where information about date and authorship is available (Charles of Orléans, John Lydgate, Humfrey Newton, Lord Thomas Howard and Lady Margaret Douglas) as the fixed frame on which to hang a tissue of conjecture, but there is no assurance that those cases are representative of evolutionary stages affecting the genre as a whole. We can speak with reasonable assurance about the period of the genre's emergence, in the second quarter of the fifteenth century, and that of its decline, in the mid sixteenth century, but the stages of its development during the century of its flowering can only be conjectured.

---

[30] *De Amasio,* pp. 107–17 and 222–31, respectively.

16

CHAPTER 2

Precursors of the Middle English Verse Love Epistle

2.1. *Salut d'amour*

Until the latter part of the fourteenth century, there is no clear evidence that the verse love epistle was recognized as a distinct poetic genre in England. Love letters in Latin verse are found already in late eleventh-century France and Germany and survive in considerable numbers from the twelfth century.[1] Although these texts are probably too widely scattered and too different in character and function to qualify as a genre,[2] the same is not true of the vernacular tradition that developed somewhat later. During the second half of the twelfth century, the verse love epistle (*salutz*) emerged as a well-defined genre of the Provençal lyric, and the *salutz* in turn gave rise to the *salut d'amour,* which flourished in northern France during the second half of the thirteenth century.[3] It seems likely that some Anglo-Norman *saluts d'amour* would have been composed during the thirteenth century. In fact, the earliest reference to the Old French *salut* (ca. 1170) is by the Anglo-Norman writer Denis Piramus, who claimed to have composed "saluz" along with the other repented love poems of his youth.[4]

Another early and especially interesting witness to the genre occurs in the *Ancrene Wisse,* a guide for English nuns written in the late twelfth or early thirteenth century (before 1221).[5] At one point in the text, Christ is

---

[1] See E. Ruhe, *De Amasio,* pp. 22–50 (notes 374–77), 81–87 (notes 385–86), 91–97 (notes 388–90). An extensive group of twelfth-century texts not covered by Ruhe is that edited by E. Könsgen, *Epistolae duorum amantium.*

[2] See especially D. Schaller, "Überlieferung und Verfasserschaft" and his review of E. Ruhe's *De Amasio,* in *Arcadia.*

[3] On the *salutz,* see especially E. Ruhe, *De Amasio,* pp. 97–119 (notes 391–96), 161–70 (notes 410–12), and 208–15 (notes 428–29), and Christiane Leube, "Salut d'amor," pp. 77–87; on the *salut d'amour,* E. Ruhe, *De Amasio,* pp. 215–53 (notes 429–42), and 271–74 (notes 446–48) (all with additional bibliography).

[4] E. Ruhe, *De Amasio,* pp. 215–16.

[5] The most recent scholarship suggests that the *Ancrene Wisse* was first composed in English, but some scholars still argue for the priority of the French version. On this and other questions regarding the *Ancrene Wisse,* see Roger Dahood, "*Ancrene Wisse,*" pp. 1–33.

allegorized as a king who "luueþ an lafdi of feorrene londe" (i.e., the Church). He first sends his messengers, "þe patriarkes and þe prophetes of þe alde testament," to her "wiþ lettres isealed," and then "on ende he com him seoluen & brochte þe godspel as lettres iopened & wrot wiþ his achne blod saluz to his leofmon, luue gretung for to wowin hire wiþ & hire luue welden."[6] The precision of the reference is striking: not only is the technical term ("saluz") employed and the function explained, but the love letter, as *epistola familiaris,* is distinguished from the two chief varieties of *epistolae negotiales*, the letters close and the letters patent. Clearly, in some English circles the *salut d'amour* was already a familiar genre in the first quarter of the thirteenth century. Nonetheless, the only extant example that was definitely intended for an English audience appears in a work composed in 1396, a century after the *salut* had gone into decline in France. Rather than the expected *saluts d'amour,* one finds a handful of thirteenth- and early fourteenth-century texts, in Latin, Anglo-Norman, and English, that collectively testify to the absence of a tradition.

2.2. Gerald of Wales, *Symbolum electorum*

The oldest surviving verse love epistle of English provenance is a poem of 30 lines, in distichs, included in Gerald of Wales's *Symbolum electorum* (Part II, #8).[7] Although Gerald probably put together the collection between 1204 and 1205, the poem could have been composed somewhat earlier. Stylistically and structurally the piece is not much different from others in the same section of the *Symbolum electorum.* Why Gerald chose to put it into epistolary form is explained in the title he attached to it:

> Ad quandam puellam litteratam nomen habentem
> Laetitiae sed non omen, sub amatoris sui specie.

["To a certain learned girl who has the name but not the appearance of Joy, in the guise of her lover."] He plays at being Laetitia's lover and plays on the fact that she is sad although her name means joy, in order to

---

[6] Ed. E. J. Dobson, *Ancrene Riwle,* p. 284 (punctuation mine). The texts in MS Cotton Nero A.XIV (ed. Mabel Day, EETS, o.s. 225, p. 177) and MS Corpus Christi College Cambridge 402 (ed. J. R. R. Tolkien, EETS, o.s. 249, p. 198) do not exhibit any significant variants.

[7] Ed. J. S. Brewer, Rolls Series, 21, pt. 1 (1861), pp. 356–57. For discussion, see E. Ruhe, *De Amasio,* pp. 95–97.

18

drive away her sadness. There are precedents for this sort of punning in some of the verse epistles by Hilarius, who, though apparently an Englishman, lived and wrote a century earlier in France.[8] But if Gerald has an epistolary model it is rather Ovid's *Heroides,* two lines from which he borrows and adapts for the *exordium* of his letter:

> Quicquid amor jussit non est contemnere tutum,
> Me tibi quae scribo scribere jussit amor.
> (II, 8: 1–2; cf. *Heroides,* iv, 10–11)

["Whatever love commands, it is not safe to disdain; what I write to you love commanded me to write."] Moreover, the poem's epistolary character is indicated only by this *exordium* and an equally brief leave-taking:

> Ecce recedit amans sed non ab amore recedit
> Pectoris in thalamo fortius ille furit.
> (II, 8: 29–30)

["Lo the lover retires but does not retire from love; in the chamber of his heart it rages ever the stronger."]

2.3. Appendix to the *Chastoiement d'un pere à son fils*

If Gerald's letter to Laetitia is an isolated example with only minimal epistolary characteristics, it is at least a free-standing poem. The next three texts to be considered have a much higher concentration of epistolary features, but their generic identity is compromised by the fact that they are embedded in larger romance narratives. Moreover, the first two have been transplanted, along with part of the surrounding narrative, from their original romance context into a didactic work, an appendix added by an Anglo-Norman author to the *Chastoiement d'un pere à son fils,* a verse translation of the *Disciplina clericalis,* found in Bibliothèque Nationale, Nouvelles acquisitions françaises 7517 (mid thirteenth century).[9] The appendix, like the *Chastoiement* written in octosyllabic couplets, consists of twelve *exempla* chosen to assist the son in distinguishing true from false love. Aside from the brief dialogues that introduce each *exemplum,* most of the text seems to have been lifted directly from contemporary (mostly unidentified) romances. Within two of these ex-

---

[8] See E. Ruhe, *De Amasio,* pp. 41–44, and p. 390 n. 84.
[9] Ed. Alfons Hilka, "Anglonormannische Kompilation," pp. 423–54.

cerpted *exempla* occur the full texts of letters from two knights each wishing to initiate a love relationship (VIII, lines 1333–54, and X, lines 1521–80).[10]

Both letters are carried to the respective lady by "un messager" (1327, 1519), and both are labeled in the text itself and in the surrounding narrative. The most frequently used terms are "lettre" (1355, 1581), "lettres" (1352, 1354), and "lettre close" (1331, 1519); but "escrit" (1328), "brevet" (1581), and "chartre" (1575) also appear. The letters are also set off from the surrounding narrative by the shift to direct address and by the presence of epistolary formulas at beginning and end. In addition, the second letter is composed in decasyllabics rather than the octosyllabics of the narrative proper. As in the poem by Gerald of Wales, the first letter employs an *auctoritas* from Ovid (*Her.,* iv, 10) in place of a *salutatio*:

> Amor me fet parescrire
> Ce qu n'os par boche dire.   (1333–34)

By contrast, the second letter extends the *salutatio* through anaphora, before concluding it with a formula that will reappear in English love epistles from Chaucer's day through the sixteenth century:

> Saluz vus di a decertes e sanz deport.
> En haute mer m'avez gité de port.
> Saluz vus di de fin quer e de voir;
> A vos me teng, en vos est mon espoir.
> Saluz vus di de voir quer e de fin;
> A vus me comant, a vos me devin.   (1521–26)

The situation is reversed in the respective conclusions: whereas the second letter closes with four lines playing on *merci* ("mercy," "thanks"), the first is more conventional in requesting a written reply and in emphasizing the letter as physical object, a keepsake to remind her of the bond into which he wishes her to enter: "Les lettres retenez en remembrance" (1354).

Both letters draw on the conventions of the courtly romance. The writer of the shorter one concentrates on a single appeal – that the lady tell him definitely whether he is loved or can hope to be loved by her (1341–53). He elaborates that appeal anaphorically (1342–47), in a manner reminiscent of the other letter's opening.[11] Nearly three times as long as

---

[10] See E. Ruhe, *De Amasio,* pp. 178, 414–16.

[11] Ruhe draws attention to the similar ways in which the two letters are introduced in the narrative and concludes that the repeated lines were contributed by the compiler

20

the first, the second letter naturally runs through a wider range of conventional themes: the suppliant has never loved before; he has been taken prisoner by the lady's beauty; the more he resists, the more tightly he is bound; he survives only on hope; etc. Twice he draws attention to the fact that he is writing rather than speaking, first to spell out the reasons why he hopes "cet brevet" will be looked at "bonement" (1563), and later solemnly to pledge his service: "A vus servir me rent par ceste chartre" (1575). Otherwise, only the elaborate greeting distinguishes this letter from the same lover's appeals to the lady when he finally speaks to her (e.g., 1621–42, 1653–67).

2.4. *Kyng Alisaunder*

Queen Candace's letter to Alexander of Macedon differs from the two Anglo-Norman letters just discussed not only because it is preserved in its full, original context but also because its context is more that of the *chanson de geste* than that of the courtly romance. Like them, it is not an independent work but rather a small part of a large narrative poem, *Kyng Alisaunder* (B version, lines 6674–6717).[12] It is worth considering briefly, however, because the *Kyng Alisaunder* poet's revisions of his source seem to be shaped in part by an awareness of both epistolary and courtly love conventions. Sometime between the end of the thirteenth century and 1330, the anonymous Middle English poet translated and adapted an interpolated version of Thomas of Kent's *Roman de toute chevalerie* (late twelfth century). Thomas was apparently responsible for converting Candace's catalog of exotic treasures offered in pledge of friendship into an explicit declaration of physical love, but his text (lines 6957–7002) is not a fully realized letter, much less a proper love epistle.[13] Only the body or *narratio* of the letter is given in Candace's own words. The *salutatio* is merely summarized in the narrator's voice, and the *conclusio* is entirely ignored. This neglect of the formal opening and close of the letter, though perfectly consistent with Thomas's thematic purposes, is striking from the perspective of medieval epistolography.

---

of the appendix: *De Amasio,* pp. 178, 416 (n. 99). The similarity could also be explained by both passages having been extracted from a common source.

[12] Ed. G. V. Smithers, *Kyng Alisaunder,* vol. 1, pp. 355–57. For a more extensive treatment of the letter's evolution and its position within the text, see Martin Camargo, "Metamorphosis of Candace," pp. 101–11.

[13] Ed. Brian Foster, with the assistance of Ian Short, *Anglo-Norman Alexander,* vol. 1, pp. 217–18.

Because the *salutatio* and the *conclusio* were the defining parts of a medieval letter, marking it off as a self-enclosed piece of writing, identifying its sender and recipient, and distinguishing it from other types of structured discourse in direct address, the fact that Thomas plays down the *salutatio* in his version of Candace's letter betrays either an ignorance of or an indifference toward epistolary form (which is belied by his treatment of letters elsewhere in the *Roman*) or, what is more likely, a purpose that is in this case better served by the breach than by the observance of epistolary decorum.

When the *Kyng Alisaunder* poet takes steps to correct the "flaws" of his source, his actions accordingly have thematic as well as formal consequences. Since the formal consequences are more obviously intentional, I shall discuss them first. Comparison of the *Roman*'s letter with the translation and adaptation in *Kyng Alisaunder* reveals several significant revisions. First, the Middle English poet expands the paraphrased opening into a conventional, four-line *salutatio* (*KA*, 6674–77). More noticeably, because there is no precedent whatsoever in his source, he eliminates the interruption of the *narratio* that occurs midway through the letter in the *Roman* (*RTC*, 6979–87). The result is a unified, rhetorically correct, and complete letter that is formally independent of the surrounding third-person narrative. In dramatic terms, Candace is permitted to say her piece from start to finish, without interruption, in her own words. The formal *salutatio* and *conclusio* strictly delimit the interval during which she holds the floor.

This formal encapsulating effect is probably felt most strongly at the letter's end; for even in the *Roman* there is no mistaking the point at which we first hear Candace *in propria voce*. But when Candace begins to speak in the *Roman,* the first words we hear are:

> Sire roy dreiturer,
> Nule rien ne coveit tant en mon desirer
> Cum vous prendre a seignur e vous mey a moiller.
> Sur toz homes vous aim ...   (*RTC,* 6959–62)

["Sir rightful king, nothing so suits my desires as (for me) to take you as husband and you me as wife. I love you above all men," etc.] Compare the first impression this leaves with that of

> To Alisaunder þe Emperoure,
> Of caysers prince, of kniȝttes floure,
> þe quene Candace, wiþ al honoure,
> Sendeþ gretynges, par amoure.   (*KA,* 6674–77)

Though the Middle English poet immediately proceeds to translate the lines with which the direct quotation in the *Roman* begins, he has already softened their effect though the indirection provided by the conventionally polite *salutatio*. Candace's first words express not powerful desire but the customary amenities, and this fact makes her seem somewhat less impetuous.

The *Kyng Alisaunder* poet's other revisions likewise suggest that the movement toward perfecting the letter's form is accompanied by, if not motivated by, a desire to ameliorate Candace's character. In other words, the poet's sense of genre is sufficiently precise for him to realize that if he is to make hers an acceptable love letter, he must make Candace a more acceptable lover. Thomas of Kent's attitude toward Candace is very clear. His handling of the entire episode, which the letter merely foreshadows, betrays a strongly moral perspective. His Candace is a sensualist and a temptress, a figure straight from the antifeminist tradition. Like her comic counterpart the Wife of Bath, she is after "maistrie," and Thomas never lets us forget how dangerous she is on this account. Her aggressive, blatantly materialistic letter accordingly prepares us for the licentious affair into which she will trick the insufficiently wary Alexander.

In reshaping her letter, however, the *Kyng Alisaunder* poet is careful to mitigate precisely those qualities of Candace's character which Thomas highlights. Most of his minor revisions in the *narratio* serve to remove language that might make Candace sound too greedy, materialistic, or overbearing. He deletes, for instance, the superlatives from her description of the treasure that she offers, perhaps for fear of emphasizing her wealth and power to the detriment of Alexander's. Though the lengthy catalog of booty remains the letter's focus, even here the poet tries to elevate the tone by adding to the end of her list a "genteel" gift of thirty thousand beautiful and courteous maidens, each of them an earl's or baron's daughter. Finally, by stressing in her *conclusio* Alexander's high station and her own eagerness to serve him, Candace confirms the positive first impression created by her modest *salutatio*. The *Kyng Alisaunder* poet thus strives throughout the letter to turn the aggressive, masterful Candace of his source into a humbler, more refined, and hence, to his audience, more sympathetic lady.[14]

The end result of his labors is nonetheless far removed from the courtly milieu of chivalric romance. Candace's almost comically extravagant "dowry" is enough to ensure that the letter will remain closer in

---

[14] For a different view, see George Cary, *Medieval Alexander,* pp. 100–101.

spirit to the *chanson de geste* or travel book than to the courtly love poem, despite any efforts to the contrary.[15] And if the Middle English Candace is less emphatically aggressive in her letter than her Anglo-Norman model is, she still initiates the affair with Alexander. Their styles are different, but their messages remain nearly identical. The Middle English poet might well have successfully shifted stereotypes in the confines of Candace's letter through his skillful use of conventional epistolary form, had not the bulk of the letter's contents stood so squarely in the way. Candace's aggressive materialism is only partially mitigated by the correctness of her letter, in which, as in the subsequent treatment of her love affair with Alexander, the tension between her character as developed in the *Roman* and the ideal type with which the *Kyng Alisaunder* poet sought to align her proves too great to be resolved through stylistic means alone. Because the poet is reluctant to make the radical changes in content that might bring his project to fulfillment, the Middle English Candace remains uncomfortably suspended between the immoral temptress of the *Roman* and the nobler Dido figure she might have become. Her letter can thus only in a problematic sense be called the earliest specimen of the English verse love epistle; but it reveals, if hesitantly and indistinctly, the shape of things to come.

2.5. Letter to "Dame Desyree"

None of these love letters counts as an example of a distinct genre, in the sense of the *salut d'amour,* though the attention to epistolary form and (in the letter from *Kyng Alisaunder*) the introduction of courtly love elements may indicate an awareness of such a genre. This awareness is more evident, however, in another Anglo-Norman text that is roughly contemporary with *Kyng Alisaunder.* The untitled letter to "Dame Desyree" (1299) is not a verse love epistle but a prose treatise in epistolary form on the choosing of a lover.[16] It nonetheless merits brief mention here not

---

[15] Ruhe comments on the unusual fact of Lavinia's taking the initiative and sending a declaration of love to Eneas in the *Roman d'Eneas* (before 1174; ca. 1160?) and relates it to the intermediate position of this work between the *chanson de geste* (and the classical epic) and the *roman courtois* (*De Amasio,* pp. 122–23). Gower used Candace as an *exemplum* of love based on covetousness in the *Confessio Amantis* (V, 2543–46) and accordingly excluded her from the company of noble lovers who comfort Amans near the end of Book VIII.

[16] Ed. John Koch, "Anglonormannische Texte," pp. 50–54. Ruhe calls it a parody of the Old French epistolary treatise on love, the only surviving example of which is Richard of Fournival's *Consaus d'amour* (before 1260): *De Amasio,* pp. 442–43. Subsequent references are marked in the text by line numbers in parentheses.

only because it observes good epistolary form and some of the conventions proper to the *epistola amandi* but also because it is the earliest example in England of the legalistic "love document," a form whose history will be intertwined with that of the verse love epistle from the late fourteenth century on.

The author, who wishes to act as "counceyler" to the lady addressed, opens with a *salutatio* that fills the requirements of both *dictamen* and the love letter: "A la tresnoble Dame Desyree, saunz nomer pur Medisaunz, le soen lige saluz, honurs e reuerences, e sey subiet a ses comaundemens!" (1–3). The placement of the lady's titles before the sender's, in the position of honor, is stressed in a way more typical of formal than of familiar letters (including love letters).[17] The writer further emphasizes the lady's high station ("tresnoble Dame") by styling himself "le soen lige" and submitting to her commandments. The analogy between a vassal's oath of fealty to his feudal lord and a lover's promise of service to his lady had of course long been conventional in Provençal love poetry. Also consistent with the conventions of love letters is his care not to reveal her name for fear of "Medisaunz." The fear of "losyngoures" and the consequent precautions lest the lover's words compromise his lady are constant features of the genre.[18] By concealing his lady's name the

---

[17] Abelard, for example, places Heloise's name before his own in the salutation of his second letter, even though he "outranks" her. She organizes her response around this breach of decorum in order both to introduce the idea that his salutation was not the only part of his letter which went against her expectations, and to remind him ironically that their relationship is indeed no longer a familiar one:

Unico suo post Christum unica sua in Christo.

Miror, unice meus, quod preter consuetudinem epistolarum, immo contra ipsum ordinem naturalem rerum, in ipsa fronte salutationis epistolaris me tibi preponere presumpsisti, feminam videlicet viro, uxorem marito, ancillam domino, monialem monacho et sacerdoti diaconissam, abbati abbatissam. Rectus quippe ordo est et honestus ut qui ad superiores vel ad pares scribunt eorum quibus scribunt nomina suis anteponant; sin autem ad inferiores, precedunt scriptionis ordine qui precedunt rerum dignitate.

J. Monfrin, ed., *Historia calamitatum*, pp. 117–18.

To her only one after Christ, she who is his alone in Christ.

I am surprised, my only love, that contrary to custom in letter-writing and, indeed, to the natural order, you have thought fit to put my name before yours in the greeting which heads your letter, so that we have woman before man, wife before husband, handmaid before master, nun before monk, deaconess before priest and abbess before abbot. Surely the right and proper order is for those who write to their superiors or equals to put their names before their own, but in letters to inferiors, precedence in order of address follows precedence in rank.

Betty Radice, trans., *Letters of Abelard and Heloise*, p. 127.

[18] See the Norfolk abbot's first two letters (discussed below) for other examples. The

suitor performs his duty of secrecy (cf. lines 52–72), a responsibility with which the perfect lover is frequently charged.

The *narratio* (3–150), predictably, constitutes by far the bulk of the letter. Some general remarks to the effect that a woman should take care when choosing a lover are followed by detailed instructions for testing a would-be paramour's suitability over a seven-year trial period. The author's didactic intent is evident in his use of *auctoritates* (in this case the romances) to confirm each of his major points.[19] The *narratio* concludes with the assurance that anyone who has passed all the tests and is willing to swear the oath provided (136–42) will be a trustworthy lover. A brief *petitio* follows, in which the lady is asked to heed these precepts of her "conseyler" whenever she is "des amours requise" (150–51). The *conclusio* preserves the effect of formal address to a superior created in the *salutatio*: "Done dens les quatre mers de Engleterre, la vyle de la seynt Johan le baptist, Le aan du reyne [le Roy Edward fiz] le Roy Henry vint e seitime" (151–53).[20] As with the salutation, the reader will recognize here the type of conclusion recommended for official letters by fourteenth-century *dictatores* such as Thomas Sampson.

2.6. MS Harley 2253

Perhaps not coincidentally, it is not until more than half a century later, when Thomas Sampson, John Briggis, Thomas Merke, and others were actually teaching the *ars dictaminis* at Oxford and composing the few indigenous treatises on the subject that have survived, that texts relevant to the genre under study are once again encountered. Before turning to the late fourteenth century, when a genuine, continuous tradition of the verse love epistle can finally be said to begin in England, we must pause to consider one last ambiguous and isolated example from the late thirteenth or early fourteenth century. Among the Middle English lyrics in MS Harley 2253 is one that probably was intended to be a love epistle, even

---

author of the present letter probably intended the epistolary form to serve as the anonymous dedication of a work written for public scrutiny. Cf. E. Ruhe, *De Amasio*, pp. 249–51. On the quasi-public nature of medieval letters in general, see G. Constable, *Letters and Letter-Collections*, p. 11. Cf. chapter 1, n. 18.

[19] Cf. the anonymous *Liber et dictamen ad dilectam sibi* (E. Ruhe, *De Amasio*, pp. 261–68).

[20] Koch (pp. 49, 56) thinks Chester, where the cathedral was dedicated to St. John, may be meant. The subscription is misprinted in the text (p. 54); I correct it from Koch's introduction (p. 21).

though in most ways it is less epistolary than any of the texts discussed so far.[21] The poem consists of five eight-line stanzas, the last two lines of which form a refrain:

> Euer ant oo for my leof icham in grete þohte;
> y þenche on hire þat y ne seo nout ofte.   (7–8)

In the manuscript, this lyric follows immediately after an identically structured poem about Christ's love, with the same *incipit* but with the refrain

> Euer ant oo, nyht ant day, he haueþ vs in is þohte;
> he nul nout leose þat he so deore bohte.[22]

Comparison of the two poems cannot reveal which was modeled on which, but information from other sources suggests that the secular lyric is the earlier composition.[23]

Although the theme of the refrain – the separation of the two lovers – is characteristic of love letters, its presence alone is usually not sufficient to distinguish a letter from a non-epistolary complaint. And the fact that the lady for whom the poet is "in grete þohte" is referred to in the third person throughout the first four stanzas violates perhaps the most basic formal requirement of a letter. However, the final stanza leaves no doubt that the poet is mindful of contemporary love epistles, and not just because he addresses his lady directly:

> Ffayrest fode vop loft,
>   my gode luef, y þe grééte
> ase fele syþe ant oft
>   as dewes dropes beþ wééte,
>   ase sterres beþ in welkne ant greases sour ant suete.
>   Whose loueþ vntrewe, his herte is seld sééte.   (30–35)

The specific form of greeting that he chooses was already such a cliché in Latin love letters by the early thirteenth century that Boncompagno felt compelled to attack its use.[24] Nor is the Harley lyric the only proof that Boncompagno's criticism fell on deaf ears: the *quot-tot* salutation, often

---

[21] Ed. G. L. Brook, *Harley Lyrics*, pp. 71–72.

[22] Ibid., pp. 70–71, lines 7–8.

[23] Ibid., pp. 87–88.

[24] See E. Ruhe, *De Amasio*, pp. 399–400. E. Könsgen, *Epistolae duorum amantium*, p. 79, and Peter Dronke, *European Love-Lyric*, vol. 2, p. 476, give further examples from Latin literature. For discussion of this extremely popular formula, see especially Hans Walther, "*Quot-tot*," pp. 257–89.

elaborated to much greater lengths than here, remained popular in both Latin and vernacular love letters until well within the period covered by this study.[25]

Does the use of an epistolary greeting, and at the end rather than in its usual position, suffice to make the poem a verse epistle?[26] The question is unanswerable, particularly in the absence of any descriptive terms and of any contemporary Middle English texts of the same sort. In fact, very few Middle English love lyrics of any sort survive before the late fourteenth century. Only one other lyric in the Harley collection could conceivably be linked with the love epistle, and then only on the very slim evidence that the lover addresses his "lemmon" directly and that he asks her to keep him in mind: "Suete lemmon, þench on me."[27] Yet the particular type of greeting selected was so closely associated with love epistles that its inclusion in the Harley poem seems at the very least a sign that in function, if not in overall form, this lyric was intended to be a letter. That conclusion is strengthened by the fact that, though the greeting occurs at the end of the poem, its appearance there does not in any sense result from constraints imposed by the verse form. The requirement that a ballade end with an envoy, for example, results in many poems with a similar shift to direct address in the last stanza, without necessarily indicating epistolary function.

Gerald of Wales's letter to Laetitia and the Harley lyric are the only free-standing verse love epistles composed in England that have come down to us from the three centuries following the Norman Conquest. During the reign of Richard II (1377–1399) we encounter for the first time significant numbers of such texts, nearly all of them written in Anglo-Norman, as well as an important work in English that contains relevant material. The embedded texts, from Chaucer's *Troilus and Criseyde* (composed 1382–1386), are best treated in a separate chapter (see chapter 3). The remainder of this chapter will address four groups of love letters, most of which draw upon long-established French genres (*salut d'amour, ballade-lettre*) and all of which date, at least in their present

---

[25] Cf., for example, the love letter from BL, MS Harley 3988, discussed below.

[26] Theo Stemmler also comments on the epistolary formula but stops short of calling the poem a letter, grouping it instead among the "carols." *Liebesgedichte des MS. Harley 2253*, pp. 164–68. However, the poem does not fit the specifications of the carol form very well (cf. *ibid.*, p. 161). According to Richard L. Greene, "Ichot a burde in boure bryht" (Brooks, #14) is "the only one of the MS Harley 2253 lyrics in full carol form." "Carols," p. 1750 (cf. also his definition of the carol, on p. 1743).

[27] Ed. G. L. Brook, *Harley Lyrics*, p. 63, line 8.

form, from the last decade of the fourteenth century. Together they provide the first unmistakable signs of the genre that would become "without doubt, ... the main conventional form during the fifteenth century."[28]

2.7. Letters of a Norfolk Abbot

Especially interesting, because it includes what may be the earliest independent verse love epistle in English, is the series of love letters ostensibly composed by an English abbot and copied on the last two leaves (fols. 146rb, 147v) of MS 54/31 of Gonville and Caius College, Cambridge, in an English hand of the very late fourteenth century.[29] The editor of these letters, Paul Meyer, has printed them as three separate Anglo-Norman texts, the second and by far the longest of which is interrupted midway by a brief passage in English. In reality there are five letters, four in Anglo-Norman and one in English. Although the scribe has in fact copied Meyer's second text as if it comprised a single item, internal evidence suggests that there are actually three distinct letters, of which the second is a Middle English love greeting, functioning here as a billet doux. The French text preceding the English lines concludes appropriately enough with the request that "Mergerete" remember the abbot and inform him of her wishes:

> E de moy donkes remembrez.
> Si rien vers moy vus plest
> Mandez m'en ceo qe vus plest,
> Com a cely a ki plest, etc.[30]

The final "etc." is further evidence that a formulaic *conclusio* is being employed.[31] The first two lines of the Middle English section, moreover, constitute a brief *salutatio*, and the final line brings the thought expressed in the piece to an emphatic close:

---

[28] R. H. Robbins, *SL*, p. 286.

[29] R. H. Robbins, *SL*, p. 274; E. Ruhe, *De Amasio,* p. 281 and n. 25. The editor, Paul Meyer, dates the texts in the first half of the fourteenth century: "Mélanges," p. 434.

[30] P. Meyer, "Mélanges," p. 437. Subsequent references are marked in the text by page and line numbers (where appropriate) in parentheses.

[31] Cf. the endings of the other letters (pp. 435 and 438). Only in the final letter is the entire formula written out. See also the discussion of Margery Brews's letter in chapter 1.

Have Godday nou, Mergerete.
With gret love y the grete
Y wolde we mizten us ofte mete
In halle, in chambre and in the strete
Withoute blame of the contre.
God zeve that so mizte hit be.   (p. 437)[32]

Finally, when the French text resumes it is with a brief formula of salutation: "Saluz cent mile feiz par celes enseignes qe vus tochates" (p. 437). Thus, we are here dealing with not three but five separate letters.

Both sender and recipient are partially identified in the text. The letters are addressed to "Mergerete la bele" by one who calls himself "vostre abe" (p. 434, lines 9, 5). The implication is that Margaret is a nun under the anonymous abbot's authority, since he reminds her several times of the obedience that she owes him (e.g., p. 434, line 6). Meyer believes, on the basis of the abbot's allusions to Margaret's replies and the abundance of circumstantial detail that he supplies, that we have here an actual correspondence rather than a mere *jeu d'esprit*.[33] As with most questions of this sort, the genuineness of the letters or, better, of the love affair between the abbot and Margaret can never be proven.[34] The whole thing could just as easily have been the satirical creation of a clerk, perhaps poking fun at a local abbot of dubious piety.

Meyer's low estimate of the author's skill as a versifier, on the other hand, is clearly incorrect.[35] What he criticizes as "des vers d'amateur" is actually perfectly acceptable rhymed prose. When the abbot does make use of verse, he does so selectively, in the way that Margery Brews did nearly a century later. At the end of the first letter, for example, he quotes the refrain of a contemporary *chanson* by way of a *conclusio*:[36]

Ey, Mergrete jolie,
Mon quer sanz fauser, etc.   (p. 435, lines 23–24)

The Middle English letter is likewise in verse and of considerably higher quality than any of the French texts. It is possible that here too the author

---

[32] Also printed separately by R. H. Robbins in *SL*, p. 148.

[33] P. Meyer, "Mélanges," pp. 435–36. The abbot is apparently from Norfolk, as he mentions two places in that county – Fakenham (p. 437) and Lynne (p. 439).

[34] Cf. Ruhe's criticism of earlier Marbod scholarship (*De Amasio,* pp. 27–28). He concurs with Meyer, however, in regarding the abbot's letters as genuine correspondence (pp. 281–83).

[35] "Mélanges," p. 435. Ruhe, *De Amasio,* p. 282 and n. 28, points out his error.

[36] Ruhe observes (*De Amasio,* pp. 282–83) that Meyer prints this very song, without recognizing the connection, later in the same article. The refrain imitated is printed on p. 439 of "Mélanges."

simply took over part of a contemporary lyric. If, on the other hand, he wrote all five letters, his skill as a poet leaves little doubt that his native language was English.[37]

Epistolary form is observed to varying degrees in each of the letters, although none of them is so strongly influenced by *dictamen* as was the thirteenth-century letter to Dame Desyree. All five open with some type of greeting, those in the fourth (quoted above) and fifth – "Saluz et chiers amystés" (p. 438) – most closely resembling the dictaminal *salutatio*. Only the first two letters possess what could be called a *captatio bene-volentiae*, though all but the English piece make use in the *narratio* of the proverbs so dear to the French *dictatores*. The first letter alone lacks a *petitio*, which in any case would have been inappropriate to its subject, while in the third and fifth letters the *petitio* also serves in place of the abbreviated *conclusiones* of the other three. The size of the *narratio*, like that of the letter as a whole, varies a good deal. The *narratio* is never less than half of the entire letter and is sometimes, as in the first and fourth letters, a much larger portion of the whole.

Both Ruhe and Meyer have discussed the Anglo-Norman letters in some detail: they are remarkable mainly for their unusually high quantity of circumstantial detail and a certain homely bluntness. Otherwise their contents are mostly conventional – e.g., the need to maintain secrecy (p. 434, lines 12–17; pp. 436–37); the idea that love is proved by deeds, not words (p. 437); etc. One can get a good idea of their general subject matter, tone, and style from the first letter's opening "lines":

> M., ma especiele,
> Vus estes bone e bele;
> Gardes qu vus seez lele
> Aval la mamele,
> Ceo vus mand vostre abe de grant reverence.
> Loke nou that hit so be in obedience.
> Vus estes mout naturele
> Pur ceo l'en vus apele
> Mergerete la bele;
> Vus ne estes pas pucele
> Pur ceo qc vus estes frele.   (p. 434, lines 1–11)

Since all four Anglo-Norman pieces are mainly in prose, albeit consciously artificial rhymed prose, they do not fully qualify as verse love

---

[37] Cf. also the occasional English interjections in two of the French letters (p. 434, line 6, and p. 438). Meyer draws attention to the superiority of the author's "anglais très limpide" over his French (p. 436).

epistles. At best, particularly if they are genuine love letters, they provide evidence of reception similar to that offered by Margery Brews's Saint Valentine's Day letter. In this case the abbot's use of rhyme and of extracts from contemporary love poems (including love epistles?) would indicate a consciousness of the love letter as a distinct literary form. The Middle English poem presents a different sort of problem in that it is too brief to permit much elaboration of epistolary elements. It is clearly a greeting, but the strongest argument for classifying it as an *epistolary* greeting is the fact that it occurs in the company of four longer texts that are obviously epistles.

2.8. Anglo-Norman Formulary (MS Harley 3988)

The role of the *ars dictaminis* in the emergence of the love epistle in England is difficult to estimate. Even though most of the texts examined so far obey the rules taught by the *dictatores,* their authors could have learned those rules by imitating contemporary usage just as well as through formal training. It does seem significant that the reception of the *ars dictaminis,* like that of the verse love epistle, was belated in England and that the period during which *dictamen* was most carefully observed in English documents and most assiduously taught in English schools (ca. 1350-ca. 1425) corresponds exactly to the "incubation period" of the verse love epistle. On the other hand, the English *dictatores* almost never included love letters in their collections of models, unlike their predecessors in twelfth- and thirteenth-century France and Italy.[38] The single exception, from a formulary compiled to instruct Englishmen in the art of composing French letters, is thus all the more valuable as a witness to the "official" status of love letters in England around the turn of the fifteenth century.

The authorship and date of the collection are not certain. Stengel, who edited the letters that concern us, believed that it was the work of a transplanted Englishman, namely, the same "M. T. Coyfurelly, canonicum, Aurilianum doctorem utriusque juris" (p. 16) to whom he attributed the version of *La maniere de language* (1396) that precedes it in BL, MS Harley 3988.[39] If the parallels between the *Maniere,* a phrasebook for

---

[38] See especially E. Ruhe, *De Amasio,* pp. 61–90, 127–60, 185–203, etc. See also Jürgen Kühnel, *Du bist min,* and Josef Purkart, facs. ed. and trans., *Rota Veneris.*
[39] Ed. E. Stengel, "Anleitungsschriften," pp. 7–8.

students of French, and some of the letters set a *terminus post quem* of 1396 for the collection, the date of the manuscript (early fifteenth century) sets a *terminus ante quem*. Perhaps on the basis of the manuscript, Vising dates the letters in the first quarter of the fifteenth century.[40] Stengel edited a series of six "charakteristische Briefe" from the collection (fols. 57v–60r), the last two of which – "De viro ad eius uxorem" and "Littera amorose composita" – are of interest.[41]

Neither the letter from a man to his wife nor the one from a lover to his "amie" contributes much to our genre. The former is neither about love nor in verse, while the latter is a thoroughly conventional exercise that Ruhe has called a "sehr ferne Echo einer Gattungsform …, die auch auf dem Kontinent völlig in Vergessenheit geraten war."[42] Much more important is the deliberate juxtaposition of the two – unlike the letters preceding them, they are not accompanied by replies – and what the contrast implies about the reception of love letters. That the "Littera amorose composita" draws heavily on the *saluts d'amour* for its contents and, even more important, that it is written in the octosyllabic couplets preferred in the *saluts* rather than in prose underscore its fundamental difference from the other models in the formulary. It is therefore not surprising that this is the only known vernacular love letter from an English formulary. Adulterous love was a subject for the lyric poet; the practical-minded English *dictatores* generally treat only such love as has been sanctified by matrimony. The formulary in MS Harley 3988 is unique in providing examples of both types, thus making comparison possible.

The husband's letter is more circumstantial than the lover's and a better example of the typical form taught by contemporary English *dictatores*. He begins by greeting his "treschiere et tresamee fame" as often as he knows how or is able. After expressing his desire to hear good news of her and her health, he informs her that at the time of his writing he was himself in good health. The requisite formalities completed, he gets down to business, which is to report on his activity and request that she discharge a debt "pour l'amour de moy." He asks her to greet everyone back home in his name and to behave well in his absence. The *conclusio*, in typical fashion, commends her to God and is followed by a

---

[40] Johan Vising, *Anglo-Norman Language & Literature*, p. 76.
[41] Ed. E. Stengel, "Anleitungsschriften," pp. 9–10.
[42] *De Amasio*, p. 271. Earlier dictaminal love letters in the vernacular also exist: for example, those by Brunetto Latini (in Italian) and "Simon" (in Old French). See E. Ruhe, ibid., pp. 196–203.

subscriptio that is simply an abbreviation of the form used a century before in the didactic letter discussed earlier in this chapter: "Treschiere et tresamee compaigne, Dieux vous eit en sa garde et vous doint grace de bien faire. Escript en hast etc."[43] We shall encounter the opening and closing formulas of this letter again, notably in the "Litera Troili" and in the "Litera Criseydis."

The love letter that follows in the manuscript is organized in much the same way, though the tone is naturally much different. The opening formulas should by now be familiar:

> A m'amie tres belle et chiere
> En qui est toute ma pansere.
> Saluz vous mande milles cent
> Et moy a vostre commandement,
> (pp. 9–10, lines 49–50, 1–2)

The lover praises his lady's beauty, declares his affection for her, sends greetings, and submits to her commands all within four lines. He goes on to elaborate the brief salutation of the third line by means of the *quot-tot* formula favored by Guido Faba but censured by Boncompagno (p. 10, lines 3–6).[44] He does not ask about his lady's health (nor does he mention his own), concentrating instead on the love greeting. The *narratio* (p. 10, lines 7–14), which is equal in length to the *salutatio/captatio benevolentiae*, introduces only one new idea, the lover's desire to speak with his lady (lines 13–14). He repeats his declaration of love (7–10) and reaffirms his willingness to do her bidding (11–12). A brief *petitio* (15–18) follows, in which the lover asks that his lady think of him as he thinks of her,[45] that the love between them be "loyal," and that Jesus Christ give her honor and preserve her from evil.[46] By way of a *conclusio* he states that he has no more to say and commends her to the "filz Marie." Once again the *subscriptio* – "Escript. etc." – is indicated only cursorily.

---

[43] Ed. E. Stengel, "Anleitungsschriften," p. 9, lines 45–47. Subsequent references are marked in the text by page and line numbers in parentheses.

[44] The husband also uses a shorter version of this formula in his letter: "je vous salue si souvent fois comme je say ou puis" (p. 9, lines 35–36), as does the Norfolk abbot: "Saluz certes vus mand / A(u)tant cum erbes sunt / Entre nous cressant" (P. Meyer, "Mélanges," p. 435, lines 18–20); and the Harley lyric discussed earlier. Cf. also E. Stengel, "Anleitungsschriften," p. 10, line 1, and the first line of the abbot's fourth letter (quoted above).

[45] Cf. the final four lines of the abbot's second letter (quoted above), which also express the desire to know of the woman's wishes.

[46] Cf. the "Litera Troili": *Troilus and Criseyde*, V, 1359–65; for the *conclusio* (p. 10, lines 19–20), cf. ibid., 1408–14.

34

Essentially a pastiche of conventional phrases from the earlier French *saluts d'amour* and courtly romances, this love letter is like a boiled-down version of the longer letter from the appendix to the *Chastoiement*.[47] It differs from the other verse love epistles discussed so far above all in the closeness with which it follows correct dictaminal form, and it was doubtless selected for inclusion in the formulary for that very reason. In fact, it would be tempting to regard the letter as one of those "lost" thirteenth-century Anglo-Norman *saluts d'amour* whose existence was conjectured earlier, were it not less than half as long as the shortest surviving *salut*.[48] Few fourteenth-century French verse love epistles, most of which are also *poèmes à forme fixe*, obey the rules of the *ars dictaminis* so well as this, though most have some elements of form or content in common with it.

2.9. John Gower, *Cinkante Balades*

Paradoxically, as the epistolary function became more established in French courtly love poetry, the epistolary form seems to have become progressively looser.[49] The process was doubtless affected by the vogue of the *poèmes à forme fixe* beginning in the fourteenth century: the "surface structure" of the verse form increasingly took priority over the epistolary "deep structure," without altering the epistolary function. Among the fixed forms, the ballade was especially receptive to the epistolary function, particularly with the addition of the envoy (through the influence of the fixed-form chant royal). Yet it would be an oversimplification to say that every ballade that employed formulas of greeting in the envoy was *ipso facto* intended to function as a letter. Moreover, the French lyric poets of the fourteenth and early fifteenth centuries were usually careful to distinguish the letter proper from the often quasi-epistolary ballade. In Machaut's *Voir Dit* (1363–1364), for example, the forty-six "lettres" are all in prose and thus formally distinct from the ballades and other fixed-form poems that accompany them and that are,

---

[47] For example, page 10, lines 9–10 ("Vous estez ma mort, vous estez ma vie, / En vous est toute ma druerye"), may intentionally echo the Anglo-Norman *Tristan* (1155–1170?) of Thomas. See M. Dominica Legge, *Anglo-Norman Literature*, p. 350 (she quotes the parallel lines on p. 54). The same expression occurs in Marie de France's *Eliduc* (671–72).

[48] See E. Ruhe, *De Amasio,* p. 222.

[49] On this tendency, see especially E. Ruhe, ibid., pp. 271–74, 446–48.

functionally speaking, an equally essential component of the written correspondence between Machaut and Peronnelle.[50] While Deschamps and Christine de Pisan sometimes composed letters in the form of ballades, when they wished to write a *verse* epistle they typically employed octosyllabic couplets, the verse form associated with French verse epistles since the thirteenth-century *saluts d'amour*.[51] That the undeniable affinity between ballade and letter was therefore complex and variable is well illustrated in John Gower's *Cinkante Balades,* which includes the most extensive group of love poems explicitly identified as letters that was composed in England during the last half of the fourteenth century.

The overlap between letters and ballades is to a certain extent unproblematic, since the ballade is not only a genre but also a form that is longer, more complex, more variable, but nonetheless capable of being employed in much the same fashion as, say, a rime royal stanza. In other words, although the ballade normally comprised an entire short poem, while the rime royal stanza was normally a component of a larger work, beginning in the late fourteenth century the ballade also served occasionally as an unusually elaborate "stanza." The different roles of the ballade can be seen clearly in Gower's two sequences of French ballades. In the *Traitié pour essampler les amantz marietz,* a treatise on virtuous love in marriage consisting of eighteen ballades, the ballade form functions much like an enlarged stanza: each ballade consists of three rime royal stanzas, without envoy. The single envoy, following ballade #18, is really an envoy to the treatise as a whole. The other sequence, the *Cinkante Balades,* is by contrast a collection of distinct if similar poems: all but two of the fifty-two ballades in the collection have a four-line envoy. While these ballades are still characterized by a fixed form, they evidence greater flexibility than those of the *Traitié*. Three stanzas is the norm, but along with the seven-line rime royal pattern (ababbcc), the eight-line

---

[50] Machaut, in fact, insists on the distinction when, early in the work, he defends his decision to include "nos escriptures, / ... Que l'on doit appeller epistres, / (C'est leurs drois noms & leurs drois titres,)." *Le livre du Voir-dit,* ed. Paulin Paris, p. 16. The "lettres" in Christine de Pisan's *Le livre du duc des vrais amans* are also set in prose and distinguished from the ballades that accompany them. See, e.g., *Oeuvres poétiques,* ed. Maurice Roy, SATF, vol. 22, pt. 3 (1896), p. 132: "doulces et amoureuses lettres et ballades." On the ballade, see especially Daniel Poirion, *Le Poète et le prince,* pp. 361–95.

[51] For Deschamps, see *Oeuvres complètes,* ed. Gaston Raynaud, SATF, vol. 9, pt. 7 (1891), pp. 343–47, and pt. 8 (1893), pp. 3–73; for Christine, see SATF, vol. 22, pt. 2 (1891), pp. 295–301 (her *L'Epistre au dieu d'amours* is in decasyllabic couplets).

"Monk's Tale" pattern (ababbcbc) is permitted. And one ballade (#9) has five eight-line stanzas (= chant royal).

The envoy is important not only for providing closure; it is also the only place where Gower applies descriptive labels to the poems. Such labels are found in thirty-seven of the fifty envoys:

> *balade, balade escrite:* #5, 8, 10, 13, 14, 16, 17, 29, 30, 31, 33, 36, 41, 45, 46 (= 15)
> *lettre:* #2, 3, 4, 15, 18, 20, 22, 27, 38, 39, 44 (= 11)
> *escrit, escris, escript:* #1, 2, 11, 26, 34 (= 5)
> *compleignte:* #9, 42, 43 (= 3)
> *dit:* #23, 28 (= 2)
> *supplicacion:* #24
> *chançoun:* #35

> no label: #4*, 6, 7, 12, 19, 21, 25, 37, 40, 46, 48, 49, 50 (= 13) (#32 and 51 lack envoys)

Not surprisingly, *balade* is the single most frequently used term. The less precise terms *dit* and *chançoun* reveal nothing about the specific verse form or genre. *Supplicacion* and especially *compleignte* are thematic designators frequently applied by fourteenth- and fifteenth-century poets to a broad range of poems and even to parts of poems. Although both terms could be and often were applied simultaneously with *balade* to the same poem, it is interesting that Gower chooses to keep these and all the other terms separate. Indeed, he only once employs two labels in the same envoy, when he calls #2 both a *lettre* and an *escrit*. And even this apparent exception proves the rule, since the two terms in question are virtual synonyms both in Anglo-Norman and in contemporary Middle English. Thus, the majority of the labeled poems fall into two groups – those identified as compositions in verse (*balade, dit, chançoun*) and those identified as epistles (*lettre, escrit*) – while only four out of thirty-seven are identified by theme (*compleignte, supplicacion*).

The fact that Gower never mixes terms in labeling a single poem is in itself interesting. How motivated, one wonders, were his choices among the seven different terms that he uses to describe poems that we would have little trouble assigning to one and the same genre? As far as I can determine, the themes of complaint and supplication are not unusually prominent in the poems so labeled. More significant seems to be the fact that in the supplication and in one of the complaints (#42) the label occurs in rhyming position. Also called a complaint is the only poem that exhibits the five-stanza form of the chant royal rather than the three-stanza form of the ballade: in this case the thematic designation may be motivated by the formal difference. But while complaint and supplication are the substance of most of the poems, the terms themselves are of secondary rank in Gower's classifying scheme. Clearly the principal choice was between calling a poem a ballade or an epistle, and we stand to learn much about Gower's understanding of genre if we can discover the rationale behind that choice or, at the very least, the relationship between the two categories.

Are the fifteen *lettres* and *ecrits* more "epistolary" than the rest of the *Cinkante Balades?* This is a more precise question than "Is there more complaining in the *compleigntes?*," because the medieval epistle is a well-defined genre in its own right, with a distinctive structure and vocabulary. Its classic five-part form, as set down in the textbooks of the *ars dictaminis,* has been described in chapter 1, where it was also pointed out that, in actual practice, there was considerable variety. What remained most stable, what defined epistolary form at the deepest level was the greeting and, to a lesser extent, the farewell. Underscoring the primacy of these two parts was the clustering of the most formulaic language in just those positions. Lexically and even syntactically, letters varied least at beginning and end.

The formal prominence of the greeting is particularly evident in verse letters, where poetic conventions often displace those epistolary conventions that are least essential. This prominence is explicitly recognized, for example, in the names that earlier vernacular poets most commonly used to designate verse love epistles: the twelfth-century Provençal *salutz* and its descendant, the thirteenth-century northern French *salut d'amour.* For the practice of the later poets writing in fixed forms, Deschamps is again instructive. The ballades that he chooses to call letters differ from his other ballades in little other than their marked tendency to begin with a formal greeting, often complete with epistolary set phrases.[52]

However, Gower's ballade-letters are less conventional than those of Deschamps in this crucial feature. Of the fifteen ballades that are explicitly identified as letters, only one begins with a true *salutatio. Cinkante Balades,* #26, is in fact a near-perfect match of ballade form with the classic epistolary structure of the *ars dictaminis:*[53]

---

[52] See, e.g., SATF, vol. 9, pt. 4 (1884), pp. 351–52; pt. 6 (1889), pp. 13–14; and pt. 7 (1891), pp. 15–16, 122–25. For the same technique in Christine de Pisan's poems, see especially the series of New Year's greetings in ballade form, addressed to noble patrons: SATF, vol. 22, pt. 1 (1886), pp. 225–33, 248–49.

[53] Ed. G. C. Macaulay, *Complete Works,* vol. 1 (1899), p. 359. Subsequent references to Gower's works are to this edition and are marked in the text by abbreviated title,

Salutz honour et toute reverence,	*salutatio*
Com cil d'amour q'est tout vostre soubgit,	*captatio*
Ma dame, a vous et a vostre excellence	*bene-*
Envoie, s'il vous plest, d'umble espirit,	*volentiae*
Pour fare a vous plesance, honour, profit:	
De tout mon coer entier jeo le desire,	
Selonc le corps combien qe j'ai petit,	
Sanz autre doun le coer doit bien suffire.	

Qui donne soi, c'est une experience	*(exordium)*
Qe l'autre bien ne serront escondit:	
Si plein com dieus m'ad de sa providence	*narratio*
Fait et formé, si plein sanz contredit	
Soul apres lui, ma dame, en fait et dit	
Vous donne; et si Rois fuisse d'un Empire,	
Tout est a vous: mais en amour perfit	
Sanz autre doun le coer doit bien suffire.	

Primer quant vi l'estat de vo presence,	
En vous mirer me vint si grant delit,	
Q'unqes depuiss d'ascune negligence	
Mon coer pensant vostre bealté n'oublit:	
Par quoi toutdis me croist celle appetit	*petitio*
De vous amer, plus qe ne porrai dire;	
Et pour descrire amour en son droit plit,	
Sanz autre doun le coer doit bien suffire.	

A vous, ma dame, envoie ceste escript,	*conclusio*
Ne sai si vo danger le voet despire;	
Mais si reson soit en ce cas eslit,	
Sanz autre doun le coer doit bien suffire.	

As is so often the case, it is difficult to draw a sharp line between the salutation proper and the securing of goodwill, but together the formalities of address take up the entire first stanza. The epistolary nature of the greeting is signaled not only by the key first word but also by the lover's explicit reference, in line 4, to his "sending" the lady his wishes for her "Salutz honour et toute reverence," together with the gift of his heart. The first two lines of the second stanza form a kind of *exordium*, stating a general truth – that he who gives himself will not refuse to give anything

---

section or item and line numbers in parentheses. In drawing attention to the "logical and argumentative" wording of this poem, Lynn W. Hagman reveals an unconscious awareness of its precise rhetorical structure: "Study of *Cinkante Balades*," p. 66. Ruhe maintains (*De Amasio,* p. 272) that the ballades of, e.g., Gower and Deschamps were probably not perceived as letters merely because they are in direct address, but only when they are explicitly so called and provided with formulas of greeting and other epistolary features.

else – as an introduction to the substance of the letter, the lover's declaration that all of him, and especially his heart, belongs entirely to his lady. Although the second half of the third stanza is more a summation than a request, it is formally set off with the "Par quoi" that is among the most common formulas for beginning epistolary *petitiones*. More problematic is the equation of the envoy with the epistolary *conclusio*, first, because the envoy is an all but obligatory constituent of the ballades in this collection, and, second, because this envoy contains none of the formulas of farewell that characterize most epistolary *conclusiones*. The nearest thing to a *conclusio*-formula is the reference to sending a written document, in the first line of the envoy, but similar statements occur in several of the ballades that are not called letters.

Although none of the other fourteen ballade-letters opens with a genuine *salutatio*, many do open in one of the ways recommended for the second part of a letter – for example, with a simile, often drawn from popular or learned lore.[54] For example, in *Cinkante Balades, #15*, the lover compares his affection to a tethered sparrowhawk, or, in #18, he contrasts his futile prayers with the drops of water that eventually pierce even the hardest stone,[55] or, in #38, he compares the power of his lady's "douls regard plesant" over him to the natural attraction "Diamand" exercises on iron. Unfortunately, this type of opening is not peculiar to the ballades identified as "letters"; indeed, it predominates in the *Cinkante Balades* by a ratio of more than 3:2.[56] The same problem arises in those poems that might be said to begin with a *captatio benevolentiae*, compounded by the fact that praise of the lover, the most popular means of securing goodwill, is also a favorite theme for an entire poem.

If the sorts of beginnings that are usually the surest indicator of epistolary form do not distinguish Gower's ballade-letters, it is reasonable to expect the ending to carry more of that burden. But the fact that

---

[54] Already in the late twelfth century, the *dictator* Bernard de Meung had introduced this technique, beginning each model letter in his collection with a *prouerbium*, and Gower's contemporary Thomas Merke recommended the use of a *prouerbium*, an *auctoritas*, or an *exemplum* at the head of a letter in his *Formula moderni et usitati dictaminis*, composed at Oxford around 1390. However, since the same techniques are recommended for beginning poems in the *artes versificandi* of teachers such as Geoffrey of Vinsauf, their use does not automatically distinguish letters from other types of text.

[55] He calls this an "essample" (line 3).

[56] Only *CB*, #3–4*, 6, 9–11, 14, 23–25, 28–29, 31, 33, 39, and 44 (i.e., 17 of 50 – *CB*, #1, lacks the opening stanzas) do not make use of a simile, proverbial expression, or literary convention such as the *reverdie* at the beginning, and even a number of these begin with a general reflection.

Gower's envoys do have much the same summarizing and missive force as the epistolary *conclusio* does not in itself indicate an attempt to imitate epistolary form, unless one is willing to argue that all ballades with envoys are epistles. More suggestive is the occasional displacement into the envoy of something like the missing *salutatio*. In *Cinkante Balades, #4*, for example, the lover omits any greeting and starts off with a *captatio benevolentiae,* an assertion of his complete devotion. However, the envoy fills equally well the roles of *salutatio* and *conclusio:*

> Au flour des flours, u toute ma creance
> D'amour remaint sanz nulle departie,
> Ceo lettre envoie, et croi me sanz doubtance,
> Vostre amant sui et vous serretz m'amie.   (22–25)

More emphatic still is #39, where the lover sends his lady "Mil et Mil et Mil et Mil salutz" (27) in the envoy. But these are isolated, if significant, exceptions; the great majority of the envoys to the ballade-letters are distinctive only in employing the terms *lettre* and *escrit.*

Thus, while the example of *Cinkante Balades, #26*, clearly demonstrates both Gower's familiarity with classic epistolary form and the compatibility of that form with ballade form, there is only sporadic and inconclusive evidence that Gower sought to distinguish the ballades that he identified as letters from those that he did not. If he could call #18 a "lettre," even though it does not even employ direct address, much less any epistolary conventions, then he could have called all the poems in the collection letters. But while it is to some degree arbitrary which ballades Gower chose to call letters, his decision to call so many of them letters was not unmotivated. Rather, in the *Cinkante Balades* Gower seems to have assigned letters the status of genre not at the level of form but at the level of function. In other words, the ballades are envisioned as being sent and read rather than, say, being sung and heard, and the use of terms such as *lettre, escrit,* and even, in #10, *balade escrite* is one of the ways in which this function is indicated.

Other indications of epistolary function are not difficult to find and are equally common in poems called letters, ballades, or something else. For example, there are frequent references to the act of *writing* and especially in the envoy, to the act of *sending* what one has written to one's lover. The poem's status as a *physical object* is emphasized, for example by associating it with a gift or by addressing it as a messenger. In #28, which Gower calls a *dit,* the lover complains that his lady doesn't send him "un soul salutz" (4) or "un mot" (13) and asks her to keep his poem as a reminder of him and to send him poems of hers. Many of the *Cinkante Balades* take as their central theme the physical separation that makes it impossible for the lover to communicate in any way other than by writing (e.g., *CB,* #6–9, 29). Usually the separation of the lovers is simply a given, but in #25 the "mesdisantz" are blamed for keeping the lover from his lady, forcing him to send his heart in his place.

Through such themes, together with the epistolary labels and the occasional epistolary formulas discussed earlier, Gower consistently foregrounds the epistolary function of his *Cinkante Balades*. But only once, in #26, does he allow epistolary function to merge with epistolary form. Certainly his choice of the ballade form rather than the more "open" octosyllabic couplets of the *salut d'amour* must have influenced his approach to writing verse love epistles: the strict limitations of space leave little room for developing the central theme, if one must also accommodate the formal greeting and conclusion; and the formulaic beginnings and endings of medieval epistles would have made monotonous reading if observed strictly in a collection of relatively short poems. The calculated balance between the "musique naturelle" of the ballade and the insistent textuality of the letter is essential to the particular pleasure that the *Cinkante Balades* have to offer. Although Gower was perhaps only intermittently concerned with the formal principles of epistolography, he clearly had a strong sense of the love letter as a literary category. In fact his ballades differ most from those of his French contemporaries precisely in their insistence on calling themselves *letters.*

The themes and motifs of the *Cinkante Balades* are those that typify medieval literature of *fin amour*, epistolary or not[57] – the lady's beauty, both physical and spiritual; the sufferings of the lover and the lady's indifference to them; the fear of "mesdisauntz" with their "fals jangle" (*CB*, #25); the desire to serve faithfully so noble a lady, coupled with the fear that she will think him unworthy of so high an honor; to name but a few. The conventional motif of sending the heart to the lady is especially suited to the love letter and is very popular with Gower (*CB*, #25, 26, 33, 44). Somewhat atypical is Gower's interest in married love, a topic rarely treated explicitly in the context of "courtly" literature.[58] He marks off the

---

[57] See L. W. Hagman, "Study of *Cinkante Balades*," chapter III.

[58] See William G. Dodd, *Courtly Love*, pp. 89–90; John H. Fisher, *John Gower*, pp. 81–82; and J. A. W. Bennett, "Gower's 'Honeste Love,'" pp. 107–21. Douglas Kelly observes that the language of courtly love was the only one available to medieval poets who wished to describe "good love," whether marital or extramarital. *Medieval Imagination*, pp. 192–93, and 234–35.

first six ballades as a kind of "marriage group" with a gloss to *CB*, #5 (4 is repeated in the numbering): "Les balades d'amont jesqes enci sont fait especialement pour ceaux q'attendont lours amours par droite mariage." He returns to the subject of proper love – i.e., that which accords with reason – at the end of the sequence (*CB*, #48–50) and concludes with a ballade renouncing the service of all other ladies in favor of the Virgin Mary. Gower's only other ballade sequence, be it remembered, is the *Traitié pour essampler les amantz marietz*. Less unusual but also noteworthy is his concern with allowing the woman to present her viewpoint. Five of the ballades (#41–44, 46) are written in a female persona.

Though not all critics agree on the literary merits of the ballades,[59] most agree that their function was the one announced by Gower himself in the dedication to Henry IV: "Por desporter vo noble Court roia(l) / Jeo frai balade" (p. 337). Even if, as many scholars believe,[60] most of the poems date from Gower's youth rather than from the end of his life when he dedicated them to the new king, it is nonetheless clear that they were written solely as literary exercises and not as autobiographical testimonies. Gower's goal was not accuracy in depicting the psychology of love (except insofar as it had already been systematized in the poetic practice of his predecessors) but rather elegance in expressing a set of conventional themes within the limits of a highly artificial verse form.

---

[59] The harshest judgment is Albert B. Friedman's:

Gower's two balade sequences in French, the *Cinkante Balades* and the *Traitié pour Essempler les Amants Marietz,* are dilute in thought and strained in execution – the work of a foreigner, or perhaps better, provincial, attempting a complicated verse pattern in a language whose resources are not readily at hand. He reaches for rimes with noticeable effort; the dynamics of the French *balade*, particularly the graceful pivoting on the central couplet in the seven-line (ababbcc) and eight-line (ababbcbc) stanzas, elude him. His *balades* show, however, that the French fashion was at least appreciated in England, if only indifferently practised. It remains for Chaucer to introduce the *genre* into English with his 'sovereyn ballades' modelled on those of his admirer Deschamps.

"Late Mediaeval Ballade," p. 98. His objections are ably fielded by J. H. Fisher, *John Gower*, p. 344. The opposite extreme is represented by M. D. Legge, *Anglo-Norman Literature*, pp. 358–60. G. C. Macaulay comes close to expressing the consensus view when he says that

There is indeed a grace and poetical feeling in some of them which makes them probably the best things of the kind that have been produced by English writers of French, and as good as anything of the kind which had up to that time been written in English.   (p. lxxv)

See L. W. Hagman, "Study of *Cinkante Balades*," pp. 34ff, for a survey of the *Cinkante Balades*' critical reputation.

[60] Macaulay and a few others consider them late work. See L. W. Hagman, "Study of *Cinkante Balades*," p. 43.

Gower's ballades, along with the condensed *"salut d'amour"* from MS Harley 3988, comprise the entire corpus of Anglo-Norman verse love epistles. By the last quarter of the fourteenth century, French was already being challenged by English as a written medium and by the end of Henry V's reign had been abandoned even by trained clerks.[61] Driven by forces as diverse as the "linguistic nationalism" aroused by the Hundred Years' War and the "vernacular consciousness" of an increasingly literate and increasingly powerful lay middle class, the shift manifested itself most clearly in widespread use of English in letter writing, beginning around 1420.[62] The tremendous popularity of the Middle English verse love epistles, which begins to be noticeable at about the same time, was doubtless fueled in part by this fairly sudden and thus all the more self-conscious interest in English letters among all levels of literate Englishmen. Whether Gower's Anglo-Norman ballades founded the genre in England is thus difficult to determine, not only because fixed forms such as the ballade never took strong hold in England but also because Gower's "successors" must be sought among poets writing in English at a time when most Englishmen were deliberately turning away from the language in which he wrote.[63]

Gower's fondness for the love letter is not matched in the shorter love poems attributed to his friend Chaucer, who was the first to write ballades in English. None of Chaucer's love lyrics call themselves letters, though *To Rosemounde* and *Womanly Noblesse* meet at least the minimal requirements of direct address to the lady.[64] A better case can be made for the "epistolary" character of the more conventional *Womanly Noblesse*, but on very slight evidence indeed: the lover's talk of "remembrance" (1, 31) and "souvenaunce" (13) underscores his separation from his lady, that most characteristic theme of love letters, and his "envoye" proceeds from complimentary greeting, to apology (for his poor writing?), to what could be interpreted as a reference to his sending the poem to the lady:

---

[61] See especially Rolf Berndt, "Final Decline of French," pp. 341–69. On the relationship of French to English (and Latin) during the period preceding the fourteenth century, see Michael T. Clanchy, *Memory to Written Record*, pp. 151–74.

[62] See Malcolm Richardson, *"Dictamen* and Its Influence," pp. 207–26 (especially pp. 208–19), and Charles L. Kingsford, "English Letters," pp. 22–47. On the few personal letters in English surviving from the period before 1420, see John Taylor, "Letters and Letter Collections," pp. 66–69.

[63] On the relatively small influence of romance literature on the Middle English lyric, see, e.g., H. Bergner, "Frage der Gattungen," pp. 47–52.

[64] The similarities between the two poems may not be coincidental. See Jörg O. Fichte, *"Womanly Noblesse* and *To Rosemound,"* pp. 181–94.

44

Auctour of norture, lady of plesaunce,
Soveraigne of beautee, floure of wommanhede,
Take ye non hede unto myn ignoraunce,
But this receyveth of your goodlihede,
Thynkyng that I have caught in remembraunce,
Your beaute hole, your stidefast governaunce.   (lines 27–32)[65]

Three of the questionable attributions included in the third Riverside edition of Chaucer's works are fixed-form love poems in direct address (*Against Women Unconstant*, *Merciles Beaute*, and *A Balade of Complaint*), none of which shows evidence of epistolary intent. Though the other poem in this group (*Complaynt d'Amours*) calls itself a "compleynte" (68, 85, 88) and a "song" (88) and alternates between referring to the lady in the third person (1–7, 33–63, 85–91) and addressing her directly (8–32, 64–84), it does include a request that the lady "wolde ones rede" the poem (67) and is dated "on Seint Valentynes day" (85), already in late fourteenth-century England one of the most suitable occasions for sending verse love epistles.[66] But none of these love poems, it must be admitted, has as good a claim to the title "verse epistle" as *Lenvoy de Chaucer a Scogan*. The next chapter will show that Chaucer was quite familiar with the form, function, and even the classical prototypes of the verse love epistle. But unless fate has simply deprived us of his contributions to the genre, he apparently did not embrace the form with the same enthusiasm as the next generation of English versifiers.

2.10. *De amico ad amicam* and *Responcio*

This chronicle of the genre's prehistory concludes with a pair of verse love epistles (*Index* 16, 19) that are rare on at least three counts: they are macaronic, they form a paired letter and response, and they are preserved in more than one manuscript. They may also be somewhat later in date than the other poems discussed in this chapter,[67] with which they nonetheless belong generically if not chronologically. Their mixture of Latin, French, and English and their careful observance of epistolary form may

---

[65] Ed. Larry T. Benson et al., *Riverside Chaucer,* p. 650. All subsequent citations of Chaucer's works are from this edition and are identified by line numbers in the text.
[66] Cf. Gower, *CB,* #34 (which calls itself an "escript") and 35.
[67] R. T. Davies places them in the early fifteenth century: *Medieval English Lyrics,* #70; but R. H. Robbins, "Satiric Love Epistles," p. 420, thinks that they may have been written as early as the late fourteenth century.

indicate a more or less conscious phase of transition between an established (Anglo-Norman) French tradition and an emerging English tradition.[68] The combination of unusual features, together with the poet's deft handling of a difficult verse form, may have earned the poems a wider than usual audience, as is perhaps suggested by the fact that they are preserved in two manuscripts.[69]

Like their counterparts in dictaminal collections, the two letters are paired to form a brief dialogue. The resemblance is further strengthened by their Latin titles in the colophon, "De amico ad amicam" and "Responcio." Although they treat only the conventional themes of the amatory complaint and that in a general fashion, they manage to do so with skill and grace, especially given the constraints imposed by the use of three languages and the epistolary form.[70] The man's letter in particular masters the verse form while scrupulously observing epistolary decorum. Its first stanza illustrates the poet's skillful adaptation of the *salutatio* to fit his chosen metre:

> A Celuy que pluys eyme en mounde,
> Of alle tho that I have found,
> > *Carissima*
> Saluz od treyé amour,
> With grace and joye and alle honour,
> > *Dulcissima.*

The lover's subsequent statement that he is in good health, for which he thanks God, is also a regular feature of fifteenth-century letters. Not before the third stanza does he come to tell the pains that he suffers for love. Each of the next five stanzas of the *narratio* alternates between

---

[68] The only other macaronic love letter to survive (*Index* 724) is shorter (36 lines), simpler (French alternating with English), and probably later than these: it occurs in a manuscript of the second half of the fifteenth century (MS Douce 95, fol. 68), in which two more verse love epistles are also preserved. Although paired love letters are quite common on the continent and are virtually the rule in the model letter collections of the *dictatores* (in prose, of course), there is likewise only one other English example, also in a manuscript from the second half of the fifteenth century (*Index* 3832, 2437: MS Rawlinson poet. 36, fols. 3v–5r).

[69] Cambridge University Library, MS Gg.4.27, fols. 10v-11r (first half, fifteenth century) and BL, MS Harley 3362, fols. 90v–91r. Ed. E. K. Chambers and F. Sidgwick, *Early English Lyrics*, pp. 15–19 (#VIII and IX). See also Leo Spitzer, "Emendations," pp. 150–55. On the infrequency of Middle English lyrics in multiple copies, see J. Boffey, *Manuscripts of Lyrics*, pp. 88–89.

[70] Spitzer, "Emendations," pp. 151–52 n. 1, goes so far as to argue that each of the poem's three languages has its "specific climate" – "conventional courtesy" (French), "genuine feeling" (English), and "epigrammatic terseness" (Latin) – and that the three levels are carefully and deliberately sequenced to produce the right effect. Carol J. Harvey rejects this theory, in "Macaronic Techniques," pp. 78–80.

46

expressions of suffering and of request or praise. The strongly binary character of this particular stanzaic form encourages such complementarity, the clearest manifestation of which is the following:

> Saches bien par verité
> Yif I deye I clepe to thee
> > *Causantem*;
> Et par ceo jeo vous treser
> Love me well withouten daunger
> > *Amantem.*   (25–30)

Next comes a stanza of praise (43–48) and then two stanzas of request concealed by the conditional. The *petitio* proper is organized exactly as the stanza quoted above. It stands out only by virtue of the line that introduces the second element or the actual request – "Et pur ceo jeo vous pry" (64), which is the equivalent of the signal words like "Ergo" or "Igitur" recommended by the *dictatores*. The same structure is repeated at the beginning of the final stanza, leaving only the last two lines for the *conclusio*: "O à Dieu que vous gard! / *Valete*." (71–72). The requests themselves – that the lady retain him in her thoughts and that she take his words to heart – are the usual ones.

The woman's reply resembles the man's letter in all respects save length (nine stanzas as opposed to twelve). She too greets him and promises to tell him of her "stat." Her letter echoes the complaint and the concern with fidelity that were the central themes of her lover's letter but dwells more on the desire to be reunited – a topic that gets explicit mention only once in his letter (35–39). She begins the *narratio* by promising to come when she may (10–15) and, after recalling her sufferings on his account (to be allayed only if he loves her "sikerlie") and reaffirming her own affection for him, later returns to the subject emphatically with "Wolde God in youre armes I were / *Sepulta*!" (35–36). The remainder is closer in sense than in form to the end of the first letter. There is nothing that corresponds, on the formal level, to the man's *conclusio*. Rather she concludes with three stanzas in which a declarative statement is coupled with a request. The first of the three illustrates the principle (and echoes the wording of the man's final stanza):

> Jeo a vous pleyne grevousement
> That thine love hath me schent
> > *Amando.*
> De moy, jeo pry, avez peté;
> Turneth your herte and loveth me
> > *Letando.*   (37–42)

She also asks him to tell her whether she may trust him and to take her words to heart (cf. lines 67–70 of his letter). The opening line of the last stanza, "Vous estes ma morte et ma vye" (49), echoing a phrase that originated in the Anglo-Norman *Tristan,* strengthens the impression that these poems represent as much the end of one tradition as the beginning of another.[71]

---

[71] Cf. n. 47 above.

CHAPTER 3

Chaucer's *Heroides*

3.1. Chaucer and Ovid's *Heroides*

In his shorter love poems Chaucer consistently thinks in terms of the complaint rather than the epistle. Though the complaint iself may derive historically from Ovid's epistolary elegies, though the *complainte d'amour* and the epistolary *salut d'amour* were very closely intertwined, and though the "complaints" of Chaucer's French contemporaries sometimes took the form of love epistles,[1] Chaucer's complaints are no more epistolary than most poems in direct address. Like his French contemporaries, when Chaucer thought of lyric *form,* he thought of fixed verse forms such as the ballade and the rondeau (see "The Franklin's Tale," 946–48). Nonetheless, he was very much aware of epistolary form and of the role that love letters played in the ritual "game" of courtly love. His treatment of both in *Troilus and Criseyde* would in fact proye to be the decisive stimulus to the emergence of the verse love epistle as a lyric genre.

The "Litera Troili" (*T&C,* V, 1317–1421) is the direct model for the poems to be discussed in the next chapter, poems that established the "classic" form of the English love epistle that was to endure for more than a century. But in two ways Troilus' letter of complaint resembles Candace's letter in *Kyng Alisaunder* rather than the elegant epistles associated with Charles of Orléans. In the first place, it is part of a larger narrative, and has a different effect when it is considered apart from that larger context. However, the "Litera Troili" is less firmly "embedded" than Candace's letter or even the "Litera Criseydis" (*T&C,* V, 1590–1631), either of which becomes incomprehensible when detached from the larger narrative. The "Litera Troili," by contrast, was rich enough in

---

[1] See Nancy Dean, "Chaucer's *Complaint,*" pp. 1–27, and E. Ruhe, *De Amasio,* pp. 222–31. Ruhe goes on to observe that the *salut* and *complainte* blend into a single form during the fourteenth century (pp. 274–75), a tendency already visible in the mixed form, which he calls *salut–complainte,* that occurs during the late thirteenth century (cf. pp. 229–31).

conventional expressions to permit imitators to ignore the "irrelevant" circumstantial details.

A second point of resemblance is the identity of the sender and recipient: like Candace and Alexander, Troilus and Criseyde are famous lovers from pagan antiquity, whereas the verse love epistles of the fifteenth and sixteenth centuries are addressed by contemporary ladies and gentlemen to each other. But again the contrast with *Kyng Alisaunder* is more important. Despite the pagan setting and despite the narrator's protests to the contrary (*T&C*, II, 22–48), Troilus and Criseyde speak and act in ways that are thoroughly familiar to Chaucer's audience, while Candace and Alexander derive much of their appeal from their association with the exotic. Furthermore, Candace's letter and the ensuing affair with Alexander are mere detours from the high road of action and adventure, whereas the love between Troilus and Criseyde is the real subject of Chaucer's poem, and the "Litera Troili" is an important expression of the courtly ethos that shapes it.[2] The last words that each lover addresses to the other, or at least the last ones that the narrator records, the "Litera Troili" and "Litera Criseydis" also acquire a dramatic prominence unequaled even in Chaucer's immediate source.

An epistle of complaint addressed by a famous lover of antiquity to the loved one whose absence has caused a crisis and sent at the moment of maximum dramatic tension, the "Litera Troili" shares many distinctive features with Ovid's *Heroides,* the main classical precedent for the verse love epistle. In the light of Chaucer's extensive use of the *Heroides* in *The Legend of Good Women* (ca. 1387), a work "motivated" by *Troilus and Criseyde,* it would not be surprising to discover that Ovid's heroic epistles were in some way the model for his own.[3] Pandarus' reference to Oënone's letter to Paris (*Her.*, v; *T&C*, II, 652–65), not long before he instructs Troilus in the techniques of love–letter writing, seems to suggest as much. However, Chaucer's direct borrowings from the *Heroides* in *The Legend of Good Women*, like Gower's in the related and roughly

---

[2] See, e.g., Winthrop Wetherbee, *Chaucer and the Poets*, pp. 176–78.

[3] John Norton–Smith briefly discusses the possible connection in "Chaucer's Epistolary Style," pp. 157–60. Norton–Smith notes the lack of epistolary features in the *Heroides,* comparing them to the letters in *T&C,* V, which he finds stylistically indistinct from amatory complaints except for their use of epistolary formulas at beginning and end. He also perceives a close resemblance between Chaucer's epistolary style and that of certain *ballade–lettres* by Deschamps. His argument is not very detailed, however, as his main goal is to demonstrate the Horatian quality of *Lenvoy de Chaucer a Scogan* and *Lenvoy de Chaucer a Bukton.*

contemporary *Confessio Amantis*,[4] are limited to extracts, usually translations of passages that contain striking language or images.[5] Epistolary
form is ignored in both works: in no case does the excerpted material
comprise a complete and unified letter.[6] Rather, the primary interest is in
the "historial" matter to be gleaned from Ovid's heroic epistles.[7] Like the
allusions to *Heroides*, vii (Dido to Aeneas) in the *House of Fame* (376–
82) and *Anelida and Arcite* (346–48), the more extensive borrowings in
The Legend of Good Women are relevant to this study chiefly as evidence
that Chaucer could have had Ovid's verse epistles in mind as he reworked
Boccaccio's text.

Chaucer's direct borrowings from the *Heroides* in *The Legend of
Good Women* were far less important for the subsequent history of the
verse love epistle in England than were the earlier, indirectly Ovidian
love letters in *Troilus and Criseyde*. The "Litera Troili," in particular,
synthesizes the Ovidian, the courtly, and the dictaminal and thus prepares
the way for the genre that flourished in the following century.[8] Boccaccio's original is, by contrast, more uniformly Ovidian in tone. The general
pattern that Chaucer established in adapting the material from the *Filostrato* was to govern most subsequent productions of the type. His initial
achievement was the more remarkable in that it was never equaled by any

---

[4] According to Fisher, the first version of the *Confessio Amantis* was probably completed between 1390 and 1392, though portions date from as early as 1385: *John Gower,*
pp. 116–27.

[5] The relationship between the *Heroides* and *The Legend of Good Women* has been
studied by Edgar Finley Shannon, *Chaucer and Roman Poets*, pp. 169–301; Sanford
B. Meech, "Chaucer and *Heroides*," pp. 110–28; Eleanor Winsor Leach, "Sources
and Rhetoric"; John M. Fyler, *Chaucer and Ovid*, pp. 99–115; and Lisa J. Kiser,
Telling Classical Tales, especially pp. 120–46. See G. C. Macaulay's notes (pp.
461ff) and M. Bech, "Quellen und Plan," pp. 313–82, for Gower's borrowings from
the *Heroides*.

[6] Chaucer once even cuts his translation short in the middle of a thought (*LGW*, 2254;
Her., ii, 137). However, later readers of *LGW* sometimes singled out the epistolary
passages. See J. Boffey, *Manuscripts of Lyrics*, p. 57.

[7] Beginning in the third quarter of the fifteenth century, the *Heroides* became extremely popular in France, and were often translated and imitated. Before this time
they were influential only as sources of mythological information, and were generally translated and/or excerpted within much larger compilations. See E. Ruhe, *De
Amasio*, pp. 286–88, and H. Dörrie, *Der heroische Brief*, pp. 340ff (esp. 355–57).
Ruhe attempts to explain the obstacles to the *Heroides'* reception in the Middle Ages
on pp. 48–50 and 59–60.

[8] J. Norton–Smith, "Chaucer's Epistolary Style," p. 159: "Chaucer's polite, graceful
and conventional style in these letters sets the tone for the vast number of amatory
verse epistles which was to be written in England in the fifteenth century." Cf. Arthur
K. Moore, "Middle English Verse Epistles," pp. 86 and 87.

of its many imitators: the highpoint of the English tradition is also its point of origin.

To what extent was Chaucer aware of the verse love epistle as a genre? The answer to this question is complicated in interesting ways by two obvious but important facts about the letters in *Troilus and Criseyde.* First, Chaucer worked from a source, chiefly Boccaccio's *Filostrato,*[9] supplemented by other texts.[10] Second, as in its source, the letters in *Troilus and Criseyde* are embedded in a larger narrative and, though capable of being appreciated as autonomous lyric passages,[11] have a distinct function within that narrative context. The fact that Chaucer's poem is a translation and an adaptation of a known original turns out to be more an advantage than not, since the changes that Chaucer made both in general conception and in specific details are perhaps the single most valuable index of his intentions.[12] One such change is the fuller integration of the first set of letters into the surrounding context. Like the excerpts from the *Heroides* in *The Legend of Good Women,* the letters in Book II of *Troilus and Criseyde* derive their importance from the larger narrative to which they belong: they do not even speak for themselves, as do their models in the *Filostrato,* but are paraphrased by the narrator. Though the two letters in Book V are far more self–contained than those in Book II or any of the "letters" in *The Legend of Good Women,* nonetheless the "Litera Criseydis," in particular, is not fully comprehensible without an awareness of what lies behind it. But Chaucer handles his source differently in *Troilus and Criseyde* than in *The Legend of Good Women.* Though he always alters the epistolary passages from the *Filo-*

---

[9] See William Michael Rossetti, *Chaucer's Troylus and Cryseyde*; Hubertis M. Cummings, *Indebtedness*, pp. 50–122; and especially B. A. Windeatt, ed., *Troilus and Criseyde*. Although Cummings claims that it is impossible to overestimate Chaucer's debt to Boccaccio (p. 50), he has obviously done so. For the opposite extreme, see W. F. Schirmer, "Boccaccios Werke," pp. 288–305.

[10] In "Chaucer and *Le roman de Troyle et de Criseida*," pp. 509–39, Robert A. Pratt maintained that Chaucer also used Beauvau's French translation of Boccaccio; but this has since been shown to be chronologically impossible. See B. A. Windeatt, *Troilus and Criseyde*, pp. 19–24, and David Wallace, *Chaucer and Boccaccio*, pp. 106–7. Also irrelevant to the present study are minor sources such as Guido de Columnis and Benoît de Sainte–Maure.

[11] On the relationship between the lyric and the narrative aspects of *Troilus and Criseyde*, see James I. Wimsatt, "Lyric Element," pp. 18–32.

[12] See especially C. S. Lewis, "What Chaucer Really Did," pp. 27–44; Sanford B. Meech, *Design*; Ian C. Walker, "Chaucer and *Il Filostrato*," pp. 318–26; and D. Wallace, *Chaucer and Boccaccio*, pp. 73–140. Thomas A. Kirby also compares *Troilus and Criseyde* with the *Filostrato*, but makes no judgments of his own, in *Chaucer's 'Troilus'*.

strato, and though his innovations generally draw those passages more tightly into the narrative, at the same time they frequently have the effect of underscoring either epistolary form or epistolary function. Thus, Chaucer seems to have exploited the generic potential of the epistle (and possibly even the verse love epistle) without making that genre his principal concern. Chaucer probably did not intend to create a model for a "new" lyric genre: for him, the love epistle was a discrete but integral component of a larger design – a means rather than an end.

3.2. Epistolary Function:
The Letters of *Troilus and Criseyde*, Book II

In both the *Filostrato* and *Troilus and Criseyde* there are two separate series of correspondence between the lovers – one in the early stages of the love affair and one when it is already doomed. Both poets further agree in presenting a single, representative pair of letters from each series, while merely indicating that there were others (*T&C,* II, 1342–44, 1350: *Fil.,* ii, 131; *T&C,* V, 1583–86: *Fil.,* viii, 3). However, while Boccaccio quotes the entire text of Troiolo's first letter to Criseida (*Fil.,* ii, 96–106), as well as that of her reply (121–27), Chaucer summarizes both letters in indirect discourse, drastically reducing their length in the process (*T&C,* II, 1065–84; 121–25).[13] In treating the second exchange of letters, which begins after Criseyde has been among the Greeks for two months, Chaucer both follows his source more closely and departs from it more radically than he had in the previous instance. He preserves Troiolo's elaborate epistolary complaint, though he reduces its length by nearly half (*T&C,* V, 1317–1421; *Fil.,* vii, 52–75); but whereas Boccaccio only alludes briefly to Criseida's reply (*Fil.,* vii, 105), Chaucer expands this hint into a full–scale letter (*T&C,* V, 1590–1631).

Chaucer's alterations in both cases correspond to the general difference in conception between *Troilus and Criseyde* and *Il Filostrato*. To see how this is true, it will be necessary to look closely at each text in turn while simultaneously keeping in mind the broader context of the work as a whole. The advantages of this approach become immediately obvious when the first exchange of letters is considered. By reducing Troiolo's lengthy, elegantly conventional courtship letter to a rather prosaic para-

---

[13] Troilus' letter is reduced from eighty–eight lines to twenty, Criseyde's from fifty–six lines to five.

phrase, Chaucer transforms the effect of the episode in at least two ways: (1) the role of Pandarus is enhanced and that of Troilus diminished; and (2) the pace of the action is stepped up.

If there is a single book of *Troilus and Criseyde* in which Pandarus occupies center stage, it is the second. He is constantly before our eyes as he hurries back and forth between Troilus and Criseyde, personally fostering their budding affair. From his first embassy to Criseyde to his final success in bringing the two together, it is he alone who provides the impetus. Without him Troilus probably would never have progressed beyond the lovesick paralysis into which his first vision of Criseyde had cast him. Though the general outline of Pandarus' role is the same in the *Filostrato,* Chaucer makes a number of changes that give him even greater prominence.[14] The scene in which Pandarus advises Troilus to put his feelings in writing illustrates the pattern perfectly. Where Pandaro acts in response to Troiolo's immediate desires, Pandarus, once set in motion, provides the initiative that carries Troilus forward in spite of himself. Troiolo is impetuous where Troilus is timorous. After Pandaro returns from his first visit to Criseida and tells Troiolo of his success, Troiolo immediately rushes to Criseida's house to verify the news with his own eyes (*Fil.,* ii, 81–82).[15] All Troiolo's talk is then of how the fires of his desire have been intensified (86–89) and how he would give anything to satisfy them. Pandaro sympathizes and suggests that Troiolo write a letter, which he will then deliver to Criseida, along with his own pleas in his friend's behalf (90–92). Troiolo expresses some misgivings (93), but Pandaro quickly lays them to rest (94), and Troiolo retires to his chamber to write (95).

Although the account of the events leading up to the letter writing occupies approximately the same amount of space in *Troilus and Criseyde* (126 lines) as in *Il Filostrato* (136 lines), Chaucer both adds to and deletes material from his source. Gone are the impulsive visit to Criseida's house and its immediate consequences (*Fil.,* ii, 81–85) – Chaucer shifts these elements to a later position in the story. Troiolo's passionate outcries (86–89) are condensed from four stanzas into one (*T&C,* II, 981–87). Pandarus' role, on the other hand, is proportionately greater. His

---

[14] E.g., the stratagem he devises to bring the lovers together at Deiphebus' house. There is no model for this in the *Filostrato,* where Criseida's scruples are less tender and the direct approach ultimately succeeds (ii, 133–43).

[15] The corresponding incident in *Troilus and Criseyde* – when Troilus rides by Criseyde's house (II, 1247–74) – takes place during Pandarus' second interview with Criseyde and is arranged by his contrivance (II, 1009–22).

words, which fill five of seventeen stanzas in Boccaccio's version, account for twelve of the eighteen stanzas in Chaucer's. Pandaro had wasted no time delivering his message to Troiolo. Pandarus, by contrast, puts Troilus off with japes and hauls him off to dinner before finally relieving his suspense. It is Troilus who is being manipulated at this stage: while Pandarus is talkative and lively, Troilus can respond only with a feeble "Dowe as the leste" (945). Even after Pandarus breaks the news to him, Troilus remains far more passive than Troiolo was in the same situation. His expressions of gratitude to Pandarus, like the flower simile and the offering of thanks to Venus, are also in the *Filostrato* (ii, 80–81), but Chaucer emphasizes them by eliminating most of Troiolo's subsequent words and actions. Hardly has Troilus managed to make known his impatience to see Criseyde again when Pandarus, cutting him short, unfolds a fully thought–out plan.[16]

The purpose of this plan is to bring Troilus and Criseyde together as quickly as possible, but Pandarus is clever enough to recognize that "every thing hath tyme" (II, 989) and that excessive haste will scare off the timorous Criseyde. Therefore, he decides to administer a carefully controlled dose of Troilus' physical presence during his second interview with Criseyde. Unaware that this technique had already worked spectacularly well on an earlier occasion (II, 610–51), Pandarus arranges for Troilus to ride past Criseyde's house while he is with her, "sittynge / At som wyndow, into the strete lokynge" (II, 1014–15). His excuse for visiting Criseyde and thus "presenting" Troilus to her – at a distance, to be sure – will be the delivery of a love letter.

Chaucer's linking of the letter to the staged personal appearance of Troilus, for which there is no precedent in the *Filostrato*, underscores the function of the letter within an elaborate game of seduction. By contrast, Pandaro's suggestion that Troiolo write a letter for him to carry to Criseida seems much more spontaneous (*Fil.*, ii, 91–92). Moreover, he offers only a few general hints as to the contents, while Pandarus specifies not only the contents but also the style and even the physical appearance of the letter that Troilus should write (II, 1005–7, 1023–43). Nor do we read Troilus' actual words, as we do Troiolo's (*Fil.*, ii, 96–106). Along

---

[16] Pandarus constantly draws attention to his control over Troilus with remarks to the effect that if Troilus will not follow his advice he can look elsewhere for help –

Do now as I shal seyn, and far aright;
And if thow nylt, wit al thiself thi care!
(II, 999–1000; cf. 993–94 and 1051–57)

– and by his authoritative tone in general.

with Pandarus' detailed instructions, we get only the narrator's summary of what Troilus wrote (V, 1065–84). The letter is less important as discourse than as an object to be manipulated and interpreted by Pandarus.

Indeed, the letter's function has more to do with what it is than with what it says. By a kind of well–understood metonymy the letter becomes a surrogate Troilus, physically present to beg his lady's mercy. Pandarus strives to intensify the identification between Troilus and his letter, to join synecdoche with metonymy, when he advises him to write the letter with his "owen hond" (II, 1005) and to "Biblotte it with [his] teris ek a lite" (II, 1027). The erotic implication of this advice to mark the letter with a bodily fluid is obvious. Troilus himself is aware of the intimacy that awaits the letter but is so far denied to him. Though he only allows himself to imagine Criseyde "seeing" the letter, his delicacy is at odds with the erotically charged images of the stanza in which he prepares the letter for sending:[17]

> And with his salte teris gan he bathe
> The ruby in his signet, and it sette
> Upon the wex deliverliche and rathe.
> Therwith a thousand tymes er he lette
> He kiste tho the lettre that he shette,
> And seyde, "Lettre, a blisful destine
> The shapyn is: my lady shal the see!"   (II, 1086–92)

This stanza is fairly closely translated from *Filostrato,* ii, 107. The chief changes are the substitution of "ruby" (1087) for the less–precise "gemma," and the linking of the letter's happy fate to its being "seen" by Criseyde (1092) rather than its passing into her hand ("in man di tal donna verrai").[18] Whether due to confusion between "will come" (*verrai*) and "will see" (*vedrai*), or to a conscious decision on Chaucer's part, the latter change in particular introduces a tension between Troilus' delicate sentiments and the more sensual subtext that is never far from Pandarus' mind. There can be no doubt of Chaucer's deliberately exploiting that tension a few stanzas later, when Pandarus delivers Troilus' letter.

---

[17] For the erotic significance of the ruby and the ring in this passage and elsewhere in *Troilus and Criseyde* (i.e., II, 585, and V, 549), see Thomas W. Ross, *Chaucer's Bawdy*, pp. 103–5, 196–98. The possible metonymic association between the pliant Criseyde and the warm wax into which Troilus presses his ruby is suggested by Chaucer's more obvious use of the same metonymy in "The Merchant's Tale," 1429–30.

[18] Vincenzo Pernicone, ed., *Il Filostrato*, p. 108. Subsequent references are to this edition.

In Boccaccio's text, the eroticism is closer to the surface and less problematic. Though Criseida is initially reluctant to accept Troiolo's letter, she is rather easily persuaded to change her mind and, smiling, takes it from Pandaro and puts it in her bosom (*Fil.*, ii, 113: "Criseida sorrise lui udendo, / e quelle prese, e miselesi in seno"). Criseyde's resistance to Pandarus is more strenuous, and Pandarus' "persuasion" is correspondingly more forceful. In fact, he does not wait to see whether his words convince her to accept Troilus' letter:

> "But for al that that ever I may deserve,
> Refuse it naught," quod he, and hente hire faste,
> And in hire bosom the lettre down he thraste,   (II, 1153–55)

Even without bearing in mind the letter's function as stand–in for Troilus, one recognizes in this scene a surrogate rape. Here, Pandarus does by means of synecdoche what he does more literally one dark and stormy night in his own bedchamber: he overcomes Criseyde's scruples by "thrusting" Troilus himself upon her (cf. III, 1095–97).

The letter functions as rhetorical discourse as well as proxy, but in this respect too Chaucer has altered his source so as to diminish in favor of Pandarus Troilus' role as origin of the discourse. Pandarus is not content merely with proposing that Troilus communicate his suffering to Criseyde in a letter; he insists on describing the sort of letter that Troilus should write. His instructions do not betray any obvious or direct influence of the *ars dictaminis* (*T&C*, II, 1023–44).[19] While none of his remarks contradicts the teachings of the *dictatores,* and while similar advice could be found in many *dictamen* manuals, nothing that he says is so closely tied to *letter writing* that it could not as easily come from any other type of rhetorical or indeed grammatical treatise.[20] The best evi-

---

[19] Bartlett J. Whiting, *Chaucer's Use of Proverbs,* p. 57: "No one as yet has accused Chaucer of taking the precepts which Pandarus gives from some rhetorician's treatise on *dictamen,* and no one is likely to find them there. Ovid was more to the point, and after Ovid the occasional common sense of love." Meech's statement that Pandarus gives Troilus "pedantically detailed instruction in the *ars dictaminis*" (*Design,* p. 45) is probably not to be taken too literally. He does not, in any case, develop the idea further. Even John McKinnell, who makes the most detailed case for dictaminal influence on the letters, suggests that Pandarus' remarks serve to undermine conventions that had been taken seriously in the *Filostrato.* See "Letters as Type of Formal Level," p. 81.

[20] Traugott Naunin, "Einfluss der Rhetorik," p. 49: "Er hält ihm hier einige allgemeine Regeln der Rhetorik vor." Though the nature of Chaucer's education is uncertain, he probably came into contact with the rules of *dictamen.* He could hardly have served as King Edward's envoy to France and Italy and still have managed to remain

dence for dictaminal influence comes from the actual love letters in Book V.

To the extent that they have direct sources, Pandarus' precepts derive mainly from the Latin classics. The image of the harper (1030–36) and the remarks on suiting style to content probably come from Horace's *Ars poetica* (lines 355–56, 1–5), and the passage as a whole is reminiscent of Ovid's *Ars amatoria,* i, 455–68.[21] Ovid's authority in the matter of writing love letters had already been tacitly acknowledged in Book I, when Pandarus alluded to *Heroides,* v:

> I woot wel that it fareth thus be me
> As to thi brother, Paris, an herdesse,
> Which that icleped was Oënone,
> Wrot in a compleynte of hir hevynesse.
> Yee say the lettre that she wrot, I gesse.   (652–56)

and quoted several lines – (*Her.,* v, 151–52), now considered spurious – from it to Troilus (*T&C,* I, 659–65). And several of Ovid's heroical epistles are echoed in both Pandarus' precepts and in the summary of the letter's contents.[22]

Pandarus recommends above all a simple and straightforward style. He does not oppose variety, so long as it does not interfere with the unity and congruity of the letter, and warns against excessive repetition. Also stressed is the need to preserve decorum, to suit form to content:

---

ignorant of the literary style which then prevailed in the royal foreign correspondence. The Host's warning to the Clerk in the *Canterbury Tales* may contain an allusion to Chaucer's former service and reflect a firsthand knowledge of this kind of style:

> Youre termes, youre colours, and youre figures,
> Keepe hem in stoor til so be that ye endite
> Heigh style, as whan that men to kynges write.
> Speketh so pleyn at this tyme, we yow preye,
> That we may understonde what ye seye.
> ("The Clerk's Prologue," 16–20)

If Chaucer studied at St. Paul's School, Oxford University, or the Inns of Court, the possibility that he knew the type of *dictamen* taught by Thomas Sampson becomes much greater.

[21] Naunin believes that Chaucer knew the *Ars poetica* firsthand: "Einfluss der Rhetorik," pp. 49–50. See also S. Meech, *Design,* p. 45 and n. 26, and Stephen A. Barney's notes (*Riverside Chaucer,* p. 1035).

[22] Cf. *T&C,* II, 1027, and *Her.,* iii, 3. McKinnell notes the similarity between *T&C,* II, 1213–14, and *Her.,* xvii, 143–44 ("Letters as Type of Formal Level," p. 82). I would add *T&C,* II, 1074–75, which paraphrases the first half of *Fil.,* ii, 97, but also echoes *Her.,* iv, 10–11.

> Ne jompre ek no discordant thyng yfeere,
> As thus, to usen termes of phisik
> In loves termes; hold of thi matere
> The forme alwey, and do that it be lik;   (II, 1037–40)[23]

Pandarus even outlines the approach that Troilus ought to take, advising him to tell Criseyde how he "ferde amys, and hire biseche of routhe" (1007). In counseling an appeal to pity rather than the equally popular appeal to vanity,[24] Pandarus speaks from a firsthand acquaintance with Criseyde's personality. She is not the kind of simple creature whom mere flattery can sway.

By paraphrasing the contents of the letter, Chaucer has still further diminished Troilus' role in directing the course of his own romance. He has, in effect, dealt with the letter as quickly as possible in order to get back to Pandarus and on with the real action. In the *Filostrato* the narrative is brought to a halt by Troiolo's letter, an imposing rhetorical set piece (eighty–eight lines) that runs through all the conventions of the epistolary invitation (*Fil.*, ii, 96–106). Not only does Troiolo speak for himself, but he speaks eloquently and at considerable length.[25]

Herbert Wright noticed this contrast and used it to support his contention that Chaucer made a "man of action" out of Boccaccio's wordy Troiolo.[26] His argument is curious given the crucial role that language plays in achieving the lover's goal. It is, after all, Pandarus' ready tongue more than Troilus' strong right arm that ultimately wins Criseyde over. And after Pandarus' first, modest success in persuading Criseyde to make Troilus "bettre chiere," one of her first questions about her noble suitor is "kan he wel speke of love?" (II, 503). The strong, silent type so dear to the modern romantic imagination comes across as a dolt in the courtly

---

[23] The ingenious biographical critic might catch in line 1038 a derogatory allusion to Gower's practice in the *Cinkante Balades* (provided, of course, that Gower wrote the ballades in his youth), though the same stricture is found in Ovid's *Ars amatoria*, i, 463–66.

[24] The appeal to vanity is employed to a much greater extent in the *Filostrato* than in *Troilus and Criseyde*, especially by Pandaro (e.g., ii, 54–55).

[25] He draws attention, in conventional fashion, to the danger of prolixity near the letter's end:

> El mi restava molte cose a dire,
> ma per non farti noia le vo' tacere.   (ii, 106)

McKinnell emphasizes the conformity of this and the other two verbatim letters in the *Filostrato* to the patterns taught by the *ars dictaminis:* "Letters as Type of Formal Level," p. 80.

[26] *Boccaccio in England*, p. 75. Troilus is frequently tongue–tied in the presence of his lady (e.g., III, 78–84 and 1081–92).

milieu, as Troilus himself points out before he is smitten by love (I, 190–96). A sophisticate like Chaucer's Diomede is never at a loss for words. Hence, in terms of the poem's central action, Chaucer makes Troilus less a man of action by making him less "wordy" than Troiolo.

The paraphrase does, on the other hand, heighten the pace of the narrative action. Instead of dwelling on what exactly Troilus says, Chaucer hastens to bring Pandarus and Criseyde back together. Pandarus' gloss (II, 1121ff) is more important than the text of the letter.[27] Later in the poem, in answer to those of his readers who would know every word that the lovers said or wrote, the narrator states outright that he intends to include only what is essential:

> But now, paraunter, som man wayten wolde
> That every word, or soonde, or look, or cheere
> Of Troilus that I rehercen sholde,
> In al this while unto his lady deere.
> I trowe it were a long thyng for to here;
> Or of what wight that stant in swich disjoynte,
> His wordes alle, or every look, to poynte.

> For sothe, I have naught herd it don er this
> In story non, ne no man here, I wene;
> And though I wolde, I koude nought, ywys;
> For ther was som epistel hem bitwene,
> That wolde, as seyth myn autour, wel contene
> Neigh half this book, of which hym liste nought write.[28]
> How sholde I thanne a lyne of it endite?   (T&C, III, 491–504)

Like his narrator, who is himself no lover, Chaucer is a sympathetic but detached observer of the events depicted. By contrast, Boccaccio identifies personally with Troiolo, and this difference helps explain why he includes the full text of the letter. The initiates of love will be able to vivify the conventional contents from their own experience, even as they appreciate the skill and grace with which the courtly (and epistolary) commonplaces are expressed.

An outsider, Chaucer's narrator cannot penetrate beneath the con-

---

[27] This reflects the contemporary practice of transmitting letters, especially when an important or confidential subject is involved. See G. Constable, *Letters and Letter–Collections*, pp. 53–54.

[28] Lines 501–3: Boccaccio makes no such statement, but Chaucer may have had the two letters from *Filostrato*, ii, in the back of his mind. Both authors indicate that the lovers exchanged numerous letters (*T&C*, II, 1342–44, 1350: *Fil.*, ii, 131), and if they all were as lengthy as the first pair in the *Filostrato* they would indeed fill half of Chaucer's book.

ventional and apparently redundant language of his source and is impatient to "get on with the story":

> First he gan hire his righte lady calle,
> His hertes lif, his lust, his sorwes leche,
> His blisse, and ek thise other termes alle
> That in swich cas thise loveres alle seche;
> And in ful humble wise, as in his speche,
> He gan hym recommaunde unto hire grace;
> To telle al how, it axeth muchel space.   (II, 1065–71)

And when he comes to the lover's self–deprecation and abasement before his lady, the narrator responds to the surface content of Troilus' statements, which is *literally* untrue, rather than to the emotions that motivate them, before he again excuses himself from repeating Troilus' interminable complaints:

> And after that he seyde, and *leigh ful loude,*
> Hymself was litel worth, and lasse he koude;
>
> And that she sholde han his konnyng excused,
> That litel was, and ek he dredde hire soo;
> And his unworthynesse he ay acused;
> And after that, than gan he telle his woo;
> But that was endeles, withouten hoo;   (II, 1077–83; my italics)

Criseyde's response to the letter is more discerning. Aware that the letter is at least as important for what it represents as for what it says, she is less inclined to judge it in terms of its literal accuracy or its originality. She rejects the letter *before* she reads it, in refusing her uncle's request that she permit the greater intimacy with Troilus that accepting his letter would constitute. Her vehemence and even some of the expressions that she employs betray her sensitivity to the letter's synecdochic function as a physical, tangible surrogate for Troilus himself:

> scrit ne bille,
> For love of God, that *toucheth swich matere,*
> Ne bryng me noon; and also, uncle deere,
> To myn estat have more reward, I preye,
> Than to his lust!   (II, 1130–34; my italics)

Whether her resistance is feigned or not, once Pandarus has forced her to put aside "this nyce fare" (II, 1144), she can scarcely conceal her eagerness to read what Troilus wrote (II, 1172–76). And having read the letter carefully, "word by word in every lyne," she "fond no lak, she thoughte he koude good" (II, 1177–78).[29] However hackneyed its sentiments, the letter has the desired effect, since Criseyde, like Boccaccio's Criseida, offers less resistance to Pandarus' requests once she has read it.

After the letter has been thrust upon her, but before she has had an opportunity to retire to her private chamber to read it, Criseyde playfully resists Pandarus' urging that she send Troilus "som goodly answere" (II, 1125).

> "Em, I preye,
> Swich answere as yow list, yourself purveye,
> For trewely I nyl no lettre write."
> "No? than wol I," quod he, "so ye endite."   (II, 1159–62)

Here again the status of the letter as physical object is preeminent: Pandarus responds, if jestingly, not to her refusal to "answer" Troilus but to her refusal to "write" an answer with her own hand. Moreover, in offering to perform that function for her, he is reasserting the role of preceptor. With Troilus he had placed almost equal emphasis on the letter as object and as message; with Criseyde he seems to be more concerned that she not say anything negative. His instructions to Criseyde are not nearly so detailed as those that he gave Troilus (II, 1208–9). Though his most insistent offer of assistance again involves preparing the physical object rather than supplying Criseyde with words, there is something suspicious about the division of labor:

> "Aquite hym wel, for Goddes love," quod he;
> "Myself to medes *wol the lettre sowe.*"
> And held his hondes up, and sat on knowe;
> "Now, goode nece, be it nevere so lite,
> *Yif me the labour it to sowe and plite.*"   (II, 1200–1204; my italics)

The implication that Pandarus' eagerness to fold and sew up the letter personally is motivated by his desire to verify the suitability of its contents is strengthened by the parallel with Troilus, who *read his letter over* immediately before folding and sealing it (II, 1085).

Pandarus does not push his offer, and Criseyde does not accept it. She seals the letter herself (II, 1226), after writing it in her own hand. In fact, she emphasizes the novelty of her actually *writing* (rather than dictating) a letter when she finally gives in to Pandarus' urging:[30]

---

[29] The wording echoes line 1078, and further undercuts Troilus' protestations of spontaneous artlessness. Boccaccio's Criseida puts up a less spirited resistance to receiving the letter and is more obviously pleased by its contents (ii, 109–17).

[30] Criseyde's claim that this is the first time that she has ever done anything of this sort is echoed by Diomede in Book V, 155–61.

"Depardieux," quod she, "God leve al be wel!
God help me so, this is the firste lettre
That evere I wroot, ye, al or any del." (II, 1212–14)

More than likely the end result is the one that Pandarus was after all
along. His methods are different with Criseyde, but he has orchestrated
her behavior just as thoroughly as he had Troilus'. Even the exclamation
with which she prefaces her assent to Pandarus' proposal ("Depardieux")
is identical with the one that Troilus used in the same situation (II, 1058),
reaffirming by linking the two scenes the key part that Pandarus plays in
both.

Once again Chaucer chooses to paraphrase the letter (II, 1221–25),
rather than quote the full text as Boccaccio does (*Fil.,* ii, 121–27).
Comparison of Chaucer's abstract with Boccaccio's letter reveals, besides even greater condensation than in the previous instance, some fairly
significant discrepancies in content. Criseyde's letter, as the narrator
summarizes it, makes three points: (1) she thanks Troilus for his good
intentions, but (2) she will not bind herself to him in love, although (3)
she will consent to love him as a sister. The letter in *Il Filostrato* is
concerned above all with Criseida's refusal to grant Troiolo's request.
The world, Criseida says, is not as it should be, and there is no way for her
to satisfy his desire (or hers) without suffering the loss of her good name.
She mitigates the finality of the rebuff somewhat in the final two stanzas
(*Fil.,* ii, 126–27) but never makes her meaning quite clear. The cautious,
deliberately ambiguous tone of her letter is already evident in the *salutatio:*

> A te amico discreto e possente,
> il qual forte di me inganna Amore,
> come uom preso di me 'ndebitamente,
> Crisëida, salvato il suo onore,
> manda salute, e poi umilemente
> si raccomanda al tuo alto valore,
> vaga di compiacerti, dove sia
> l'onestá salva e la castitá mia. (ii, 121)

She is unwilling to give anything away, to commit herself the least bit:
even her greeting is conditional on the preservation of her "onore,"
"onestá," and "castitá."

Chaucer's paraphrase removes the letter's ambiguity. Instead of
quoting Criseyde's own words, he describes what he takes to be the
thoughts behind them. Seen in this light, the words that introduce the
letter take on an otherwise unsuspected significance. Criseyde

> ... sette hire down, and gan a lettre write,

> Of which to telle in short is myn entente
> Th'effect, as fer as I kan understande.   (II, 1218–20)

Boccaccio's text makes no mention of her thanking Troiolo, but, as Troiolo is quick to recognize (*Fil.*, ii, 129), the very fact that she is willing to reply at all indicates that his overtures are not repugnant to her.[31] Chaucer probably took Criseyde's offer of "sisterly" love from the conversation between Pandaro and Criseida later in Book ii of the *Filostrato* (stanza 134).[32] By taking subsequent developments into account, Chaucer uncovers what remains veiled in the Italian letter and tells the reader what Troilus saw

> On which hym thoughte he myghte his herte reste,
> Al covered she the wordes under sheld.   (II, 1326–27)

In the *Filostrato* it is Criseida herself who is shielded and not her words:

> ... Se io costei intendo,
> amor la stringe, ma sí come rea,
> sotto lo scudo ancor si va chiudendo;   (ii, 129)

Her protection is the ambiguity of her words. Chaucer converts this metaphor into an expression of the "fruyt and chaf" idea: the literal sense is like a shield that conceals the *sententia* or true meaning. Troilus reads the letter like a good exegete, just as Chaucer had in paraphrasing it, and "to the more worthi part he held" (II, 1328).

The first exchange of letters begins a correspondence that lasts until Pandarus arranges the affair's consummation. Of these other letters we know only that Troilus wrote one nearly every day and sent it by Pandarus (II, 1342–44), that Criseyde's answers were sometimes favorable and sometimes not (II, 1350–51), and that by Chaucer's estimate they would fill half the book were they copied out (III, 501–3). We do not need to know more about these letters because the distinctive function of the letter within the carefully graded process of courtship that Pandarus enacts through Troilus and Criseyde had already been fulfilled by the first two. The fact that Chaucer provided only summaries of those two letters is further testimony that their significance is more functional than for-

---

[31] Cf. Ovid, *Ars amatoria*, i, 479–86, and Boncompagno, *Rota Veneris*, iii (ed. and trans. J. Purkart, pp. 78–79).
[32] This offer is again paralleled by Diomede's, in Book V, 127–40.

64

mal.[33] Troilus' and Criseyde's exact words in their first letters to each other are less important than the fact that those letters come after Pandarus has spoken for each of the future lovers (II, 78–595, 939–66) but before they first speak directly to one another at Deiphebus' house (III, 64–182). Each step moves Troilus and Criseyde closer to that night of "hevene blisse" in Pandarus' very own bedchamber.

3.3. Epistolary Form: The "Litera Troili"

When next we encounter the lovers writing letters the circumstances are entirely different. Fortune, which had long favored them and allowed them to enjoy the fruits of their love, has turned against them and forced Criseyde to leave Troy. Troilus is now more helpless than he was before he won Criseyde's love, since even Pandarus can do nothing for him. Though it is again Pandarus who persuades Troilus to write a letter (V, 1292–1309), this time his personal involvement in the letter's transmission and reception extends no farther.[34] The kinesis of Book II gives way in Book V to profound stasis: Pandarus' constant shuttling between Troilus and Criseyde, his inexhaustible resourcefulness, and his lively conversation are replaced by Troilus' increasingly hopeless waiting, his (and Pandarus') utter frustration, and his futile complaints.

Chaucer's treatment of the letters in Book V accords with this contrast: each of the salient features of the previous letter–writing scene is reversed. The subject is now Troilus' tragedy, and he is the sole focus of attention. It is Troilus alone who suffers the unforeseen consequences of his desire and experiences the treachery of Fortune. Denied any opportunity for action, Pandarus can neither help Troilus overcome his misfortune nor show him how to transcend it. He already suspects the truth

---

[33] McKinnell remarks the "cheerful detachment" with which the reader is encouraged to view the two letters, which, with their errors and insincerities, "are all part of a game" into which the lovers have entered without a great deal of forethought ("Letter as Type of Formal Level," p. 83). The sequence in which they operate, the set of rules for this game, is so fixed that Chaucer could later disrupt it to produce deeper irony in "The Merchant's Tale," where, for example, May receives and then reads Damyan's love letter *after* she has visited his bedside and spoken with him in person.

[34] Boccaccio permits Troiolo to retain the services of Pandaro even after Criseida's departure. He sends him to the Greek camp at every truce:

> mandovvi Pandar, qualora tra essi
> o triegue o patti alcun furon promessi.   (viii, 3)

The lovers' separation is more absolute in *Troilus and Criseyde*.

when he once again advises Troilus to write Criseyde a letter; this time he has no well–laid plan but is merely grasping at straws.

Nothing indeed can be done; Troilus can only wait and hope. With no possibility of effective action, words alone remain: Troilus puts his sorrows in words (in his complaints and letters) and gets only more words in return. Chaucer therefore not only reproduces Troilus' letter verbatim but also includes a reply from Criseyde that has no precedent in his source. Here there is no action to be interrupted, and Chaucer's procedure emphasizes that fact. By allowing the letters to speak for themselves, as the lovers once had face to face, he portrays more vividly the distance that now separates Troilus from Criseyde and that renders other communication impossible. There is no give and take, no physical allurements, only the words themselves.

While Chaucer quotes Troilus' letter in full, he shortens Boccaccio's version from 192 to 105 lines. By comparison with the text in the *Filostrato,* the "Litera Troili" has been streamlined and unified. Chaucer adds little that is completely new – although that little is highly significant – but reduces and expands, deletes, and rearranges freely.[35] Most modern critics agree that Chaucer's modifications of the letter, in Meech's words, "perfect the hero in loverly decorum."[36] This judgment rests largely on his elimination of the suspicion and accusation that at points become explicit in Troiolo's letter (*Fil.,* vii, 53, 56–59, 73). In so doing Chaucer makes the tone of the letter more consistent with the basic dilemma facing the courtly lover who would criticize his lady's conduct:

> If any servant dorste or oughte of right
> Upon his lady pitously compleyne,
> Thanne wene I that ich oughte be that wight,
> Considered this, that ye thise monthes tweyne
> Han taried, ther ye seyden, soth to seyne,
> But dayes ten ye nolde in oost sojourne, –
> But in two monthes yet ye nat retourne.
>
> But for as muche as me moot nedes like
> Al that yow liste, I dar nat pleyne moore,   (V, 1345–53)[37]

---

[35] See B. A. Windeatt, *Troilus and Criseyde,* pp. 522–29 (also Rossetti, *Chaucer's Troylus and Cryseyde,* pp. 280–83).

[36] *Design,* p. 125. Cf. T. A. Kirby, *Chaucer's 'Troilus',* p. 272. The ultimate source of this view is Lewis's highly influential article.

[37] Chaucer frequently underscores Troilus' loss of sovereignty: he renounces his high station (I, 432–34), Criseyde takes pleasure in the thought that she is master of so glorious a prince's fate (II, 652–65, 736–49, and 1581–94) and informs him that he must renounce his superior rank insofar as he is her lover (III, 169–75). Such instances, which could be multiplied, have no precedent in the *Filostrato.*

The stanzas on which these lines are based (*Fil.,* vii, 54–55) immediately precede Troiolo's voicing of his suspicion that Criseida has taken a new lover, first as only one of several possible explanations for her tarrying (vii, 56), then as the most probable reason:

> Ma forte temo che novello amore
> non sia cagion di tua lunga dimora.   (vii, 58)[38]

Troilus' complaints about Criseyde's uncourtly behavior are by comparison fewer, milder, and always heavily qualified. The passage quoted above is the strongest criticism that he permits himself in the entire letter.

Even though his accusation is already deeply undercut by the conditional, Troilus sees fit to balance it with a stanza (not found in the *Filostrato*) in which he prays God to increase Criseyde's well–being "In honour":

> The whos welfare and hele ek God encresse
> In honour swich, that upward in degree
> It growe alwey, so that it nevere cesse.
> Right as youre herte ay kan, my lady free,
> Devyse, I prey to God so moot it be,
> And graunte it that ye soone upon me rewe,
> As wisly as in al I am yow trewe.   (V, 1359–65)

Although the ironic overtones of these lines are evident to the reader who knows the truth, their ostensible purpose is to soothe Criseyde after his presumptuous questioning of her behavior. For the rest he confines himself to reminders of her promise – "yet thynketh on youre trouthe" (1386), "And to youre trouthe ay I me recomande" (1414) – while relying mostly on the power of his sufferings to arouse her compassion, just as they had at the outset of the romance. He focuses on the consequences of her actions rather than their cause. His inability to admit the possibility of betrayal excludes, in any case, all but the vague and improbable explanations that he warily offers:

> And if so be my gilt hath deth deserved,
> Or if yow list namore upon me se, ...   (V, 1387–88)

---

[38] He had alluded to this fear as early as the second stanza of the letter:

> El non dovrá, *come che divenuta*
> *sia quasi Greca,* la lettera mia
> da te ancor non esser ricevuta   (vii, 53; my italics)

Chaucer eliminates these lines.

His refusal to speculate more deeply about Crisyede's motives may make him more "courtly" than Troiolo, but it also reemphasizes the fixation on his own fate from which only death will release him.

Chaucer also changes the letter to make its epistolary quality more prominent and to bring it more into line with contemporary epistolary standards. This he accomplishes both by expanding and revising the letter's most important parts and by deleting superfluous material. Troiolo's second letter is even more a rhetorical set piece than his first: like Ovid's *Heroides,* it is as much an elegy as an epistle. This is not to say that Boccaccio has neglected to employ the traditional structure of a letter. On the contrary, Troiolo's epistle breaks down rather neatly into the five–part pattern taught by most of the medieval *dictatores: salutatio* (52); *exordium* or *arenga* (53);[39] *narratio* (54–68); *petitio* (69–72); and *conclusio* (73–75). Moreover, the narrative context, as well as internal references to "la lettera mia" and to the fact that Troiolo is writing to Criseida (vii, 55) identify it as a letter. But the epistle's great length and the disproportionate space devoted to the long *narratio* of complaint (fifteen of twenty–four stanzas) dilute the effect of the specifically epistolary language in the first and in the last three stanzas.

An important step in Chaucer's revision is thus to reduce the letter's dimensions so that they more closely resemble those of an actual letter that might be sent in such a situation. Chaucer preserves most of the basic contents, but eliminates whatever merely elaborates without adding anything new. Hence he removes the list of pleasures in which Troiolo no longer delights and reduces four stanzas of complaint (*Fil.,* vii, 60–63) to one (*T&C,* V, 1373–79). Troiolo's evocation (and envy) of the parts of nature privileged to gaze upon Criseida (vii, 64–66) and of the Greek camp (67–68) are also deleted, allowing Troilus' complaint to lead directly and logically to his request that Criseyde return and change his woe to joy. The balance between these two thoughts is thus much clearer in Chaucer's version than in Boccaccio's, where they are separated by seven stanzas of *amplificatio.* Similar examples of compression, though on a smaller scale, can be found throughout the letter.

Chaucer also expands parts of his model, sometimes simply stressing points already present in the Italian, sometimes adding new material of

---

[39] These terms, which alternate with *captatio benevolentiae* and even *proverbium* in the *artes dictandi* and are especially favored by the Italian teachers, seem best to describe the second part of Troiolo's letter. McKinnell maintains that all three verbatim letters in the *Filostrato* follow the same pattern, which is that of the *ars dictaminis* ("Letters as Type of Formal Level," p. 80).

his own. This technique is used to make Troilus a more perfect lover, as noted above, but serves simultaneously to perfect the letter in epistolary decorum. This is best seen in the way Chaucer treats one of the most significant parts of any letter, the opening formulas. Troiolo's *salutatio*, though based in part on a popular convention of the literary love letter,[40] reveals more than anything his impatience to get on with the complaint:

> Giovane donna, a cui Amor mi diede
> e tuo mi tiene, e mentre sarò 'n vita
> mi terrá sempre con intera fede,
> per ciò che tu nella tua dipartita
> in miseria maggior ch'alcun non crede
> qui mi lasciasti, l'anima smarrita
> si raccomanda alla tua gran virtute,
> e mandarti non può altra salute.   (vii, 52)

The formal greeting is interrupted midway by three lines of complaint.

Chaucer borrows only a few ideas from this stanza and part of the penultimate stanza of Troiolo's letter (vii, 74) for his expansion of the letter's opening:

> Right fresshe flour, whos I ben have and shal,
> Withouten part of elleswhere servyse,
> With herte, body, lif, lust, thought, and al,
> I, woful wyght, in everich humble wise
> That tonge telle or herte may devyse,
> As ofte as matere occupieth place,
> Me recomaunde unto youre noble grace.

---

[40] Norman Davis, "*Litera Troili*," pp. 239, 240. The ultimate source is the play on the ambiguity of *salus* (i.e., "greeting" and/or "health, well–being") popular among Latin epistolographers of the Middle Ages. Ovid uses this pun in *Heroides*, xvi, 1–2:

> Hanc tibi Priamides mitto, Ledaea, salutem,
> quae tribui sola te mihi dante potest.

["I, son of Priam, send you, Leda's daughter, this wish for welfare – welfare that can fall to me through your gift alone."] Grant Showerman, ed. and trans., *Heroides and Amores*, pp. 196–97. See also E. Ruhe, *De Amasio*, pp. 101–2. Davis fails to notice that Boccaccio uses this very device in the stanza from *Il Filostrato* (vii, 52) that he quotes on the first page of his article (233). Boccaccio had used the same typical opening for Troiolo's first epistolary complaint in Book ii, 96:

> Come puó quei che in affanno é posto,
> in pianto grave ed in stato molesto
> come sono io per te, donna, disposto,
> ad alcun dar salute? credo chesto
> esser non dee da lui; ond'io mi scosto
> da quel che gli altri fanno, e sol per questo
> qui da me salutata non sarai,
> perch'io non l'ho se tu non la mi dai.

Liketh yow to witen, swete herte,
As ye wel knowe, how longe tyme agon
That ye me lefte in aspre peynes smerte,
Whan that ye wente, of which yit boote non
Have I non had, but evere wors bigon
Fro day to day am I, and so mot dwelle,
While it yow list, of wele and wo my welle.

For which to yow, with dredful herte trewe,
I write, as he that sorwe drifth to write,
My wo, that everich houre encresseth newe,
Compleynyng, as I dar or kan endite.
And that defaced is, that may ye wite
The teris which that fro myn eyen reyne,
That wolden speke, if that they koude, and pleyne.

(V, 1317–37)

The element of complaint has all but disappeared from the *salutatio* proper (1317–23), to be replaced by the declarations of humility and loyalty characteristic of the formal greeting in letters addressed to superiors.[41] The only hint of what is to come is Troilus' description of himself as a "woful wyght." He saves the complaint from Troiolo's *salutatio* for the second stanza of his letter, where he expands it and uses it to introduce his excuse for writing. Only after this elaborate prelude, and not without profuse apologies, does Troilus finally present his first petition: that Criseyde deign to read his letter (1338–44). Within a much longer letter, Troiolo reaches the same point in half the space.[42]

Norman Davis has thoroughly and convincincly shown how Chaucer reworked the letter's opening to incorporate the seven–part sequence of conventional phrases with which fifteenth–century English letters of a formal, respectful sort normally begin.[43] Though the "Litera Troili" is the

---

[41] Cf. the briefer but similar formulas in Thomas Sampson's *Modus dictandi*, BL, MS Royal 17B.xlvii, fols. 42v–43r (lines 55–112 in my forthcoming edition). See also Henry G. Richardson, "Oxford *Dictatores*," pp. 329–450, for many more examples.

[42] The disproportion is not due simply to the expansion which normally accompanies translation: both poets handle the subsequent section in two stanzas (*Fil.*, vii, 54–55: *T&C*, V, 1345–58).

[43] N. Davis, "*Litera Troili*," p. 236. The pattern, which he illustrates on pp. 236–39, is (1) "Right" plus an adjective and an appropriate noun; (2) a formula commending the writer to the reader, often accompanied by an expression of humility and/or a request for a blessing; (3) a wish to hear of the recipient's welfare; (4) a prayer for the continuation or increase of that welfare; (5) an offer of news regarding the writer's welfare; (6) an assertion of the writer's good health at the time of writing; and (7) thanks to God for the writer's present good health. Davis notes syntactical regularities in these formulas as well.

70

earliest surviving letter in English to exhibit this pattern, the same sequence of phrases is found in fourteenth–century Anglo–Norman letters and, as early as the thirteenth century, in French letters written on the continent.[44] Not mentioned by Davis is the fact that Chaucer also echoes the *quot–tot* construction so popular in Latin epistles, especially those of lovers (lines 1320–23). Chaucer's revisions would have straightaway informed the members of his audience that they were here dealing with a *letter*. He wished the "Litera Troili" to be perceived as qualitatively different from the dialogues between Troilus and Criseyde in the earlier books. The treatment of the letters in Book II does not share this concern because then Troilus and Criseyde were both in Troy and, at least theoretically, able to see and converse with one another. The distance that now separates them is real, and the fact that Troilus can address Criseyde only in a letter helps to emphasize that physical separation.

Chaucer's restructuring of Boccaccio's text is still more complex than the usual five–part models of the *dictatores*.[45] Since Davis does not carry his discussion beyond the opening formulas, a brief glance at the overall design of the letter in the perspective of contemporary teaching and practice is in order. Even the *dictamen* manuals of the twelfth and thirteenth centuries provide for altering the position of the letter's parts (except, of course, the *salutatio* and *conclusio*) or even eliminating some of them as the occasion demands. One might, for example, stress the need for immediate action by transposing *petitio* and *narratio*. A *petitio*, on the other hand, has no function in a simple report, nor is a *captatio benevolentiae* appropriate in a letter to an enemy. By Chaucer's day the exception had become the rule: letters constructed like those in Bernard de Meung's or Guido Faba's textbooks are rare even in the dictaminal collections of the fourteenth century. The terms are retained and occasionally even expanded by the introduction of new distinctions,[46] but the

---

[44] Ibid., pp. 240–43. Davis is unsure as to the role of the *ars dictaminis* in the development of these formulas; but it is clear that contemporary *dictatores* promoted their use. For example, the formulas dealing with the health of recipient and writer (parts 3–7) are called the *status affectus* in Sampson's treatise, fol. 42r (lines 19–30).

[45] McKinnell notices some of the same "deviations" from the normal pattern that I do but interprets them differently. He regards the alternation of *narratio* and *petitio* as "merely confused" and, like the stylistic ineptitude that he detects in the first half of the "Litera Troili," part of Chaucer's deliberate representation of Troilus' disordered mental state. "Letters as Type of Formal Level," pp. 84–87. My more positive response to the irregular structure of the letter's interior is shared by Davis Taylor, "Terms of Love," pp. 84–88.

[46] See, e.g., T. Sampson, *Modus dictandi*, fol. 42r (lines 9–12), and W. A. Pantin, "Treatise on Letter–Writing," p. 338.

corresponding parts are no longer so rigidly distinguished in practice. The *salutatio* and *captatio benevolentiae* or *exordium* are characteristically combined and elaborated along the lines that Davis describes, while the *conclusio* is generally augmented with, for example, a wish for the recipient's good fortune. Otherwise the contents are subject to wide variation, especially in the hands of poets.

In fact, the "Litera Troili" fits the traditional pattern surprisingly well. Chaucer's major departure from the strict five–part format is the interruption of the *narratio* at two points by minor *petitiones*.[47] Troilus' central concern in the *narratio* is to recount the suffering that he has undergone as a result of Criseyde's absence, while in the *petitio* proper he requests that she put an end to this suffering either by returning to Troy or by writing him a letter. Chaucer revises Boccaccio's text to make the letter as effective as possible in accomplishing these two tasks. This requires that rhetoric be linked to psychology; a delicate balance must be maintained between the bestowal of praise and the evocation of sympathy, on the one hand, and the cautious criticism and the disguised demands, on the other.

The *salutatio*'s single goal is to make Criseyde well–disposed toward Troilus. His humility and fidelity, his perfection in love's service are accordingly stressed. The functions, in short, of *salutatio* and *captatio benevolentiae* are combined in the letter's first stanza.[48] In the next two stanzas, which begin the *narratio*, Troilus increases Criseyde's sympathy even further by showing how strongly her absence has affected him. His inability to restrain his tears from falling and staining the parchment as he writes proves that his grief is real. In quantity and quality these tears are different from those with which Troilus had earlier moistened the ruby in his signet before pressing it into the wax that sealed his first letter to Criseyde. His infusion of that letter was more superficial and at least somewhat contrived, even if he was not simply following Pandarus' instructions (II, 1027). Here Troilus' weeping is sincere, spontaneous, and copious: he literally "pours himself" into his letter. His awareness of the letter as synecdoche for himself is correspondingly intense. The tears that instill his physical presence in the parchment "wolden speke, if that they koude, and pleyne" (V, 1337), as he would, could he but trade places

---

[47] There is an early precedent for this technique in the *salutz* of Arnaut de Maroill. See E. Ruhe, *De Amasio*, pp. 111, 394–95 n. 108.

[48] The normal means of securing goodwill is through praise (cf. the first letter). Chaucer, realizing the impossibility of this approach (short of insincerity) in a letter of complaint, chooses a subtler means of accomplishing the same end.

with the letter. However, they have become mere stains that have "de-faced" the letter to the point that Criseyde may not recognize him in it (cf. V, 1402–4) and turn away her "eyen clere," the openings through which love enters (cf. I, 295–308), lest they be "defouled" by looking upon it/him:

Yow first biseche I, that youre eyen clere,
To loke on this, defouled ye nat holde;   (V, 1338–39)

The very physical image of Criseyde's refusing to "take him in" by refusing to read the letter because he has left his mark on it is a powerful projection of Troilus' deepest fears. By moving the apology from the end of the letter, where Boccaccio put it,[49] and by developing a synecdochic dimension that is unacknowledged in his source, Chaucer increases the letter's psychological realism as well as its rhetorical effectiveness.

The preliminary assault on Criseyde's sympathy gives way to a first, innocent *petitio*. All Troilus asks at this point is that she read his letter and overlook its artlessness, a small request in the light of his present con-dition, but warily proferred nonetheless:

And over al this, that ye, my lady deere,
Wol vouchesauf this lettre to byholde.
And by the cause ek of my cares colde,
That sleth my wit, if aught amys m'asterte,
Foryeve it me, myn owen swete herte!   (V, 1340–44)

Up to this point all his "complaint" has focused on himself, on the effects rather than on the causes of their continued separation. Now, when he has done his utmost to arouse her sympathy and has placed her securely in a position of power tempered by benevolence (she has already granted one request), he introduces his only real criticism. Though he borrows the conditional directly from Boccaccio, Chaucer takes steps to increase its significance. Besides dropping the stronger criticisms with which Troiolo augments this one, Chaucer has Troilus shift almost immediately to a second minor *petitio*, this time a wish for Criseyde's increased well–being:

But for as muche as me moot nedes like
Al that yow liste, I dar nat pleyne moore,
But humblely, with sorwful sikes sike,
Yow write ich myn unresty sorwes soore,
Fro day to day desiryng evere moore

---

[49] Chaucer's model for this change could have been *Heroides*, iii, 3, though no source is needed to explain his motives.

To knowen fully, if youre wille it weere,
How ye han ferd and don whil ye be theere;

The whos welfare and hele ek God encresse
In honour swich, that upward in degree
It growe alwey, so that it nevere cesse.
Right as youre herte ay kan, my lady free,
Devyse, I prey to God so moot it be,
And graunte it that ye soone upon me rewe,
As wisly as in al I am yow trewe.   (V, 1352–65)

The first of these stanzas translates fairly closely *Il Filostrato,* vii, 55, but the second is all Chaucer's. One of Chaucer's most inspired additions to the letter, it is a *petitio* masquerading as a *captatio benevolentiae*.[50] Of the two prayers that Troilus addresses to God, the second is structurally subordinate to the first. The first three lines of the stanza introduce the initial request and the next two repeat it, leaving only the final two lines for the second request. The fact is, however, that the accomplishment of his first wish – that her "welfare and hele ek God encresse / *In honour*" (my italics) – is conditional on her granting the second. The well–being of the two lovers, given the oaths that they have sworn to one another, must be mutual. As long as Criseyde plays by the rules, she cannot possibly be happy apart from Troilus. A wish for the honorable increase of her well–being is hence equivalent to a wish for her speedy return. As it turns out, the essential condition, underscored in the stanza's final line,[51] is violated by Criseyde, a creature less of "honour" than of fortune and "slydynge corage."

The wish for Criseyde's (and Troilus') betterment leads naturally to a contrasting description of Troilus' actual condition – presumably the same as hers – with which the *narratio* resumes:

And if yow liketh knowen of the fare
Of me, whos wo ther may no wit discryve,
I kan namore but, chiste of every care,
At wrytyng of this lettre I was on–lyve,

---

[50] It corresponds to the part of the letter that Sampson calls *status affectus* (cf. n. 44 above), which Davis discusses in "*Litera Troili,*" pp. 238–39.

[51] Cf. *T&C*, V, 1386, 1414. The mutual obligation of feudal lord and vassal – the dominant metaphor of the courtly relationship – lies behind these references to "trouthe" and is the basis of Troilus' appeal. Criseyde has accepted his fealty, he has served faithfully, and therefore she is obliged to carry out her part of the contract. The appeal to honor in this context becomes ironic, if one recalls that Troilus has abjured the sphere wherein honor is truly operative and feudal obligations truly binding.

> Al redy out my woful gost to dryve;
> Which I delaye, and holde hym yet in honde,[52]
> Upon the sighte of matere of youre sonde.　　(V, 1366–72)

Some mention of the writer's own health is a regular feature of contemporary letters, but it usually occurs at the beginning, as in Boccaccio's original (*Fil.*, vii, 52).[53] By shifting it to the middle of the letter, Chaucer not only manages a graceful transition but also reemphasizes the epistolary situation for his audience. Chaucer plays on the predictable expectations that the first line of the stanza (1366) would have created in the members of his audience. Instead of the usual "At writing of this letter I was in good health," Troilus can claim only that he was "on–lyve." Chaucer thus turns a familiar epistolary convention to dramatic use and sets the stage for the only passage of sustained rhetorical complaint in the letter:

> Myn eyen two, in veyn with which I se,
> Of sorwful teris salte arn woxen welles;
> My song, in pleynte of myn adversitee;
> My good, in harm; myn ese ek woxen helle is;
> My joie, in wo; I kan sey yow naught ellis,
> But torned is, for which my lif I warie,
> Everich joie or ese in his contrarie.　　(V, 1373–79)

This renewed appeal to Criseyde's pity restores the mood of the letter's opening and prepares the way for the main *petitio*. Troilus is again more subtle than Troiolo, who states his request after spending two full stanzas (*Fil.*, vii, 70–71) appealing to Criseida in the name of her beauty, her promises, and the pleasures (and hardships) that she once shared with him. There is no mistaking the approaching *petitio*. Troilus, by contrast, makes the main point of his *petitio* before Criseyde can realize that she is being importuned. He simply sets alongside the fresh depiction of his present sufferings a picture of what still might be. The talk of reversals and the final word "contrarie" in the stanza of complaint prepare the reader for the opposition, as does, in a less obvious way, the repetition in both stanzas of the key words (virtually equated in Troilus' present state of mind) "joie" and "lif." Things are the reverse of what they used to be, says Troilus, but they may yet be reversed again. Having first shown

---

[52] Troilus' phrase "holde ... in honde" almost certainly conceals a *double entendre* signifying his self–deception. Criseyde uses the same expression in her letter, when she suggests that Troilus has been deceiving her (V, 1615).

[53] Cf. also Troiolo's first letter (ii, 96) and Margery Brews's letter (quoted in chapter 1).

Criseyde what she is capable of bringing about, he goes on to remind her
gently but firmly of her obligation to do so:

> Which with youre comyng hom ayeyn to Troie
> Ye may redresse, and more a thousand sithe
> Than evere ich hadde, encressen in me joie.
> For was ther nevere herte yet so blithe
> To han his lif as I shal ben as swithe
> As I yow se; and though no manere routhe
> Commeve yow, yet thynketh on youre trouthe.   (V, 1380–86)

The parallel between this stanza and the earlier *petitio*/*captatio benevolentiae* is striking. In both instances the rhetorical structure defuses a
potentially explosive statement. Criseyde is first tempted with an at-
tractive possibility and then, apparently as an afterthought, reminded that
the capacity for realizing that possibility resides entirely in her and that
indeed she is honor–bound to take action.

Language more typical of *petitiones* first appears in the subsequent
stanzas, where Troilus asks a favor somewhat easier to grant. He would
clearly prefer her return, but he will settle for a letter; anything is better
than agonizing uncertainty. Lest she forget his real desire, he returns one
last time to the theme of the *narratio* before bringing his letter to a close:

> Iwis, myne owene deere herte trewe,
> I woot that, whan ye next upon me se,
> So lost have I myn hele and ek myn hewe,
> Criseyde shal nought konne knowen me.
> Iwys, myn hertes day, my lady free,
> So thursteth ay myn herte to byholde
> Youre beute, that my lif unnethe I holde.   (V, 1401–7)

Chaucer has once again shifted an element from Boccaccio's text (*Fil.,* vii,
75) to a position where it will have greater psychological effectiveness.

Chaucer's treatment of the *conclusio* is formally, thematically, and
dramatically significant. He constructs the penultimate stanza of the letter
by the rules of the conventional *conclusio*, thereby formally signaling the
reader that the letter is approaching its end. Troilus' statement that he has
said what he intends to say and his farewell in God's name are typical
ways of concluding and do, in fact, conclude Troiolo's letter in the
Filostrato (vii, 75). In choosing to extend the *conclusio* through another
stanza Chaucer discloses other motives beyond the formal ones:

> I say namore, al have I for to seye
> To yow wel more than I telle may.

> But wheither that ye do me lyve or deye,
> Yet praye I God, so yeve yow right good day!
> And fareth wel, goodly, faire, fresshe may,
> As ye that lif or deth may me comande!
> And to youre trouthe ay I me recomande,
>
> With hele swich that, but ye yeven me
> The same hele, I shal non hele have.
> In yow lith, whan yow liste that it so be,
> The day in which me clothen shal my grave;
> In yow my lif, in yow myght for to save
> Me fro disese of alle peynes smerte;
> And far now wel, myn owen swete herte!
>   le vostre T.   (V, 1408–21)

Had Chaucer been guided by purely epistolary considerations he would have ended the letter at line 1411 or 1413. Indeed, that is precisely what his fifteenth–century imitators will do. He chose instead to attach a final summation of the theme central to the entire letter. Troilus recommends himself to Criseyde's "trouthe" because, as we have already seen, her promise is about the only hold that he has on her. In plighting her his troth he resigned his fate into her hands. She became his feudal overlord and accepted his loyal service in return for the promise to protect and provide for him. So long as he fulfills his part of the contract, and he has, she is obliged to fulfill hers. Nor can either of them simply terminate the agreement unilaterally without incurring serious guilt. Troilus has, as he discovers at the poem's end, disastrously misplaced his faith; but within the limits of his viewpoint he is correct. He is mistaken not in his interpretation of the code of courtly love, but in the belief that such love is subject to reason and governed by laws to the same degree as fealty relationships are.

Troilus' farewell is only the final touch to the dramatic irony that pervades the "Litera Troili." Behind his parting words is the hope that Criseyde will respond as she did the last time he put his life in her hands. From now on, he concludes, everything depends on her. We need not wait for Criseyde's answer to discover that he hopes in vain – indeed her first reply disguises the fact, for the betrayal has already been acted out. Her decisive interview with Diomede took place on the very day set for her return (V, 842), weeks before Troilus wrote. Even as Troilus lingered atop the city wall that night and mistook a "fare–carte" for her, she lay in her father's tent,

> Retornyng in hire soule ay up and down
> The wordes of this sodeyn Diomede.   (1023–24)

Before the night was over she "took fully purpos for to dwelle" (1029) among the Greeks and quietly forgot what she had firmly resolved only the night before (750ff). We already know what the full extent of her falseness will be some two hundred lines before we read Troilus' letter, and this knowledge cannot help but color our response to his words. Troilus' farewell to Criseyde, in particular, echoes ironically Criseyde's own farewell apostrophe to him, which she prefaces with similar talk of "trouthe":

> But syn I se ther is no bettre way,
> And that to late is now for me to rewe,
> To Diomede algate I wol be trewe.

> "But, Troilus, syn I no bettre may,
> And syn that thus departen ye and I,
> Yet prey I God, so yeve yow right good day,
> As for the gentileste, trewely,
> That evere I say, to serven feythfully,
> And best kan ay his lady honour kepe"; –
> And with that word she brast anon to wepe.

> "And certes, yow ne haten shal I nevere;
> And frendes love, that shal ye han of me,
> And my good word, al sholde I lyven evere.
> And, trewely, I wolde sory be
> For to seen yow in adversitee;
> And gilteles, I woot wel, I yow leve.
> But al shal passe; and thus take I my leve."   (V, 1069–85)

The irony deepens when this passage, with its almost naive candor, is juxtaposed with Criseyde's shameless dissimulation in her next and final appearance, the "Litera Criseydis."

3.4. The "Litera Criseydis"

The pattern of the man's address followed by the woman's response is already familiar from the paired letters that conclude the *Heroides* (xvi–xxi) and characterizes the letters in Book ii of the *Filostrato* as well. If Chaucer had the *Heroides* in mind, he would surely have noticed the irony of Troiolo filling the role of the abandoned lover. Paris (xvi), Leander (xviii), and Acontius (xx) are ardent and, except for Leander, underhanded suitors. Ovid reserved the role of forsaken lover for the women whose letters Chaucer excerpted in the course of performing his penance. Thus in yet another way, the excerpts from the *Heroides* in *The*

78

Legend of Good Women reassert legitimate *auctoritas* in opposition to the heresies of "Lollius."

The "Litera Criseydis" is not, strictly speaking, a direct response to the "Litera Troili." Chaucer follows his source in summarizing Criseyde's initial response, which arrives more promptly than in Boccaccio's version but contains the same message:

> This lettre forth was sent unto Criseyde,
> Of which hire answere in effect was this:
> Ful pitously she wroot ayeyn, and seyde,
> That also sone as that she myghte, ywys,
> She wolde come, and mende al that was mys.
> And fynaly she wroot and seyde hym thenne,
> She wolde come, ye, but she nyste whenne.
>
> But in hire lettre made she swich festes
> That wonder was, and swerth she loveth hym best;
> Of which he fond but botmeles bihestes.   (V, 1422–31)[54]

The letter that Chaucer quotes in full (V, 1590–1631) is written by Criseyde "for routhe" only after Troilus

> To hire ... wroot yet ofte tyme al newe
> Ful pitously, – he lefte it nought for slouthe, –
> Bisechyng hire, syn that he was trewe,
> That she wol come ayeyn and holde hire trouthe.   (V, 1583–86)

The letter that she writes, however, contains only the same stale excuses and "botmeles bihestes" as the previous one, which, in general content, it strongly resembles. Chaucer probably made this change in order to help characterize Criseyde's prevarication. After all Troilus' agony, she is moved to send him only the same empty assurances. The literal sense of the letter is less important than its affective meaning, which can best be understood through comparison with the "Litera Troili," which dramatically, though not literally, it answers.

We cannot determine how far the relationship between Criseyde and Diomede had progressed by the time Troilus wrote his letter; the narrator refuses to speculate about this crucial matter (V, 1086–92). It is at least certain that Criseyde has long since accepted Diomede's "friendship,"

---

[54] Cf. *Fil.*, vii, 105. Boccaccio says that her reply was some time in coming:

> Quinci la diede a Pandar suggellata,
> che la mandò: e la riposta invano
> da essi fu per piú giorni aspettata   (vii, 76)

denied that she ever had a lover in Troy (977–78), and abandoned for the time being any plans to steal back to the city. Perhaps she could still half–believe in the reassurances that she sends in reply (V, 1424–30), even if neither the reader nor the narrator (1431–35) can. There is even less room for doubt when she comes to write the "Litera Criseydis." Considerable time has passed since Troilus first wrote and she swore "she loveth hym best" (1430) in reply: in the interim, Hector has been killed and mourned; Troilus has had his fateful dream, has languished long in doubt (1569–82), and has written many more letters. Therefore, when Criseyde plays the same tune a second time – minus, significantly, the passionate protestations of her affection – the irony is no longer simply dramatic but verbal as well. We know not only that she is "falsing" Troilus but also that she knows it herself. Although in these, her final words in the poem, she is still too fearful to tell the truth, even the best–disposed reader, Troilus himself, cannot fail to see through her subterfuges. As in Book II, he obstinately hopes for the best (V, 1635–38; cf. II, 1324–30), but his hope carries little conviction. Every statement that she makes is suspect on the literal level and demands to be viewed in another light. The letter is truly a "kalendes of chaunge," for in her refusal to commit herself one way or another Criseyde displays the vacillation that made Diomede's task relatively easy.[55] By inventing this second letter, Chaucer permits Criseyde one last and especially vivid display of her "slydynge corage."

Despite the tawdriness of its sentiments, Criseyde's letter does not lag behind Troilus' in skillful use of the conventions. The difference is that in his letter they were always used sincerely, whereas in hers they are everywhere undercut by irony.[56] She opens, for example, with the combined *salutatio* and *captatio benevolentiae* that typifies epistolary complaint and that derives from the double meaning of the Latin *salus*. How can one, she asks, who is herself deprived of health by his absence send him health (i.e., greeting)?[57]

---

[55] The narrator's statement that no one knows how long it was before Criseyde forsook Troilus for Diomede (V, 1086–92) must be read ironically, given that he has just shown her encouraging Diomede and repudiating Troilus on the very day set for her return to Troy (V, 960–1008).

[56] On Criseyde's "disingenuous style" in this letter, see Monica McAlpine, *Genre of Troilus and Criseyde,* pp. 210–12. McKinnell finds her rhetoric too perfect, her arguments too balanced to be anything but contrived. "Letters as Type of Formal Level," pp. 87–89.

[57] Cf. *Fil.,* ii, 96, and n. 40 above. Meech (*Design,* p. 131) points out further resemblances between *T&C,* V, 1599–1600, and *Fil.,* ii, 122, lines 7–8, and *T&C,* V, 1625–30, and *Fil.,* ii, 126, lines 1–6.

80

Cupides sone, ensample of goodlyheede,
O swerd of knyghthod, sours of gentilesse,
How myght a wight in torment and in drede
And heleles, yow sende as yet gladnesse?
I herteles, I sik, I in destresse!
Syn ye with me, nor I with yow, may dele,
Yow neyther sende ich herte may nor hele.   (V, 1590–96)

These lines may be read on one level as courtly convention and as an appropriate elaboration on the theme of the mutuality of the lovers' well–being that Troilus stressed in his letter. Criseyde even practices a sort of amatory one–upmanship by sounding the note of complaint less hesitantly than Troilus did. But her haste to protest her sorrow and the artful cliché to which she resorts only magnify her insincerity. Her rhetoric betrays her: unable to send Troilus either "herte" or "hele," she is truly "herteles" and "heleles," lacking both compassion and integrity.

The irony intensifies in the *narratio*, where she will presumably explain why she has put off returning for so long. Criseyde opens the *narratio* in a businesslike, dispassionate style sharply distinguished from the rhetoric of the previous stanza. This is only the first of the abrupt shifts that will characterize the body of the letter. The style suits the subject matter, for in a few strokes she informs Troilus that she has read his letters, feels sorry for him, but regretably cannot comply with his wishes as yet (V, 1597–1600). Fast on the heels of this (to Troilus) crushing news comes yet another familiar convention of the love letter, which, as Criseyde uses it, completely subverts the ostensible purpose of her writing:

Youre lettres ful, the papir al ypleynted,
Conceyved hath myn hertes pietee.
I have ek seyn with teris al depeynted
Youre lettre, and how that ye requeren me
To come ayeyn, which yet ne may nat be.
But whi, lest that this lettre founden were,
No mencioun ne make I now, for feere.   (V, 1597–1603)

The fear of discovery, a regular feature of medieval love letters from the very beginning, has already been noted more than once in the previous chapter. However, Criseyde invokes secrecy not in its conventional role of concealing her love for the person whom she addresses from the eyes of outsiders, but to delude the very person who normally would share the secret. Before Troilus realizes what she has done, she has freed herself from the responsibility of accounting for her delay, which was to have been the purpose of the entire letter.

Nor does she give him a chance to catch his breath. Now that the pressure is temporarily off her, she is free to put it on him. She accuses him of impatience, of opposing the gods, and of thinking only about his own "plesaunce" (V, 1604–8). Originally the injured party, Troilus is suddenly compelled to defend his own actions. Her sudden shift to the offensive effectively diverts attention from her questionable sleight of hand at the end of the previous stanza.[58]

Any doubt that Criseyde is easily Troilus' match at psychology should be dispelled by her next move. She seems to reconsider for a moment and even offers a tentative explanation for her tarrying:

> But beth nat wroth, and that I yow biseche;
> For that I tarie is al for wikked speche.   (V, 1609–10)

Troilus would inevitably understand her to mean that she was still concerned about her reputation, and she encourages that interpretation in the next three lines:

> For I have herd wel moore than I wende,
> Touchyng us two, how thynges han ystonde;
> Which I shal with dissymulyng amende.   (V, 1611–13)[59]

Then once again she abruptly turns the tables on him –

> And beth nat wroth, I have ek understonde
> How ye ne do but holden me in honde   (1614–15)

– but just as quickly recants:

> But now no force, I kan nat in yow gesse
> But alle trouthe and alle gentilesse.   (1616–17)

There is no need to dig for the irony that pervades her touching reluctance to believe evil rumors of him. Her presumption in even mentioning his possible fickleness seems as outrageous to the reader as it probably did to Troilus.[60]

---

[58] Her strategy is precisely the one recommended by the Wife of Bath, in her "Prologue," 379–92.

[59] These last two lines describe precisely what she is doing in the letter itself and as such are thoroughly ironic.

[60] In fairness to Criseyde, it should be pointed out that she is only making Troilus fry in his own grease. In order to remain with her in bed, he had allowed her to believe that he was actually jealous of her alleged attention to Horaste (III, 1149–62). The foreshadowing is made clear in Criseyde's reply to Pandarus' account of the rumor (and Troilus' response) that he had fabricated for the occasion: "in thought ne dede untrewe / To Troilus *was nevere yet* Criseyde" (III, 1053–54; my italics).

This manipulation is perhaps less deliberate on Criseyde's part (though certainly not on Chaucer's) than my analysis suggests. Her "strategy" could just as easily be explained as desperate recourse to "graceless expedients" in a last attempt to save face.[61] The point is that her expedients, whether desperate or calculated, are effective. Nothing suits her purposes better at this point than to shake Troilus' self–righteousness, and she could hardly have found a better way to do it. By the time she gives her vague promise to return sometime, though she knows not "what yer or what day / That this shal be" (1619–20), Troilus is reduced to taking whatever crumbs he can get.

The *narratio* is misnamed in this case, since the letter is all dissimulation: Criseyde is determined at all costs to avoid saying anything substantial, since there is really nothing that she can say. Hence she does not satisfy even Troilus' minimum request (V, 1387–1400) but leaves him just unsure enough so that he can still pretend that there is hope (1635–38). What she might have said had she the courage to stand behind her actions and accept their consequences is what she did say, *sotto voce,* in the apostrophe to Troilus quoted earlier in this chapter. There can be no questioning the connection between the letter and the apostrophe, which Chaucer clearly echoes in the brief *petitio* dramatically situated immediately after Criseyde's indefinite postponement of her return:

> But in effect I pray yow, as I may,
> Of youre good word and of youre frendship ay.
> For trewely, while that my lif may dure,
> As for a frend ye may in me assure.   (V, 1621–24)

Her offer of "frendship" and her concern about his "good word" point unmistakably to the earlier passage (cf. V, 1079–81). In the light of Criseyde's lament for her reputation (V, 1054–68), one might trace in her desire to retain Troilus' "good word" the reason why she bothers to write to him at all. But it is also possible to find her motive in the wistful ending of the apostrophe (1082–85), in her sincere regret for Troilus' innocent suffering on her account and her consequent desire to give him time to recover from his infatuation with her.

Criseyde is fully aware of what poor recompense she gives Troilus for his devotion. She constantly reveals her guilt in such unconscious ways as the "beth nat wroth" (1609, 1614) with which she feels compelled to soften the blows of her false accusations. Her clearest expression of the

---

[61] S. Meech, *Design,* p. 131.

disproportion between Troilus' letter and her reply occurs in the *conclusio:*

> Yet preye ich yow, on yvel ye ne take
> That it is short which that I to yow write;
> I dar nat, ther I am, wel lettres make,
> Ne nevere yet ne koude I wel endite.
> Ek gret effect men write in place lite;
> Th'entente is al, and nat the lettres space.
> And fareth now wel, God have yow in his grace!
>   La vostre C.   (V, 1625–31)

The literal sense is again conventional for this part of the letter and might be paraphrased by two sayings still current: "Good things come in small packages," and "It's the thought that counts." It is hardly necessary to point out the irony. This sort of apology may be an epistolary commonplace, but it also springs, in the present case, from Criseyde's genuine sense of guilt. Quantitative inequality on the literal level is made to serve as a correlative for qualitative inequality on the intentional level, and, as Criseyde observes, "Th'entente is al." The last two lines sum up the whole letter, had Troilus but eyes to see.

Even the simple signature at the letter's end, "La vostre C.," contributes to the ironic contrast. On hearing Troilus' words echoed exactly, we cannot help but feel intensely the difference in the emotions behind them. The formulaic *subscriptio* thus acquires a poignancy out of proportion to its thorough conventionality. Though it may well have been supplied by a later scribe or editor rather than by Chaucer himself, this final touch is nonetheless typical of Chaucer's ability to transform epistolary clichés into powerful emotional statements.

The "Litera Troili" and the "Litera Criseydis" show how even the most time–worn conventions can take on new life in the hands of a master poet like Chaucer. Both letters are integral to the narrative, but the "Litera Troili," in particular, could easily be detached from its context and was capable of standing on its own as an independent lyric. Chaucer's synthesis of courtly language and epistolary formulas at the beginning and the end of the "Litera Troili" became the formal paradigm for what quickly evolved into a new variety of English love lyric. In this sense it can justly be compared to Ovid's heroical epistles, which had spawned numerous imitations during the twelfth century and would do so again at the close of the Middle Ages.

But in emphasizing the potential autonomy of the "Litera Troili" as a factor in the emergence of the Middle English verse love epistle, I do not

84

mean to discount the equally important influence of *Troilus and Criseyde* as the supreme *ars amandi* for fifteenth–century England. Chaucer supplied not only a new form but also a detailed and fascinating picture of the love letter's social function. The writing of love letters in verse was but one aspect, if an especially well documentable aspect, of a more comprehensive imitation of Troilus. The popularity of the whole model of behavior must have had a great deal to do with the popularity of the literary genres closely associated with it. Although in developing both form and function Chaucer "translated" what was already available in French and Italian literature, from his synthesis rather than from his sources came the voice and the vision of English love poetry for the next hundred years and more.

CHAPTER 4:

The Emergence of the Verse Love Epistle

4.1. The Context of the Genre's Emergence

Historical study of medieval English love lyrics has long been inhibited by their anonymity. While the French lyrics have come down to us in large, well-organized collections with clear indications of authorship, the English lyrics are more typically copied singly or in small groups, to fill the odd blank space in a codex whose contents are unrelated to them, and without any mention of author, place, or date of composition.[1] The few "anthologies" that survive are mostly commonplace books, often compiled by many hands over periods as long as a century (e.g., the Findern Anthology). Even when the date for their compilation can be more narrowly specified, as with such major collections as MS Rawlinson C.813 (1527–1535), the Devonshire MS (1532–1541), and the Bannatyne MS (1568), one is left with only a *terminus ante quem* for the poems that they contain, some of which will turn out to have been composed a century or more prior to the compilation. Such habits of collection and transmission make it very difficult either to establish clearly the relationships among the various lyric kinds at any given point during the fifteenth century or to trace with any precision the changes that occurred within a given kind during that same period.[2]

The verse love epistle is no exception to this rule, particularly as regards the period of its greatest popularity, from the mid fifteenth through the mid sixteenth centuries. However, for the fifty years following Chaucer's death – the crucial period during which the genre developed the essential form and functions that would distinguish it throughout its subsequent development – fate has been kinder to the genre historian. Only the five verse love epistles from MSS Harley 682 and Fairfax 16 can be dated with certainty to the period before 1450 (*Index* 2182, 2184,

---

[1] See J. Boffey, *Manuscripts of Lyrics*.

[2] On these and other difficulties inhibiting the historical study of Middle English lyrics, see especially G. Kane, "Short Essay," and H. Bergner, "Frage der Gattungen."

2230, 2823, 4192);[3] but their numbers are inversely proportional to their importance. They are unique in being preserved in well-organized, clearly labeled collections associated with a well-known poet, and they have in common a careful observance of epistolary form and better than average poetic skill.

By contrast with those discussed in chapters 2 and 3, the poems that are the focus of this chapter are the work of aristocrats who were amateur men of letters. The large collection of English lyrics in MS Harley 682 and the two smaller ones in the last booklet of MS Fairfax 16 (both mid fifteenth century) are two of only three surviving anthologies exclusively devoted to love poems in English.[4] Considering how rare such collections were in England, it is probably no coincidence that both anthologies have French connections. At one time or another, in fact, all the more than 250 English lyrics preserved in the two anthologies have been ascribed to Charles of Orléans, who remained as prisoner in England from his capture at Agincourt (1415) until his release in 1440. Most Anglo-American scholars accept Charles's authorship of at least those portions of the Harley collection that have French counterparts in Charles's *Le livre de la prison,* while several continental scholars regard the entire English version as the work of a translator/adapter.[5] Despite the presence of one poem definitely by Charles, and despite similarities to the poems in Harley 682, the second group of lyrics in Fairfax 16, comprising twenty poems, has been less widely accepted as Charles's work. Henry N. MacCracken, who first edited the poems, attributed them on rather slim evidence to Charles of Orléans's English friend and onetime "host," William de la Pole, first duke of Suffolk (1396–1450), whom he also thought responsible for the poems in Harley 682.[6] For our purposes it is

---

[3] This number could be increased many–fold if the formal restrictions were sufficiently loosened to admit some of the ballades in MS Harley 682 into the canon. The reasons for not doing so are discussed later in this chapter (4.5).

[4] J. Boffey, *Manuscripts of Lyrics,* p. 7. For the possibility that the two collections in Fairfax 16, booklet 5, are really a single sequence, see R. H. Robbins, "Court Love Lyric," pp. 230–31 n. 71.

[5] Norma L. Goodrich has devoted an entire book to proving their authenticity on thematic grounds (*Charles of Orléans*). She surveys the previous scholarship on pp. 20–31. For the most recent summation of the issue see Cecily Clark, "Charles d'Orléans," pp. 254–61, and "Postscript," pp. 230–31. The best arguments against Charles's authorship appear in Daniel Poirion, "Création poétique," pp. 185–211, and Theo Stemmler, "Verfasserfrage," pp. 458–73. Also see D. Poirion, "Charles d'Orléans," pp. 524–25. Additional bibliography is listed by Edith Yenal, in *Charles d'Orleans: A Bibliography,* pp. 32–37.

[6] "English Friend," pp. 142–80. MacCracken's edition has now been superseded by J. P. M. Jansen, ed., *'Suffolk' Poems.* For a rejection of the attribution of the Harley 682

unnecessary to decide how many of these poems were composed in English by Charles himself; it is sufficient to recognize that they are all associated with the captured duke and a rather small group of English aristocrats who shared his literary avocation and that they were probably composed and collected during the second quarter of the fifteenth century.

The association of Harley 682 and Fairfax 16 with the higher aristocracy is significant, since that class is one of the very few in England at this period to retain an active interest in French language and literature. Indeed, Julia Boffey has shown that most of the anthologies of courtly lyrics produced for or owned by English aristocrats during the period from 1400 to 1450 consisted mainly of poems in French.[7] Thus, while the verse love epistle can be said to emerge as a distinct form of the Middle English lyric during this period, it is shaped within a matrix that is still a projection of contemporary French literature. Yet none of the five epistolary poems, two in Harley 682 and three in Fairfax 16, can be traced to a French model, and four out of five are composed in a flexible but homogeneous verse form (three to six stanzas, rime royal) that does not correspond to any of the *formes fixes* used by the French courtly lyricists, including Charles of Orléans. Despite the undeniable French connections of the five verse love epistles associated with Charles and his circle of English acquaintances, the form seems already to be separating itself during the first half of the fifteenth century from the constraints evident a generation earlier. In form, Gower's love epistles were ballades first and letters second; and though they are never unambiguously designated as

poems to Suffolk, on stylistic and other grounds, see Robert Steele, ed., *English Poems,* vol. 1, pp. xxiff; Martin Crow, "John of Angoulême," p. 89; and T. Stemmler, who also denies that Suffolk wrote the poems in Fairfax 16 ("Verfasserfrage," pp. 459–60). More recently, J. P. M. Jansen has concluded that the poems in Harley 682 and those in Fairfax 16 were not composed by the same person, based on differences in subject matter and imagery, formal aspects (especially prosody), and language: "Charles d'Orléans," pp. 206–24. Poirion seems receptive to the idea that the poems in Harley 682 are the work of Suffolk and other members of his circle, such as Roos and Moleyns: "Charles d'Orléans," p. 517. Poirion had earlier demonstrated that several of the French poems that MacCracken ascribed to Suffolk are actually known works by poets like Chartier and Deschamps: "Création poétique," pp. 193–94. Enid McLeod is one of the few scholars persuaded by MacCracken's arguments for both attributions: *Charles of Orleans,* p. 390. See also n. 52 below. On the relationship between Fairfax 16 and Harley 682 (and other collections of Charles's poetry), also see J. Boffey, *Manuscripts of Lyrics,* pp. 9–11, 74–76. The first sequence of lyrics in booklet 5 of Fairfax 16, *Venus' Mass* (*Index* 4186) contains nothing relevant to the present study.

[7] *Manuscripts of Lyrics,* p. 9. V. J. Scattergood makes a similar point about the later fourteenth century, in "Literary Culture," pp. 29–43.

letters, many of the ballades of Charles of Orléans's *Le livre de la prison* (and their English versions in Harley 682) are epistolary in the same sense as Gower's. The defining structure of the five English poems (and the macaronic pair discussed in chapter 2.10) is unmistakably that of the epistle: except for length, their closest precedent is the "Litera Troili."

The role of French poetry in the emergence of the Middle English verse love epistle is probably to be sought less in models for direct imitation than in the treatment of fixed-form lyrics as written texts rather than as songs, a far-reaching change of attitude that seems to have occurred in the latter part of the fourteenth century and that is explicitly acknowledged in Deschamps's *Art de dictier* (1392). This shift of perspective allowed the epistolary function (if not the form) of the declining *salut d'amour* to be transferred onto the ballade and, less often, other *poèmes à forme fixe*. More important for the Middle English tradition, it spawned a host of new forms such as the testament, based on the public and official written documents that had always been the primary concern of the *ars dictaminis*.[8] The number and variety of such "documents of love" increased rapidly during the last quarter of the fourteenth century, and by the fifteenth century they were virtually obligatory components of courtly love sequences, especially those employing the allegorical and dream-vision conventions.[9] This development in French literature anticipated by a generation or two the dramatic increase in the use of English for public documents and private letters that England witnessed during the early fifteenth century. While love documents had already entered

---

[8] See, for example, Dieter Ingenschay, *Alltagswelt*, pp. 16–17. Ruhe makes the difference between oral song and written text one of the key *differentiae* between the Provençal *canso* and *salutz: De Amasio*, pp. 108–9.

[9] Such documents are as old as the court of love tradition. For twelfth–century examples in Latin and French, see William Allan Neilson, *Court of Love*, pp. 33 and 43. But their popularity, along with that of fictional–allegorical legal documents in general, seems to have increased dramatically in both England and France around the turn of the fifteenth century. See *The Assembly of Ladies* and especially *The Court of Love* (W. W. Skeat, ed., *Chaucer*, vol. 7, pp. 380–404 and 409–47). Cf. also "The Lover and the Advocate of Venus": ed. R. H. Robbins, *SL*, pp. 169–70 (#178). On the courts of love see W. A. Neilson, *Court of Love*, and D. Poirion, *Le Poète et le prince*, pp. 37–43. See also John A. Alford, "Literature and Law," pp. 941–51. The lover's will or testament was also popular and continued to be written through the sixteenth century. See, e.g., John Lyly's *Entertainments* (1592): ed. R. W. Bond, *Complete Works*, vol. 1, pp. 469–70, and George Gascoigne's *Dan Bartholomew of Bathe*: ed. John W. Cunliffe, *Complete Works*, vol. 1, pp. 118–23. An early vernacular pseudodocument of a lover is the Provençal *salutz* by Amanieu de Sescas (late thirteenth century), which he calls "letras pendens rimadas." E. Ruhe, *De Amasio*, pp. 209–10.

English literature in works by Chaucer and Gower, succeeding generations, doubtless stimulated in part by the widespread interest in English
prose letters and documents, embraced this genre with real enthusiasm.

It is possible that the popularity of the love document helped in turn to
establish the verse love epistle proper, and that in two ways. In the first
place, most love documents carefully imitated the form of genuine
documents, which was that of the epistle. The documents were thus verse
love epistles themselves, albeit *epistolae negotiales* rather than *epistolae
familiares*. Generally speaking, they are longer than any of the fixed-form
poems, and so their structure is dictated more by epistolary norms than by
a particular verse form. The verse love epistle could thus be seen as a
smaller, more familiar complement to an already established epistolary
form: the love document provides a formal precedent. At the same time,
the love documents created a need that the love epistle could fulfill. For
the documents are nearly always either written by or addressed to
someone other than the lover. Especially popular recipients are the gods
of love, Venus and Cupid, or personifications of abstract qualities or
emotions, such as Pity. The restriction in content thus allowed and even
encouraged the creation of an epistolary form in which the lover addressed the beloved more directly and personally. Since love letters are
traditionally classified among the familiar epistles, their emergence as a
genre restores an imbalance created by the *epistolae amatoriae negotiales*.

4.2. Other Varieties of Verse Epistle

Though the love letter and the love document are the two most popular
types of secular verse epistle in England during the period covered by
this study, they are not the only types composed. Before contrasting the
two varieties of amatory epistles, therefore, brief mention should be
made of the other varieties of verse epistle. A few examples exist of
verse epistles addressed to friends or relations. At their most idealistic,
such letters can be difficult to distinguish from love letters proper. Such
is the case with a letter, or more likely the draft of a letter, in the hand
of John Paston III and probably dating from 1471 or later (*Supplement*
2267.5). A "courtly" complaint about the pains of separation, the poem
was considered a love letter by its earliest editors and is so classified in
the *Supplement* to the *Index of Middle English Verse*. But its most recent
editor has suggested, no less plausibly, that the piece may actually be

addressed to the earl of Oxford.[10] Less ambiguous examples indicate that the practice of sending verse epistles to family and friends was not unusual.[11] The form seems to have been especially popular for humorous or even scurrilous purposes.[12]

Outside the context of love, the verse epistle is most often used to teach a moral lesson, a tradition reaching back at least to Horace. The form can be handled with brevity and wit, as in Chaucer's *Lenvoy de Chaucer a Scogan*, or it can be drawn out to treatise length, as in Christine de Pisan's *Epître d'Othéa la déesse à Hector* (ca. 1400), which was thrice translated into English between 1440 and 1540.[13] As these two examples indicate, the same contrast between the direct and personal letter and the more formal, allegorical-mythological fiction seen in the amatory epistles is also observed in the moral epistles. In fact, such epistles occasionally occur in manuscripts that also contain verse love epistles,[14] and a thirteenth-century didactic treatise on love in epistolary form, the letter to Dame Desyree, was discussed in chapter 2.5. A type that seems to have been especially popular was the letter of advice to a princely patron.[15]

---

[10] Ed. N. Davis, *Paston Letters*, vol. 1, pp. 571–73. A further possibility is that John adopted a female persona to write what was essentially a literary exercise, as Humfrey Newton apparently did on occasion.

[11] A good example is the letter from a sister to her brother (*Index* 4232), found in MS Harley 2399 (fifteenth century) and printed by Thomas Wright and J. O. Halliwell, *Reliquiae Antiquae*, vol. 2, pp. 173–74. Also see Benedict Burgh's letter to Lydgate (*Index* 2284: eight stanzas, rime royal; 1433–1440), whose learning he praises: ed. Eleanor P. Hammond, *English Verse*, pp. 189–90.

[12] See especially the letter from a woman to her "loving frende, amorous Bune" (*Supplement* 2261.8), which is followed in the manuscript by a similarly humorous, though less gross letter from a man to his "welbeloved prentise" (*Supplement* 2827.5). They belong to an anthology of fifty–two poems, including at least twenty–five love epistles, in MS Rawlinson C.813 (1527–1535). The existence of such letters helps explain the more innocently humorous verses (*Index* 1360) with which Pampyng and John Paston conclude a long prose letter to Margaret Paston: ed. N. Davis, *Paston Letters*, vol. 1, p. 145 (whole letter, pp. 140–45).

[13] See Curt F. Bühler, ed., *Epistle of Othea*.

[14] A fragment from the end of a verse epistle "signed" by Pallas occurs in BL, MS Sloane 1212 (second half, fifteenth century), a manuscript that also contains a verse love epistle (*Index* 2161). See J. Boffey, *Manuscripts of Lyrics*, pp. 119–20. The Bannatyne MS contains several moral epistles, including one advising ladies on how to preserve their virtue (ed. W. T. Ritchie, IV: 73–75).

[15] See, for example, Hoccleve's double–ballade to Henry V and the Lords of the Garter (ed. F. J. Furnivall, *Hoccleve's Works*, vol. 1, pp. 41–43), and Alexander Scott's "ane new ʒeir gift to the quene mary / Quhen scho come first hame / 1562," in the Bannatyne MS (ed. W. T. Ritchie, II: 235–42). The latter may also exploit what was by the sixteenth century a long–standing tradition of composing verse love epistles as New Year's gifts.

Begging poems often took the form of epistles, as in "Lydgate's Letter to Gloucester."[16] Not surprisingly, Hoccleve is especially fond of this type of verse epistle, which he produced in its purest form in his "Balade to Henry V for Money."[17] Since the poet-petitioner often takes pains to justify the requested change in his patron's fiscal policy, some such letters are difficult to distinguish from letters of advice. Perhaps this ambiguity led George Bannatyne to group one of Dunbar's begging letters among the poems of "wisdome and moralitee."[18] Chaucer had already mixed the conventions of the appeal to the patron and the appeal to the lady in his playful-serious *The Complaint of Chaucer to His Purse*. The requirement that begging poems be witty is probably responsible for their tendency to minimize epistolary formalities, by comparison with the other varieties of contemporary verse epistles.

4.3. Love Documents in English

It is precisely the relative prominence of epistolary markers that distinguishes the love documents and love epistles from other varieties of contemporary courtly love poetry and, with few exceptions, from non-amatory verse epistles. Without such formal signals, the love epistle is often indistinguishable from the amatory complaint, a boundary problem noticed by Arthur K. Moore some thirty years ago.[19] Throughout its history, the verse love epistle remains in a clearly defined, complementary relationship to the love document. During the early, French-dominated period its autonomous identity is threatened on one level by the ballade and on another by the complaint. After the mid fifteenth century the

---

[16] Ed. H. N. MacCracken, *Minor Poems*, part 2, pp. 665–667. Cf. also his "An Epistle to Sibille" (*Index* 3321), a verse paraphrase of *Proverbs*, 31:10–31, called a "lytel pistel" to his lady "Cybille" in the envoy (lines 134–40). Ed. H. N. MacCracken, *Minor Poems*, part 1, pp. 14–18.

[17] Ed. F. J. Furnivall, *Hoccleve's Works*, vol. 1, p. 62. For verse epistles with similar purposes, less bluntly put, cf. ibid., pp. 49–51, 58, 64–66.

[18] Ed. W. T. Ritchie, II: 251–54; better text in James Kinsley, ed., *Poems of Dunbar*, pp. 123–26 (#42). It is difficult to say whether all or any of Dunbar's petitions to the king (cf. Kinsley, #19, 25, 26, 41–45) and to other noblemen (Kinsley, #46, 47) should be called epistles. Like many of his poems of praise (Kinsley, #8, 18, 24, 31, 35), they are in direct address, but they do not employ any specifically epistolary formulas (indeed, one of them – #24 – is a song). On the other hand, one of the praise poems addressed to the queen (#49) is definitely an epistle, and one of the love poems (#12) probably is, too.

[19] *Secular Lyric*, p. 146.

ballade and other fixed forms appear to have been employed less frequently by English versifiers, but the complaint continued as the love epistle's *Doppelgänger*, until a new set of fixed forms replaced both genres in the sixteenth century. The generic matrix within which the verse love epistle assumed its characteristic identity between 1400 and 1450 need not be reconstructed artificially, for it is preserved intact in the two collections associated with Charles of Orléans. In Harley 682, a pair of letters accompany three documents (plus a fourth, found only in the French version) and over one hundred ballades, while in Fairfax 16 the love letter (three examples) is the next most frequently represented genre after the complaint (eleven examples). The distinguishing features of the verse love epistle, at the outset of its independent development, can thus be isolated most effectively by a closer look at the context in which early examples are preserved.

In its typical fifteenth- and sixteenth-century form, the love document is associated with the court of love convention. Chaucer is the first poet to compose legalistic love documents in English. Though he does not set them in the conventional context of a formal court of love, he must have been aware of that convention. Indeed he seems to allude to it in the G version of the Prologue to *The Legend of Good Women,* 359–64. The closest he comes to duplicating the *form* of a document is "The Bill of Complaint" addressed to Pity, who cannot receive it because she is dead (*The Complaint unto Pity,* lines 57–98).[20] However, the effect of this document depends more on the use of legal terminology and the structure of legal bills[21] than on epistolary conventions, which are restricted to the *salutatio/captatio benevolentiae* of the first stanza:

> Humblest of herte, highest of reverence,
> Benygne flour, coroune of vertues alle,
> Sheweth unto youre rial excellence
> Youre servaunt, yf I durste me so calle,
> Hys mortal harm in which he is yfalle,
> And noght al oonly for his evel fare,
> But for your renoun, as he shal declare.   (57–63)

A more typical love document, in terms both of setting and recipient, is the "Supplicacioun" that Amans sends to Venus and Cupid in Book VIII

---

[20] For other examples of formal complaints preceded by prologues, cf. *Anelida and Arcite* (lines 211–350) and *The Complaint of Mars* (lines 155–298). Neither complaint makes much attempt to imitate epistolary form or to employ legal terminology. W. A. Davenport applies the rubric "compound complaint" to *The Complaint unto Pity*, along with *The Complaint of Venus* and *Fortune*, in *Complaint and Narrative*, pp. 15–23.

[21] See Charles J. Nolan, Jr., "Structural Sophistication," pp. 363–72.

94

of Gower's *Confessio Amantis* (lines 2217–2300). To be properly appreciated, Amans' letter, like most of the English texts discussed in the previous two chapters, must be viewed in the context of the entire work in which it appears. It comes at the dramatically significant point where, after more than 30,000 lines, the narrative reaches its climax with Genius' ultimatum:

> Mi Sone, now thou hast conceived
> Somwhat of that I wolde mene;
> Hierafterward it schal be sene
> If that thou lieve upon mi lore;
> For I can do to thee nomore
> Bot teche thee the rihte weie,
> Now ches if thou wolt live or deie.   (2142–48)

Genius has done everything in his power to fortify Amans' reason against the demands of his will and to prepare him for the final struggle, now imminent. Amans, still "*amens*," insists on sending a petition to Venus and finally persuades Genius to deliver it for him. The letter that he writes is, in effect, his actual *confessio*. In it he recognizes for the first time the real source of his malady,[22] the discord that is the theme of the entire poem. "The effect of his writing," observes Russell A. Peck, "is to formalize his dissatisfaction so that he can cope with it."[23] Once he has confessed that the kingdom of his self is divided, the process of reuniting it can begin.

The letter's formal qualities underscore its thematic and dramatic importance. Its rime royal stanzas, for example, set it off from the octosyllabic couplets of the narrative. The distinctness of the letter impressed Macaulay, and his note is perhaps the best assessment of its quality and its ultimate source:

> This 'Supplication' is a finished and successful composition in its way, and it may make us desire that our author had written more of the same kind. ... The nearest parallel in style is to be found in some of the author's French Balades.[24]

As in Gower's ballade-letters, the epistolary characteristics in Amans' letter are not distinctive. The piece consists, structurally speaking, of a nine-stanza *narratio* followed by a three-stanza *petitio*. Although the

---

[22] In his persona of author he had anticipated this confession in lines 2189–99; but in terms of the fiction this is analysis performed *ex post facto*.

[23] Ed., *Confessio Amantis*, p. xxvii.

[24] Ed., *Works of Gower*, vol. 3 (1901), p. 544.

petitio is rather interestingly organized,[25] there is little attempt to exploit the conventions of letter writing to suit the circumstances under which the letter is sent. If the definition were stretched, the letter's opening stanza might be regarded as an *exordium* of sorts:

> The wofull peine of loves maladie,
> Ayein the which mai no phisique availe,
> Min herte hath so bewhaped with sotie,
> That wher so that I reste or I travaile,
> I finde it evere redy to assaile
> Mi resoun, which that can him noght defende:
> Thus seche I help, wherof I mihte amende.   (2217–23)

and its last few lines resemble a *conclusio:*

> This wold I for my laste word beseche,
> That thou mi love aquite as I deserve,
> Or elles do me pleinly forto sterve.   (2298–2300)

A comparison with the "Litera Troili," however, will quickly reveal how loosely these terms must be interpreted to make them fit the present case. Gower does employ a variation on one familiar convention of the love letter in having Amans write his bill of complaint "with the teres of [his] ye / In stede of enke" (2212–13), but this appears outside the actual text of the letter.

Stylistically more characteristic of this particular genre is Hoccleve's *The Letter of Cupid* (1402). Here great pains are taken to duplicate the ceremonious tone and the formal conventions of royal communications. Cupid is suitably regal in character as he identifies himself in the *salutatio:*

> Cupido vn-to whos commandement
> The gentil kynrede of Goddes on hy
> And peple infernal been obedient,
> And the mortel folk seruen bisyly:
> Of goddesse Sitheree sone oonly,
> To alle tho þat to our deitee
> Been sogettes greetynges senden we.[26]

---

[25] The first stanza is a general appeal to both Venus and Cupid; this is followed by a stanza of appeal directed specifically to Cupid and then one to Venus.

[26] Ed. Sir Israel Gollancz, *Hoccleve's Works,* p. 20. The corresponding lines from Christine de Pisan's *l'Epistre au dieu d'amours* read:

> Cupido, roy par la grace de lui,
> Dieu des amans, sanz aide de nullui
> Regnant en l'air du ciel trés reluisant,
> Filz de Venus la deesse poissant,

He places his own name in initial position, stressing his superiority, and lists his domains and genealogy before sending his greetings. Hoccleve took the pattern from Christine de Pisan, whose *l'Epistre au dieu d'amours* (1399) his poem adapts and translates, and who was in turn simply following the form recommended by dictaminal treatises as well as imitating the type of salutation actually employed by contemporary kings.[27]

The body of the letter is devoted to refuting the arguments of the anti-feminists and criticizing male treachery in the process. Hoccleve follows Christine for the most part, omitting more than he adds. Among the most notable changes is his introduction of an element of humor lacking in the original, as when he has Cupid interrupt his recitation of the complaints that he has received to "flex his muscles":[28]

> But maugree hem þat blamen wommen moost,
> Swich is the force of oure impressioun,
> þat sodeynly We felle can hir boost,
> And al hir wrong ymaginacioun,
> It shal nat been in hire elleccioun,
> The foulest slutte in al a town refuse,
> If þat vs list for al þat they can muse.
>
> But hire in herte as brennyngly desyre
> As thogh shee were a duchesse or a qweene;
> So can We mennes hertes sette on fyre,
> And as vs list hem sende ioie & teene.
> They that to wommen been I-whet so keene,
> Our sharpe strokes, how sore they smyte,
> Shul feele and knowe & how they kerue & byte.   (232–45)

> Sire d'amours et de tous ses obgiez,
> A tous nos vrais loiaulx servans subgiez,
> SALUT, AMOUR, FAMILIARITÉ.

Ed. M. Roy, *Oeuvres poétiques*, pt. 2 (1891), p. 1. Most of the poems discussed in this and the following chapter are published in one or at most two modern editions. All references will be to the edition cited in the footnote to the first mention of each text.

[27] H. G. Richardson prints a parody of a royal letter, composed at Oxford in 1432, which begins in similar fashion: "Oxford *Dictatores*," p. 439. See Rymer's *Foedera* for examples of the real thing.

[28] Cf. Christine, lines 300ff. John V. Fleming stresses this point in his interesting and highly favorable, though somewhat overly ingenious interpretation of the poem: "Hoccleve's 'Letter of Cupid,'" pp. 21–40. For the relationship of Hoccleve's poem to its source, see F. J. Furnivall's comparative table: Ed., *Hoccleve's Works*, vol. 1, pp. 243–48; Jerome Mitchell, *Thomas Hoccleve*, pp. 77–84; and J. V. Fleming.

The *narratio* is very loosely organized in both Hoccleve's and Christine's versions, and in neither case do clearly epistolary features reappear before the very end of the letter. The *petitio* – here a command – occurs rather abruptly, though the wording creates the impression that it follows logically from what has just been said:

> Than thus we wolen conclude and deffyne:
> we you commaunde, our Ministres echoon,
> þat reedy been to oure heestes enclyne,
> þat of tho men vntreewe our rebel foon,
> Yee do punisshement and þat anoon;
> Voide hem our Court & banisshe hem for euere,
> So þat ther-ynne they ne come neuere.
>
> Fulfillid be it cessyng al delay;
> Looke ther be noon excusacion!   (463–71)

Christine's version (775–95) is more elaborate in its attempt to reproduce the precise terminology and dimensions of a royal edict. The same impulse led her to subjoin to the *subscriptio* a list of gods consignatory to the decree (801–26).[29] Hoccleve, who, despite his experience as a Privy Seal clerk, does not seem to share to the same degree her concern with authenticity, is content to imitate the subscription alone:

> writen in their the lusty monthe of May,
> In our Paleys wher many a milion
> Of louers treewe han habitacion,
> The yeer of grace ioieful & iocounde,
> M.CCCC. and secounde.   (472–76)[30]

4.4. MS Harley 682: Love Documents and Love Epistles

The Letter of Cupid is especially important because it attests to a contemporary perception of the love document as a distinct form – one that

---

[29] Christine seems to have had a special affinity for the epistolary form. Her *Le livre du duc des vrais amans* contains six love letters in prose and her *Cent balades d' amant et de dame* is essentially an exchange of verse love letters. The nearest analogue to the present poem, though not on the same subject, is her *l'Epître d' Othéa la déesse à Hector*. Lydgate's "An Epistle to Sibille" belongs to the same category.

[30] Compare Christine's:

> DONNÉ en l'air, en nostre grant palais,
> Le jour de May la solempnée feste
> Ou les amans nous font mainte requeste,
> L'An de grace Mil trois cens quatre vins
> Et dix et neuf, present dieux et divins.   (796–800)

is usually, but not necesssarily, enclosed within an allegorical or vision-
ary frame. Charles of Orléans combines the typical features of the two
love documents just discussed: like Christine de Pisan/Hoccleve's, his
are formally distinct poems that carefully preserve epistolary decorum,
but like Gower's, they are functionally bound to an allegorical narrative.
The collection in Harley 682 is divided into three major parts: the
romance-like accounts of two love affairs, told mainly in ballades, separated by a "Book of Jubilee." Most of the poems in the first two parts
have their counterparts among Charles's French poems, whereas all of
the third, save a few ballades, has no French equivalent. The progress of
the first love affair, which terminates in the lady's death, is recounted in
a sequence of ballades encapsulated by an allegorical frame. Although
the first gathering of MS Harley 682 has been lost, and with it 400 lines
of the allegorical introduction, the missing material can be supplied from
the French version to which it presumably corresponded.[31]

The protagonist, later identified as "Charles, duc d'Orlians" (114),
tells how he began his life under the care of Enfance but after a time
passed into the hands of Jeunesse. His new guardian persuades him,
against his better judgment, to accompany her to the castle where the
Dieu d'Amours keeps his court on Saint Valentine's Day. There they are
admitted by the porter Compaignie and led into the god's presence by Bel
Acueil and Plaisance. Jeunesse presents Charles to Amour, but the young
duke is reluctant to enter Amour's service for fear of its pains. Amour,
asserting his power, summons Beauté, who sends a dart through
Charles's eyes to his heart. Charles tries in vain to remove it and finally
collapses in misery at the feet of Amour, who mocks his weakness. After
Jeunesse fails to gain a respite for her young charge, Beauté arrests
Charles, persuades him that resistance is futile, and receives his promise
to do homage. She then pleads his case successfully before Amour and
recites the oaths of service that he will swear. Charles swears fealty, and
Amour has his secretary Bonne Foi make his "Lettre de retenue," which
Loyaulté seals. Charles is required to leave his heart as surety, but Amour
comforts him by promising that his doctor Espoir will keep him alive
until he can replace his own heart with another's. A copy of the "Lettre de
retenue" follows, at which point the English text begins.

The letter mimics beautifully the legal formalities of this type of
document and is a better example of sustained parody than the similar
piece by Christine de Pisan/Hoccleve because it does not exceed the

---

[31] Ed. Pierre Champion, *Charles d'Orléans: Poésies,* vol. 1 (1923), pp. 1–14.

dimensions of its model. The first few lines provide a good indication of
the whole:

> The god Cupide and venus the goddes
> Whiche power han on alle worldly gladnes
> We hertly gretyng sende of oure humbles
> To louers alle
> Doyng yow wite the duk that folkis calle
> Of Orlyaunce we him amytte and shalle
> As oure servaunt which hath but yeris smalle
> Of yowthe yit spent[32]

The "lettir patent" grants Charles the rights and privileges of a lover,
commands all other true lovers to aid and protect him as best they may,
and repeats the terms of his contract. Its language is "courtly" in both the
amorous and the legalistic sense. The signature, for example, makes use
of the familiar trappings of love allegory while imitating exactly the
subscriptio of a royal patent:

> Gyve on the day of seynt Valentyn þe martere,
> As in the Castelle of humbille desere
> As for the tyme oure counselle holdyng here.   (53–55)[33]

Here the ballades commence in the French version, but the English
redaction resumes the allegorical narrative. Charles thanks Cupid for the
letter and reaffirms his willingness to obey Cupid's commands. Charles
still has some doubts about the way his heart has been handled, but Cupid
puts them to rest, instructs him, and sends him on his way with a promise
of assistance. Charles immediately catches sight of "bewte," but finds her

---

[32] Ed. R. Steele, *English Poems*, vol. 1, p. 1. The French text reads:
> Dieu Cupido et Venus la Deesse,
> Ayans povair sur Mondaine Liesse,
> Salus de cueur, par nostre grant humblesse,
>   A tous amans.
> Savoir faisons que le duc d'Orlians,
> Nommé Charles, a present jeune d'ans,
> Nous retenons pour l'un de noz servans
>   Par ces presentez;   (p. 14)

[33] The French text is slightly more elaborate, adding a combined signature and complimentary close at the end:
> Donné le Jour saint Valentin martir,
> En la cité de Gracieux Desir,
> Ou avons fait nostre conseil tenir.
> Par Cupido et Venus souverains,
> A ce presens plusieurs Plaisirs Mondains.   (p. 16)

surrounded by "disdayne" and "daungere." He considers how he might best appeal to her and decides to "make a bille." Taking counsel with Hope, he then retires to "an herber grene" to write.

Thus the allegorical introduction ends and the story of the first love affair begins to unfold in a sequence of seventy-four ballades (discussed below). Suffice it to say for now that by ballade 57 the lady has died, and hence the last eighteen ballades in the sequence are tuned to the same key of lament. In order to break this stalemate, the allegorical frame is resumed, this time in the form of a dream vision. Worn out with weeping, Charles falls asleep and soon is visited by the figure of Age, sent to his aid by Nature. Age offers him the counsel of reason, reminding him that "loue and elde are falle at gret debate" (2576). He advises Charles to reclaim his mortgaged heart by asking to be released from his service to Cupid. He also warns against the blandishments of Fortune, who will use false promises to weaken his resolve.

Once awakened Charles reflects on his dream and, not coincidentally, lights on a legal metaphor to describe it: "elde had out a writt tane of dotage / To tache me with" (2647–48).[34] He reasons within himself and resolves to accept Age's counsel. Accordingly he prepares a "bille in maner of request" (2693) with which he will present Cupid when he "next holdith fest." The text of his petition, addressed "Vnto the excellent power and nobles / Of god Cupide and venus þe goddes" (2716–17), follows.

Charles pleads his case tactfully and eloquently in this relatively lengthy bill, studiously imitating dictaminal style. The English text corresponds very closely to the French (pp. 105–8) both in sense and, even more notably, in rhyme scheme. Each consists of eight twelve-line stanzas rhymed aabaabbbabba, in which the second, fifth, eighth, and eleventh lines are short.[35] This highly artificial form and the correspondingly artificial language, rather than any conventional formulas of greeting or farewell, create the illusion of authenticity. The stanza in which Charles recalls the swearing of his vow and the pledging of his heart as surety illustrates this quality very well:

---

[34] Cf. Roundel 47 (R. Steele, ed., *English Poems*, vol. 1, p. 128), where he uses the same metaphor.

[35] The English has lines of ten and four syllables where the French has seven and three. Nor is the line length as carefully observed in the English as in the French. The fourth line of the stanza quoted below, for example, has eight syllables instead of the usual ten.

101

> Wherfore that he in tyme tofore or now
> yow made a vow
> Trewly to serue yow vnto his power
> Also he left wel wot ye how
> his hert with yow
> To ben his plegge of feithfulle trewe desire
> The which that now yow humbly doth requere
> Out displesere
> Of yow to pardone him as welle ye mow
> Therof forto he beddid haue his bere
> As more to lere
> Of loue he nevyr cast him silf to bow   (2754–65)

He had begun the letter of petition by reaffirming his obedience and recalling his long and faithful service. Like Troilus, he first requests only that he be heard (2730–36). His quarrel, after all, is not with Cupid, who has granted him "Of welthe and ioy ynow him forto chere" (2738), but with Fortune. Because his lady has been taken from him and because he has promised never to love another, he is compelled to ask for absolution from his vows and for the return of his heart. His loyalty, he says, has earned him mercy; therefore let "Good trouthe" the secretary make a letter of quittance explaining why he is leaving Love's service and freeing him from responsibilities that he can no longer discharge. He concludes by thanking "bothe the god and eek goddes" in advance and wishing them well for as long as he lives.

The actual presentation of the petition, the ensuing debate, Cupid's decision to release Charles, his leave-taking of Love's court, and his journey to the Castle of No-Care hand in hand with Comfort are related in seven ballades without envoy. The first four of these agree closely with the French version and end with Charles on his knees in gratitude, heart and quittance in hand, before Cupid and his court. Between the fourth and fifth ballades, however, the French text supplies a "Copie de la Quittance dessusdicte" (pp. 112–13), which is lacking in the English. This third document is structurally and stylistically the simplest of all. Written in the octosyllabic couplets favored for long narratives, it is less artificial than the narrative ballades that surround it. The signature's final lines, containing the date and place of writing, are of interest for revealing that Charles composed the French text during his imprisonment in England (1415–1440):

> En tesmoing de ce avons mis
> Nostre seel, plaqué et assis
> En ceste presente quittance,
> Escripte par nostre ordonnance.

102

Presens mains notables recors,
Le jour de la Feste des Mors,
L'an mil quatre cent trente et sept,
Ou chastel de Plaisant Recept.   (p. 113)

The last of the four letters that pass between the lover Charles and the god(s) of love approaches the boundary between the love document and the love epistle proper. Having spent his first night in the Castle of No-Care, Charles rises before dawn to write a letter for Comfort to carry back to his master Cupid. Although the letter's tone suits the dignity of a prince, for the first time the legalistic terminology of the earlier "billes" is replaced by language more closely resembling that of familiar epistles. The formality comes mainly in the opening phrases, in which the reader will easily recognize some of the traditional formulas used, for example, by Troilus:

> To the high and myghti lord of gret nobles
> Cupide prince of alle worldly gladnes
>
> Most excellent most high & nobil prince
> Most myghti kyng in eche rewm or provynce
> As humbly as that servaunt kan or may
> Recomaunde his lord and maystir ay
> So recomaunde y me or more to yow
> And also y am he as thenke ye how
> That most desire to here of yowre nobles
> And yowre estat which god so encres
>
> To as moche honoure as y me desire
> To haue or more then y kan write yow here   (2982–93)

He begins with the typical *salutatio* in which he commends himself to Cupid and shifts smoothly into a *captatio benevolentiae* in the form of a wish for the increase of Cupid's "nobles" and "estat" coupled with a desire to be kept informed of his continued good health. The opening formulas then conclude with Charles's statement that he was himself in good health at the time of his writing. This is an exact replica of the "long sequence of conventional phrases and sentences" that Norman Davis found to typify the beginnings of "fifteenth-century letters in English of a formal, respectful kind,"[36] and that will continue to occur with varying degrees of completeness in verse love epistles of the fifteenth and sixteenth centuries. Charles thanks Cupid for allowing Comfort to accom-

---

[36] *"Litera Troili,"* p. 236. The same pattern occurs in the French text (pp. 116–17), but Davis feels that these conventions derive ultimately from French letter writing anyway (pp. 241ff).

103

pany him on his journey and recommends that he inquire of said Comfort should he desire more particular information than the letter itself conveys:

> To whom [Comfort] as plesith yow to gefe fyaunce
> Of that y trust him say yow in substaunce
> The which bi mouth kan telle it yow more playne
> Then y kan write and eek such thyng agayne
> As towchith me y pray yow him to here   (3018–22)

The practice of merely outlining one's message and leaving the bearer to fill in the details is again typical of medieval correspondence.[37] Charles then apologizes for his poor writing (3023–27) and for his poor leave-taking at the court. The *conclusio*, likewise introduced in familiar fashion with "No more as now y write yow verily . . ." (3036), consists mainly of prayers for Cupid's welfare. All that remains is to date and sign the letter (3042–45). A final ballade then concludes the first part of the collection and ushers in the second, "The Book of Jubilee," containing more than one hundred love poems, mainly roundels.

The third section of MS Harley 682, entitled by its editor "Love's Renewal" (4638ff), resembles the first in format. Its allegorical frame is even more complex than the other, but since it contains no letters, it need concern us no further. The pseudodocuments and letters in the allegory that encapsulates Charles's first ballade sequence are important for revealing the author's thorough knowledge of the rules taught by the *ars dictaminis* and his willingness to exploit those conventions in his poetry. In no other Middle English work do allegorical fictions of this sort play so prominent a role,[38] though the presenting of bills of complaint at love assemblies remains a constant feature of longer courtly love poems. Moreover, each of the three documents is clearly distinguished by the complexity of its verse form from the rest of the sequence: the forms used for the allegorical narration are simpler (twenty-one rime royal stanzas: lines 56–202; twenty-one eight-line stanzas, ababbaab: lines 2540–2715; seven ballades, without envoy: lines 2814–2981), while the events that occur in the "real world" are set in ballades with envoys (lines 203–2539, 3046–70).

A similar structuring principle is evident in the second narrative sequence, where the "setting off" of certain special forms is even more obvious. The second love affair is introduced by a lengthy narrative in

---

[37] Cf. the role of Pandarus in *T&C*, II, 1121ff, discussed in chapter 3.2.
[38] For Charles's use of legal terms, see R. Steele, ed., *English Poems*, vol. 1, pp. xxxviii–xxxix.

rime royal stanzas (4638–5351), interrupted only once, by a "bill" of complaint addressed to Fortune, in "Monk's Tale" stanzas (4680–4735). Then, just as in the first part of the collection, the love affair is recounted in a series of thirty-seven ballades with envoy. But this time the sequence of ballades is twice interrupted, at precisely symmetrical intervals, first by another poem in "Monk's Tale" stanzas (5688–5783), and then by one in rime royal stanzas (6129–70). Robert Steele labels the first of these non-ballades a "Complaint" and the second a "Letter"; in fact, both are unquestionably verse love epistles. Parts 1 and 3 of the collection thus present us with a total of six "special" texts, each of which is set off by form and often by function from the poetry that surrounds it: (a) a "Lettre de retenue," (b) a "bille of request," (c) a letter of thanks, (d) a "bille of complaint," and (e,f) two love epistles. Three of the texts (a-c) are directed by or to Cupid and belong to the love-document genre. Although also a "document" presented to a mythical personification, the fourth text (d) is less epistolary in form than the others, is written by the lover on behalf of someone else, and is not specifically concerned with love but with Fortune. Its chief function is apparently to motivate the dream vision that initiates the second love affair, since, when he has finished writing it, Charles immediately falls asleep from fatigue (4736ff). Possibly, the rather gratuitous episode that opens part 3 was chosen with the intention of balancing the three "letters" against the three love documents in part 1. In this connection, it is perhaps significant that in part 1 two official letters are followed by a more familiar one, while in part 3 an official "bill" is followed by two familiar letters. The author's attention to symmetry is in any case clear both from his telling the second love affair in exactly half as many ballades as he took to tell the first (thirty-seven versus seventy-four) and from his using the love letters to divide those ballades into groups of twelve, twelve, and thirteen.

Whether or not the poet intended it, the epistolary love documents in part 1 invite comparison with the love epistles in part 3. And despite the similarities already noted, important differences are immediately evident. Most obvious is the distinction, mentioned earlier in this chapter, between the persons involved in the "correspondence." One of the documents is addressed by Cupid, on Charles's behalf, to all lovers, while the remaining two are addressed by Charles to Cupid. By contrast, both of the love epistles are addressed by Charles to his lady love. This distinction is underscored by the context in which the two sets of letters are set: the documents are embedded in the allegorical narrative, whereas the letters form part of the "real world" action of the love affair. Moreover, though both sets of texts are distinguished by their verse forms from the surrounding poetry, the documents are more "different" in this regard than the epistles are. Each of the documents has a verse form that is unique to it, whether the long and complex stanzas of the first two or the couplets of the third. Both letters, on the other hand, use stanza forms that are paralleled either in the allegorical narrative (rime royal) or in the ballades ("Monk's Tale"). This is not the only way in which the epistles seem less artificial than the documents. Though there is no mistaking the epistolary formulas at beginning and end of both epistles, they are not emphasized through detailed elaboration as they are in the documents. The difference is unmistakable if one compares the opening greeting even from the least formal of the documents (see lines 2982–93, quoted earlier) with that of the first epistle:

> Myn only ioy my lady and maystres
> Whiche are the hope of alle my worldis wele
> Withouten whom þat plesere nor gladnes
> As may me helpe god wot right neuer a dele
> So that it lust yow witen of myn hele
> Anoyous lijf y lede in gret turment
> And so endewre it to my caris felle
> Only bi cause y am from yow absent (5688–95)

Nor is the language ever as studiously legalistic in either epistle as it is in the first two documents. Formulas of greeting and farewell aside, the poet employs the same terms of love in the epistles as in the ballades. In short, the formal contrasts are precisely those between official and familiar letters.

4.5. MS Harley 682: Ballades and Love Epistles

All the factors that guarantee the love epistle clear and well-defined identity vis-à-vis one complementary genre, the love document, have the opposite effect vis-à-vis its other close neighbors, the ballade and the complaint. In both cases it is the love epistle's more flexible form, by comparison with that of the love document, that creates the ambiguity. Further difficulty results from the double meanings of both "letter" and "complaint." Whereas "ballade" designates a fixed form, if one that admits minor variations (different stanza forms, presence or absence of envoy), "letter" can refer either to a specific form or to a broader function, while "complaint" can designate a theme or a genre. Examples can be found for every possible combination of the three: letters and complaints in the form of ballades; epistolary complaints and complaining epistles; complaints and ballades that have no epistolary features but function as epistles by virtue of being "sent"; and even ballade-letters whose theme is complaint. At the outset, one must recognize the impossibility of assigning many poems exclusively to one category or the other. Moreover, without a distinctive verse form or a defining theme, the verse love epistle is more protean than either the ballade or the complaint.

Since Harley 682 contains most of the surviving Middle English ballades (121)[39] – indeed, with its 102 roundels, most surviving Middle English lyrics in fixed forms – and since it sets two love epistles within a sequence of ballades, it offers an ideal opportunity to explore the overlap between ballade and love letter. While many of the poems have complaint as their theme, form is a more important principle in structuring this collection. Fairfax 16, booklet 5, part 2, contains as many ballades as letters (three), but more than half of its twenty poems are called "compleynt." It thus provides a perfect complement to Harley 682, permitting us at once to differentiate the "letters" from the other most closely related type of love poem and to compare them with the similarly differentiated letters from the related collection.

It is not difficult to formulate a fairly detailed definition of a verse love epistle that would be insufficient to distinguish it from most love ballades: it is a written message, in verse, addressed directly to the beloved, and intended to be read by the recipient (rather than sung by the author). Even if one further specified that the poem contain a formal greeting, at most the ballades without envoy would be eliminated. This broad overlapping is even clearer on the level of function, as Daniel Poirion observes in his *Le Poète et le prince*:

> La ballade est une sorte de lettre poètique; sa fonction est celle du *message*, un message développé, explicite, raisonné et non un simple signal tel que celui du rondeau.[40]

A work like Christine de Pisan's *Cent balades d'amant et de dame,* in which a lover and his lady alternately address ballades to one another, is functionally a correspondence in verse. Using the same kind of reason-

---

[39] Even including some questionable examples, Helen L. Cohen could find only about 220 Middle English ballades: *The Ballade*, p. 222.
[40] P. 368.

ing, Charles Kany considers Charles's *Le poeme de la prison*[41] an epistolary romance in which the story of the actual love affair is told in ballade-letters.[42] Yet the poet of Harley 682, whether Charles himself or an English imitator, pointedly distinguished the ballades from the verse epistles by using the latter to break the second series of ballades into symmetrical groups.

Unlike Gower, the poet of Harley 682 never employs the term "letter" but only its ambiguous synonym "bille," a term that was used to describe a wide variety of texts, not all of which are epistolary. He seems to understand the word as referring to a short written piece to be sent or presented to a specific person (or personification) or group of persons. The petition to Cupid (2693) and the complaint addressed to Fortune (4736) are called "billes," as are ballades 19, 31, 51, 68, 91, 120, and roundel 11. In all but one of these ballades the term occurs in the envoy, in the conventional "go ... bille" formula.[43] The single exception, ballade 68, is the lover's "testament," a form related to the love documents. Neither the roundel nor any of the other ballades shows any preponderance of epistolary features, nor do they share any peculiarities that could explain why the term was applied to them alone.

What is probably the most significant use of the term "bille" occurs at the end of the allegorical introduction to the first ballade sequence. Much too abashed to dare address his lady in person, the lover Charles decides that it is "best to make a bille" (175). Like Gower's Amans or Chaucer's Troilus, he retires to a secluded place in order to collect his thoughts and put them on paper. Thus, says Charles, "y bigan alle this trauayle" (202). The "bille" that he had resolved to make in line 175 may simply be ballade 1, but the line just quoted strongly suggests that the entire sequence ("alle this trauayle") is meant.

One must finally choose either to follow Kany and Poirion in regarding virtually all the ballades as in some sense letters or to reject them all by applying stricter criteria. Careful stylistic, thematic, and structural analysis shows that some of the ballades have more epistolary charac-

---

[41] This name is sometimes given to the poems that Charles wrote while in England (also *Le livre de prison*), to which part of the Harley collection corresponds (= P. Champion, ed., *Charles d'Orléans: Poésies*, vol. 1, pp. 1–148, 204–35, 258–68, 287–89).

[42] *Beginnings of Epistolary Novel*, pp. 32–36. See also Mary–Jo Arn, "*Fortunes Stabilnes*," p. 8.

[43] Cf. Chaucer's "Go little bok": *Troilus and Criseyde*, V, 1786ff. For the history of this device, see J. S. P. Tatlock, "Epilog of *Troilus*," pp. 627–30; A. K. Moore, *Secular Lyric*, pp. 146–48; and N. Dean, "Chaucer's *Complaint*," pp. 6–8.

108

teristics than others,[44] but nowhere is this sufficiently striking to set the poems in question apart from the rest. There is no equivalent to Gower's *Cinkante Balades*, #26. Since adopting the first alternative would necessitate a study of the ballade in general, limitations of space, if nothing else, require that the second be chosen. A brief look at the seven ballades that Brown and Robbins singled out as "love epistles" in their *Index of Middle English Verse* (p. 753) will confirm the wisdom of this choice.

It is not clear why they selected just these seven – 19, 31, 39, 91, 93, 98, 120 – from among the 121 ballades in the collection. In four of them (19, 31, 91, 120), to be sure, the envoy begins with the "go ... bille" formula; but what of ballade 51, which employs the very same formula, not to mention roundel 11, which also calls itself a "bille"? Ballades 39, 93, and 98 were also, apparently, selected on the basis of the first lines of their envoys. The first two simply modify the more usual device – "O goo thou derke fordullid rude myture" (1406) and "Now good swet hert biholdith þis scripture" (5600) – while in the third the speaker mentions the fact that he is *writing*: "What may y more yow write at wordis fewe" (5836).[45] If the first two qualify, then why not the "Go dulle complaynt my lady þis report" (5811) of ballade 97? As for the third, ballades 20, 26, 27, and 38, also identify themselves as written pieces in their envoys, and several other poems in the collection refer to the act of writing as well.[46] A final objection is that two of the ballades that Brown and Robbins call love epistles – 31 and 39 – are not even in direct address.

The lesson is not that more rigorous or more accurate methods of selection should have been used, but rather that there is no sure way of distinguishing certain ballades from others on epistolary grounds. All the ballades in Charles's collection, with the obvious exceptions of those written after the lady's death (i.e., 57–74) and those that belong to the allegorical narrative (75–84), are ostensibly written compositions meant to be sent. The fact that many of those that possess no distinctly epistolary features nevertheless treat such themes as separation and the desire for

---

[44] E.g., ballades 10, 19, 30, 36, 85, 89, 90, 98, 110, 111, 114, 120. Cf. roundels 38, 40, 42, 50, 52, 61, 64.

[45] This piece has in its favor at least the fact that the line in question is indeed a conventional opening for the *conclusio*. Cf. ballade 120, which also incorporates a convention of the love letter into its envoy:

> Goo poor bille good fortune be þi gide
> Forblot with teeris of myn eyen twayne.   (6500–6501)

[46] E.g., ballades 10, 21, 36, 54, 90, 95, 114, 117, and roundels 61 and 64. Cf. also the ballade "in Suffolk's manner" (*Index* 1237; MS Arundel 26, fol. 32v), printed by MacCracken in "English Friend," pp. 179–80.

reunion underscores this circumstance.[47] At the level of function, they are unquestionably epistles in the same sense as the two messages that are not set in ballade form.

4.6. MS Harley 682: The Love Epistles

The deviation from the ballade pattern is the most immediate signal that the two letters are to be distinguished formally, if not functionally, from the other poems addressed to the lady in "Love's Renewal." Both letters are also longer than the ballades surrounding them, most of which consist of three "Monk's Tale" stanzas, with a four-line envoy (twenty-eight lines).[48] The first love letter employs the stanza form favored in the ballades but is more than three times as long as they are (twelve stanzas; ninety-six lines). The second letter is less than half the size of the first and half again as long as the ballades, from which it nonetheless stands out by virtue of its rime royal stanzas (six stanzas; forty-two lines). If there is considerable difference in the dimensions and verse form of the two letters, there is much greater agreement in observance of epistolary conventions. What is more, each letter is carefully introduced by the ballade that precedes it in the sequence.

When the poet has finished the account of his dream vision and his first encounter with his new lady love, he initiates the courtship with a series of twelve ballades (85–96). Since she does not accept his love right away, his theme is always complaint, coupled with protestations of devotion and pleas for mercy. But in the last of these ballades (#96), a new cause of sorrow is introduced: the two "nedis must depart / And when to mete þe tyme in nonecertayne" (5660–61). The separation of the poet from his lady now a fact, she is next addressed not in a ballade but in a love letter. Along with a decorous *salutatio/captatio benevolentiae* and the customary *status affectus,* the first stanza of the letter reemphasizes this separation (lines 5688–95; quoted above).

Often the play on *salus/salutatio* (health/greeting) is no more than an empty convention, serving at best to introduce some equally convention-

---

[47] See, e.g., ballades 10–15. Poirion observes, however, that Charles's ballades are atypical because in them the communicative function gives way to the meditative. He is less concerned with importuning the lady than with revealing his inner self. The ballades are more lyrics than letters. *Le Poète et le prince,* pp. 391–92.

[48] Two employ the rime royal stanza and so are shorter by three lines (#115, 117), while two of the three that have counterparts among Charles's French poetry (#107, 113) employ eleven– and nine–line stanzas, respectively.

al complaint. Here it links the formal greeting to a *narratio* of their last meeting and leave-taking – a detailed anatomy of the poet's emotional state at the time, as he struggled to keep back the tears that might betray his feelings for her and so cause her "dishonoure" (5696–5739).[49] The recollection of past sorrow leads him to a reaffirmation of present devotion and assurance that it will continue into the future, even after he is dead (5740–48). Captivated by the image of his own death, he bequeaths to her his heart and other goods (5749–51), since he has been entirely hers since he first looked upon her beauty (5752–59). Ever at the mercy of his imagination, he next recalls that first meeting, invoking her mercy for the suffering he endured then and endures now that he cannot see her "swete visage" and other beauties (5760–75). The implicit *petitio* is followed by an explicit one, which introduces the concluding stanza:

> Bisechyng you right thus most goodly fayre
> For to bithynke me though y ben away.   (5776–77)

Such pleas for remembrance are among the most persistent components of the verse love epistle. The remaining lines provide closure not through epistolary formulas but through summation: he restates his undying devotion and his hope to "ben rewardid wel therfore" (5783).

Most of the themes developed in the long *narratio*, as should be evident from the foregoing summary, are the usual ones of the love complaint. Besides the genre-specific stanzas of greeting and conclusion that encapsulate it, this associatively structured epistolary complaint differs from its ballade cognates chiefly in its circumstantial and almost conversational quality.[50] The contrast is particularly obvious with the ballade that follows (#97), which is also a message (refrain: "Go dul complaynt my lady þis report") complaining of the woes that the faithful lover suffers during his enforced absence from the lady. In the body of the poem the complaint is tightly focused through a single conceit: the solitary anchorite is gladder and healthier than he, whom the spectacle of "fayre folkis," particularly ladies, makes all the more miserable for want of his own lady. And even though the envoy returns to the most general level of complaint, as a whole the ballade is a better poem than the letter,

---

[49] *Index* 147, a contemporary poem that though not epistolary in form probably functioned as an epistle, also dwells on the scene of the lovers' parting (e.g., lines 28–41, 174–245). See Appendix I.A.1, for bibliography.

[50] Norton–Smith finds something similar to the "conversational style" of Chaucer's "Horatian" verse epistle, *Lenvoy de Chaucer a Scogan,* in the second love epistle from Charles's English collection (to be discussed next): "Chaucer's Epistolary Style," pp. 164–65.

if measured by concentrated effect. The letter, in short, has much of the prosiness tolerable in familiar epistles but not in fixed-form poems.

By ballade 98 the lover is back in his lady's presence, full of joy and renewed hope that she will requite his love (refrain: "Welcome my leche me forto sle or saue"). But his hope is soon disappointed, and he is driven to complain even more bitterly of her cruelty and his unhappiness than he did before their enforced separation. In ballade 108 the long-suffering lover finally loses all patience and brusquely announces that he is taking his leave of love once and for all. The cause of his sudden renunciation is only hinted at in the ballade but is partially explained in the letter that follows:

> But what in haste ye did vnto me write
> And so in wikkid haste y wrot agayne   (6136–37)

Ballade 108, his response to an earlier (accusatory?) letter she had written to him, has, like the earlier separation, created a crisis in the one-sided love affair. The purpose of his letter is to make amends for the "ruggid fowle langage" that her letter had provoked him to utter and so restore matters between them to their normal level of futility.

The most noteworthy part of the letter is its opening, where the suppliant lover infuses the traditional *salutatio* with the proper mixture of abject humility and heartfelt repentance:

> With hert repentaunt of my gret offence
> I me recomaunde in eche humbil wise
> Vnto yow lo þe whiche as recompense
> Hit makith noon þat kan y wel avise
> Vnto my gilt but what I seinys twise
> Repentid haue of þat y haue mysbore
> And sory ben alak what may y more   (6129–35)

As in the previous letter, the conventional epistolary greeting is skillfully adapted to the circumstances at hand. The easy transitions from one part to the next are more striking this time, because the letter is much briefer and yet, because of its urgent rhetorical purpose, demands the same kind of tactful control masterfully demonstrated in the much longer "Litera Troili."

Having dwelled on his guilt and repentance in the opening stanza, the lover next tries to mitigate his guilt even in the act of confessing it: his lady must have written in haste and at the instigation of others, for otherwise she "nolde haue doon so fowle a dede / Without offence vnto [her] womanhede" (6141–42). But just as her "haste" in writing was nothing to his "wikkid hast" in replying, so, as soon as he has raised the

112

possibility of her "offence," he negates it, in the process reversing their normal roles. In presuming to criticize her, whose every desire ought to content him, he has been cruel, while she has been "to pacient" to rebuke him for his "gret outrage." How then is he to cry for mercy? Of course he is different from her in that his cruelty was only temporary, and his confession has a clear undertone of wish fulfillment. Even though his behavior has earned her hatred, he will love her until the end, whether she does him "wele or woo." If he may regain her "grace" he will never lose it again; if he cannot, the only reward he asks for his continued service is that she not repeat rumors about him. That request, which probably alludes to the contents of the letter that first drew his angry response, introduces the concise but effective *conclusio:*

> Say not of me but as ye knowe in dede
> And y shal yow þe same so god me spede
> And wille yow wele wher ye me wil or no
> And fare you wele thus ende y now as loo   (6167–70)

The letter's success can be deduced from the joyful gratitude of the ballade that follows it (#109).

The two verse epistles thus stand out from the ballade sequence by virtue of more than their verse form and length. Both possess the formal, even formulaic greeting that distinguishes medieval epistles from other types of discourse in direct address. While neither employs the formulas of conclusion found in the love documents of part 1, both close with stanzas that more precisely recapitulate the message than is usual in the ballade envoys. They also differ from the ballades in the greater complexity of their structure and the circumstantiality of their contents, both features probably due to their greater length but perhaps also to a real sense of what is appropriate to familiar letters as opposed to fixed-form lyrics. Perhaps most interesting of all is the fact that both letters are so carefully motivated within the sequence. The poet's care in providing occasions that call for a letter, whether physical separation or especially sharp emotional estrangement, argues for a strong sense of the genre's functional identity. By the same token, the deliberate embedding of the two letters could also suggest that, for this poet at least, the verse epistle per se, though distinct from the ballade with epistolary elements, was not yet a fully autonomous genre.

4.7. MS Fairfax 16: The Complaint and the Love Epistle

The small anthology at the end of MS Fairfax 16 (ca. 1450), roughly contemporary with the larger collection in Harley 682 and like it associated with Charles of Orléans and his English circle,[51] supplies other important details of the verse love epistle's literary affinities during the second quarter of the fifteenth century. Here there is no doubt about the love epistle's autonomy. Nineteen of the twenty poems in the collection are provided with descriptive labels, "Lettyr" (#6, 14, 17) taking its place alongside "Balade" (#1–3), "Compleynt" (#4–5, 7–12, 15–16, 18), "Supplicacion" (#13), and "Parlement" (#20). There is no way of knowing where these labels originated, whether they were provided by the poet(s), by the professional scribe who prepared the manuscript, or by some intermediary (the nobleman to whose order it was produced).[52] In any case, they provide valuable testimony of genre consciousness during the early phase of the love epistle's development.

However, it must be acknowledged at the outset that the terms are not applied with uniform precision. "Balade" seems to be attached to poems otherwise not easily labeled. As a designator of verse form it is used appropriately for #1 (without envoy), but the other two poems with refrains, #8 (four stanzas, rime royal) and #16 (three "Monk's Tale" octaves), are both called "compleynt." There is, in fact, no term to designate the verse form that characterizes the majority of the twenty poems, including the other two "balades," most of the "compleynts," the "supplicacion," and all the "lettyrs": three to four stanzas, rime royal, without refrain (or envoy). Only two poems employ any stanza form other than rime royal (#9, 16), and only three are longer than four stanzas

---

[51] Poem #8, a complaint to Fortune, is also found in Charles of Orléans's personal manuscript of his poems: BN, f. fr. 25458, p. 313. Ed. R. Steele, *English Poems*, vol. 1, p. 223.

[52] On the production and organization of the manuscript, see John Norton–Smith's introduction to the Scolar Press facsimile edition: *MS Fairfax 16*, pp. vii–viii, and J. P. M. Jansen, ed., *'Suffolk' Poems*, pp. 1–5. Norton–Smith and Jansen agree that John Stanley, Esq. (1400–?1469) commissioned the manuscript. See also Edward Wilson, "Stanley Family," pp. 308–16. Norton–Smith feels that Charles of Orléans is the best candidate for authorship of the poems in question (*MS Fairfax 16*, pp. viii, xxix), which occupy fols. 318r–329r. Jansen considers the question of authorship in greater detail, concluding that there is insufficient evidence to support the claims for any of the four candidates who have been proposed (*'Suffolk' Poems*, pp. 13–30). See also n. 6 above. Jansen believes that the twenty love poems in Fairfax 16 form a sequence and therefore numbers the lines consecutively: in citing his edition, I have first given line numbers as if the poems were autonomous (as they are treated in MacCracken's edition) and then indicated Jansen's numbering in brackets.

(#18: five stanzas; #19: twelve stanzas; #20: sixteen stanzas, plus four-line envoy). Consequently, most of the poems are classified by theme, though only two themes are accorded generic status: complaint and supplication. "How the lovere is sett to serve the flour," the title given #19 in the old table of contents, is clearly not generic. Its absence from the normal position above the text of the poem further confirms the generic force of the other terms. Significantly, there is no generic term for the poem in praise of the lady, a popular theme perfectly illustrated by one of the imprecisely labeled "balades" (#3).

Rossell Hope Robbins both recognizes the popularity of the praise poem and attempts to supply the lacking genre term when he proposes that most of the shorter fifteenth-century "love lyrics fall into two main genres: the lover's salutation (the *salut d'amour*) describing and praising his lady, and (more numerous) the lover's plea or *complaint d'amour*, complaining to or about his lady." He then goes on to spell out in greater detail what he means by *salut d'amour:*

> The basic form consists of a brief celebration of the lady, for her beauty (the *effictio)* and personality (the *notatio*), sometimes little more than a series of anaphora or a catalogue of delights. Many *saluts* are couched as epistles; the metrical pattern is variable, but most are seven- or eight-line stanzas. While they may even mention her lack of mercy, or end in a plea for favors, their essence is praise, and for any lover's sickness the lady is always herself the doctor and the medicine.[53]

The fundamental truth behind this schema is that flattery and complaint were indeed the courtly lover's chief means of earning his lady's mercy, and not only in the fifteenth century.

Robbins's schema is nonetheless vulnerable to three objections, two of which he anticipates without adequately answering them. First, *salut d'amour* has a precise medieval meaning, designating the type of verse love epistle that flourished in France during the second half of the thirteenth century. While he admits that for him *salut d'amour* is only a term of convenience,[54] the fact that "many" of the poems of praise are also letters will cause confusion. A term such as "compliment" would be just as convenient and less ambiguous than *salut d'amour.* A second problem is that praise is less often the *exclusive* theme of a love poem than is complaint. As Robbins points out, the poems that he calls *saluts*

---

[53] "Structure of Court Poems," pp. 245, 247. Cf. also R. H. Robbins, "Court Love Lyric," pp. 206–7.

[54] "Structure of Court Poems," p. 247: "It is convenient to describe this group by the French term [i.e., *saluts d'amour*], although it is actually more specialized in French."

d'amour are often thematically mixed, and so the "genre" will not only be less well represented but also far less well defined than the complaint. Finally, whereas fifteenth-century poets and their audience clearly did recognize the complaint as a distinct, if formally variable, genre, they apparently did not accord such recognition to the praise poem per se. Despite its popularity, the praise of the lady was generally subsumed under other genres, including the letter. While this does not rule out our devising a term for poems whose "essence is praise," we must recognize that such a term will be more valid empirically than historically.

The three "lettyrs" in Fairfax 16 fall together as a group not by virtue of their themes, all of which are shared by other poems in the collection, but rather because they are the only three poems whose structure and diction are in fact epistolary.[55] Like "Parlement" (#20), "Lettyr" is used precisely and consistently to describe a form-determined genre. Indeed, in their thorough conventionality the Fairfax 16 love letters are among the most perfect specimens of their kind in all of Middle English literature. Already, in its first flowering, the verse love epistle has attained its "classic" form.

The genre term corresponding to that classic form is clearly *letter,* though we have already seen that other terms could be and were used synonymously. "Byll," the most common of these synonyms, occurs twice in one of the Fairfax 16 letters (#14, lines 5, 19 [323, 337]), while another uses the more ambiguous "wrytyng" (#6, line 24 [143]), an English equivalent of Gower's "escript." Although "byll" never achieved the status of a genre term – its presence in a poem is never *ipso facto* sufficient to indicate epistolary intent – in Fairfax 16 it seems to have much the same meaning that it had in Harley 682, namely, a written document, not necessarily epistolary in form, meant to be sent or else presented to another person. It is used in this broader sense to describe three other poems in Fairfax 16 (#10, line 20 [240]; #13, line 21 [318]; #19, line 32 [479]). Moreover, in two of these (#13, 19), the term has the same kind of legal associations observed in Chaucer's "Bill of Complaint" to Pity. This latter meaning is explicit in the last poem of the collection, wherein the lover/petitioners who have assembled for Cupid's "Parlement" on February 22:

---

[55] Brown and Robbins overlooked #6 in compiling the list of verse love epistles on page 753 of their *Index*. Robbins also calls #19 a love letter – incorrectly, as I show below – in *SL,* p. 286. (He prints the poem as #188 in that collection.) Two of the French poems that MacCracken prints as by Suffolk (IV and V) can be called letters, but their attribution to Suffolk is very dubious indeed. Cf. also the first of the two "Poems in Suffolk's Manner" at the article's end ("English Friend," pp. 179–80).

> ... present up thair byllys
> Upon her knes, wyth facys pale of hewe,
> Complenyng sore for many dyverse skyllys:
>
> > (#20, lines 50–52 [581–83]; cf. line 30 [561])

The common object of their complaint is "Daunger" (63 [594]), whose banishment from the royal court of love they solemnly request (73–84 [604–15]). Like Chaucer's Nature in *The Parliament of Foules*, Cupid takes the matter under "avysement," postponing his "jugement" until such time as the parliament reconvenes, on April 29.

In the poem preceding this one, "byll" may have a similar meaning, though it is ambiguous by virtue of its placement in the text. The speaker intends to "serve this flour" (2 [449]) and, recognizing that his "symple connyng" is not "sufficiaunt this goodly flour to prayse" (15–16 [462–63]), invokes the aid first of Chaucer and then of his worthiest successor the "Monke of Bury" (26 [473]), "This byll to forthir after myn entent" (32 [479]). Though the bulk of the poem (lines 26–84 [473–531]) is addressed directly to Lydgate, its tenor changes abruptly from praise to blame at line 36 [483]. From that point on the author indicts Lydgate, in language reminiscent of other "bills of complaint," for his dispraising of love in general and of women's fidelity in particular. The legal element is most pronounced in the ten-line "summation" at the poem's end:

> O thou unhappy man, go hyde thy face;
> The court ys set, thy falshed yt is tryed;
> Wythdraw, I rede, for now thou art aspyed.
>
> If thou be wyse, yit do this after me,
> Be not to hasty, com not in presence,
> Lat thyn attournay sew and speke for the,
> Loke yf he can escuse thy necglygence;
> And forthermore yit must thou recompence
> For alle that ever thou hast sayde byfore;
> Have mynde of this, for now I wryte no more.
>
> > (75–84 [522–31])

Though the term "byll" occurs within the indictment itself (line 32 [479]), it seems to refer to the poem of praise that the author wants to write rather than to the one of complaint that he has written. Perhaps the poet had in mind to present the putative poem to the "flour" or perhaps he used the term "byll" under the influence of the genre into which he had abruptly shifted.

In one of the two shorter poems called a "byll," namely, the one titled "Supplicacion" (#13), the legal connotation is both unambiguous and appropriate. Moreover, this poem is one of two that come close to duplicating the features that distinguish the three letters in the collection. The other "borderline case" is, not coincidentally, the one complaint that is also called a "byll" (#10). We have already encountered an example of a "Supplicacioun," in Book VIII of the *Confessio Amantis*. But Gower's text resembles the bills of complaint in the "Parlement" of Cupid (Fairfax 16, #20), in setting and even in the specific request it contains (*CA*, VIII, 2285–86). Like Gower's text, and unlike most of the "love documents" that we have examined, the Fairfax 16 "supplicacion" contains no specifically epistolary formulas, relying for its effect rather on legal and feudal language. Finally, it differs from all the previously cited examples and resembles the love epistle in being addressed directly to the lady rather than to a mythological figure or personified abstraction. Also like the epistles in Fairfax 16, it is an occasional poem polished clean of any particular occasion. Each of its three stanzas contains a request, together with the reason why it should be granted: since he has long been "attendaunt" in her "servise," the "sayed bysecher" requests "sumwhat of coumfort, / That he always may to [her] grace resort" (6–7 [303–4]); since he has often been falsely accused, "Os reson wyll, lat hym be hold excusyd" (14 [311]); and since she has taken him as her man, she should be "to hym good lady and maistresse" (17 [314]). This is poetry as pure social gesture.[56]

Most of the "compleynts" are equally conventional and equally cut off from any concrete situation. An exception is poem #10, which announces its occasion in the first line: "Now must I nede part out of your presence." While its theme is indeed mostly complaint, it deviates from the other ten so-titled poems in ways that bring it close to the love letters.[57] For example, it is one of the three complaints that speak directly and exclusively to the lady. This is apparently not an accident, since in all three of these poems separation or imminent separation is the immediate cause of complaint (cf. #4, line 2 [72]; #5, lines 8–10 [106–8]). But only #10 raises the lover's enforced departure to the chief subject of the entire poem. Absence of (and distance from) the lover has already been identified as one of the relatively few characteristic themes of the love letter – indeed it was the chief motivation for the shifts from ballade to letter in Harley

---

[56] For another poem modeled on a type of legal document, in this case a "wylle," but refined out of even that identity (it is titled a "Compleynt"), see #5 in the same collection.

[57] For a contemporary "compleynt" that presents some of the same problems of overlap with the epistle, see Appendix I.A.1 (*Index* 147).

682. Likewise, all three "lettyrs" in Fairfax 16 take separation as a central theme (see #6, lines 5, 19 [124, 138]; #14, lines 11–14 [329–32]; #17, lines 15–18 [399–402]). That the theme of separation was never the exclusive property of the epistle has already been seen in the ballade following the first of the two letters in Harley 682. But the poet of Fairfax 16 makes an important distinction between the handling of this theme in "compleynts" and in "lettyrs," a distinction that underscores his sure sense of genre. In the "lettyrs" the complaint about separation is always markedly written, the physical distance already a fact; in the "compleynts" the unhappy lover usually speaks, complaining of a separation that is either not necessarily physical or, if physical, about to happen. So in poem #4, the lover says only that he "ne may unto [his lady's] speche attayn" (line 2 [72]), without explaining why, and then laments that he knows of no one who "can tell al [his] grevaunce thurughly" (line 9 [79], cf. lines 3–4 [73–74]), that is, who can act as his go-between. The lover in poem #5 is about to be separated from his lady (lines 8–10 [106–8]), to whom he speaks (line 15 [113]: "I can say no more") from a kneeling position (line 1 [99]).[58]

What makes poem #10 an especially interesting boundary case is that it is to be understood as written rather than spoken, a fact that is repeatedly stressed in the key third stanza:

> Hold me escused, I have non eloquence,
> Nor no konnyng to wryte to my purpose,
> Made in gret hast to com to your presence
> As sone os I thys wrytyng myght endose;
> Besechyng yow that ye wyll kepe yt close,
> And lat this lytyll byll with yow abyde,
> For wykkyd tongys do harme on every syde.
>
> (15–21 [235–41])

If the "I" of line 18 is to be understood as the subject of the "to com" in line 17, the poem is a perfect blend of the speech situations in the complaint about separation and the love letter – a written message personally delivered to the lady. But though the syntax is unclear, it is somewhat more natural to refer "Made" not to the maker but to his "compleynt" itself, which will "com to [the lady's] presence." In any case, it is clear from the first two stanzas that the physical separation is imminent rather than actual.

But the epistolary elements are not limited to the emphasis on the act of writing and the physicality of the poem, which, signed or addressed

---

[58] On this poem, see R. H. Robbins, "Court Love Lyric," pp. 217–19.

("endosed") by the poet, will come into the lady's presence and abide with her while he is away. Both the synonyms for "lettyr" found in texts so labeled occur together in the stanza quoted – "wrytyng" (line 18) and "byll" (line 20). Their generic force is admittedly weakened by the use of the imprecise "balade" (line 22) to introduce the envoy-like final stanza, but an abundance of epistolary motifs and formulas confirms that we are here dealing with a genuine and perhaps deliberate hybrid. Lines such as "Have mynde on hym that serveth faythfully" (6 [226]) and "Though I be far, yit have in remembraunce / My long servyse" (8–9 [228–29]), here referring to the future, express what is one of the most commonly repeated wishes in the love letters (cf. #6, lines 19–21 [138–40]; Harley 682, lines 5776–77; *De amico ad amicam,* lines 64–66, etc.). The apology for lack of eloquence, the assertion that the letter was written in haste, and the request that it be kept secret are all paralleled either in the "lettyrs" in Fairfax 16 or in other early examples of the genre (cf. *Troilus and Criseyde,* V, 1338–44). The line "Me recomawndyng to her hye noblesse" (25 [245]) employs a formula of greeting that was already prominent in the "Litera Troili" (*T&C,* V, 1323, 1414) and is apparently obligatory in the Fairfax 16 "lettyrs" (#6, line 7 [126]; #14, lines 5–7 [323–25]; #17, line 7 [391]).

Why then is this poem called a "compleynt," when it shares to such a degree the diction, the themes, and the functions of the "lettyrs"? Although the distinction between actual and imminent separation is important, it is probably not decisive. Rather the key difference between #10 and the three "lettyrs" in Fairfax 16, as well as the other verse epistles discussed in this chapter, is structural. The elements in the "compleynt" are out of place, the greeting that above all distinguishes the epistle occurring at the end rather than at the beginning. Postposed, it functions more as an envoy than as an epistolary *salutatio/captatio benevolentiae,* a fact underscored by the shift from addressing the lady directly to addressing the poem in the last stanza, by the use of a familiar envoy formula to introduce that stanza ("Go forth, balade": line 22 [242]), and by the use in that formula of a term that usually designates a fixed form that is often provided with an envoy (as are all but seven of the 121 ballades in Harley 682). Gower had no qualms about calling similarly structured poems "lettres"; but the poet of Fairfax 16 is at least uncertain about what to call this one. For the person who labeled the poems, there can be no doubt that the initial position of the formal greeting was obligatory in verse epistles. Ignoring the cluster of epistolary features in the last two stanzas, not finding that greeting in the first stanza, he reacted instead to the theme of the first two stanzas in assigning the poem to a genre. The point is not that theme overrides form as a genre determiner in this manuscript. Thematically, two of the three "lettyrs" could be called complaints, and the "Parlement" consists of complaint set in a mythico-allegorical frame. Rather, the labels in Fairfax 16 indicate that, for this poet/reader/scribe at least, epistolary "syntax" rather than epistolary "lexicon" was the formal dominant in the love letter.

4.8. MS Fairfax 16: The Love Epistles

Though essentially the same as that of the Harley 682 letters, the structure of the Fairfax 16 letters is more immediately obvious. As in Harley 682, the opening and closing formalities tend to expand to fill an entire stanza, but this produces a rather different effect in a poem of three to four stanzas than in one of twelve or even six stanzas. In the shortest of the three (#14), it is scarcely an exaggeration to say that the formal conventions of the genre are the main subject matter; like the "Supplicacion" (#13) it is poetry reduced to pure gesture:

> Myn hertys joy, and all myn hole plesaunce,
> Whom that I serve, and shall do faythfully,
> Wyth trew entent and humble observaunce,
> Yow for to plese in that I can treuly,
> Besechyng yow thys lytell byll and I
> May hertly wyth symplesse and drede
> Be recomawndyd to your goodlyhede.
>
> And yf ye lyst have knowlech of my qwert,
> I am in hele, God thankyd mot he be,
> As of body, but treuly not in hert,
> Nor nought shal be to tyme I may you se;
> But thynke that I as treuly wyll be he
> That for your ese shall do my payn and myght
> As thogh that I were dayly in your syght.
>
> I wryte to yow no more, for lak of space;
> But I beseche the only Trinite
> Yow kepe and save be support of hys grace,
> And be your sheld from all adversyte.
> Go, lytill byll, and say thou were wyth me,
> Of verey trouth, as thou canst wele remembre,
> At myn upryst, the fyft day of Decembre.   [319–39]

Comparison with the other two letters, both longer by a stanza, reveals just how stylized this gesture was.

The frame of the *salutatio/captatio benevolentiae* stanzas is absolutely fixed: the first two lines must consist of flattering epithets coupled with a declaration of service, while the last line must contain the formulaic "recomaund." In the intervening lines the poet may choose to expand his declaration of service, as in the poem quoted (cf. #6, lines 3–4 [123–24]); to anticipate the complaint of the *narratio* (#17, lines 3–4 [387–88]); or to combine one or the other with an expansion of the greeting itself, through the familiar *quot-tot* formula (#6, lines 5–6 [124–25]; #17, lines 5–6 [389–90]). The concluding stanza always begins with an announcement of approaching closure containing the formula "I wryte no more," and it always includes some form of blessing (#6, lines 26–28 [145–47]; #17, lines 22–26 [406–10]). Two of the three end with a dated *subscriptio* that incorporates a familiar formula,[59] while the exception ends with the blessing, interposing three lines in which the lady is asked "to have in mynde / This symple wrytyng" so that the lover may find "sum comfort" (#6, lines 23–25 [142–44]).

The body of the letter exhibits only slightly more flexibility than the distinctive frame. A choice is available at the outset in the treatment of the remarks on health (*status affectus*). Two letters employ the more conventional reference to the writer's health, which cannot be good as long as the lady is far away. The other (#6) praises rather than complains and so expresses a wish for the lady's welfare. Again the congruence between stanza divisions and the parts of a letter is exact. The three-stanza letter contains only the *narratio* of complaint, whereas the longer ones each add a stanza-long *petitio*. Appropriately, the *narratio* of complaint leads to a request for the lady's "presence" (#17, lines 15–21 [399–405]), while the *narratio* of praise leads only to a request for "grace" (#6, lines 15–21 [134–40]).

4.9. The "Litera Troili" and the Earliest English Verse Love Epistles

One can hardly imagine more perfect, or emptier, examples of the conventions that, manipulated in various ways, will characterize the

---

[59] Both formulas – "Go, lytill byll" (#14, line 19 [337]) and "Wrytyn in hast" (#17, line 27 [411]) – are echoed, as we have seen, in the "para–epistolary" compleynt (#10, lines 22, 17 [242, 237]).

genre for the next century or more. It is as if the poet set out to imitate the "Litera Troili," deliberately and systematically stripping it of all circumstantial detail. The prestige of *Troilus and Criseyde,* which quickly became for fifteenth-century English poets the kind of courtly love poetry manual that the *Roman de la Rose* was for the thirteenth and fourteenth centuries, may well have had much to do with the verse love epistle's sudden popularity and precocious attainment of its classic form a generation after Chaucer's death. Indeed, we shall later encounter love letters built mainly or even entirely from passages lifted out of *Troilus and Criseyde.* Many of the conventions shared by the "Litera Troili" and the letters in Harley 682 and in Fairfax 16 were of course already present in Boccaccio's original, while others were imitated from contemporary familiar letters. Since most familiar letters in Chaucer's England were still being written in Anglo-French, and since both Harley 682 and Fairfax 16 have strong French connections, the genre could have entered Middle English directly from French literature. Perhaps the prestige of the Duke of Orléans and his English friends, rather than that of Chaucer, sparked the genre's popularity.[60] But those collections themselves distinguish letters from ballades, the most common verse form for epistolary love poems in French, in part by setting most of them in the very rime royal stanzas that Chaucer employed in *Troilus and Criseyde.*

It is also telling that the opening stanzas of all three Fairfax 16 "lettyrs" (described earlier), duplicate exactly the order and content of the first stanza of the "Litera Troili" (*T&C,* V, 1317–23). So close is the modeling that one poem even takes over the flattering epithet ("Right fresshe flour") with only a change of adjective: "Ryght goodly flour" (#6, line 1 [120]). If the Fairfax 16 poet had combined this stanza with two more from the "Litera Troili" (*T&C,* V, 1366–72, 1408–14), without changing a single word, the resulting "lettyr" would fit the foregoing description precisely as well as the poem quoted in full earlier. The imitation of the conventions is less slavish and the poetry less polished in the letters from Harley 682, which are nonetheless more like the "Litera Troili" and "Litera Criseydis" in length (105, 42 lines versus 96, 42 lines), circumstantial detail, and rhetorical strategy.[61] Neither Gower's

---

[60] A further wrinkle is the fact that the first two booklets in Fairfax 16 contain many works by Chaucer, including most of his authentic shorter poems.

[61] The letters in Harley 682 occasionally resemble those in Fairfax 16 fairly closely. For example, the epithets in the first line of the first letter – "Myn only ioy my lady and maystres" (line 5688) – combine those from two of the Fairfax 16 letters: "Myn hertys joy, and all myn hole plesaunce" (#14, line 1 [319]) and "My best bylovyd lady and maistresse" (#17, line 1 [385]).

nor Charles of Orléans's ballade-letters but rather Chaucer's stanzaic letters are the immediate ancestors of the English verse love epistle. That the genre's roots are on the continent will prove less important than that it was born in England.

The poets of Harley 682 and Fairfax 16 may well have been the first to model independent lyrics on the "Litera Troili," but the prominent role that letter writing plays in that work made it almost inevitable that someone would eventually have the idea.[62] Lydgate may have had the "Litera Troili" in the back of his mind when he composed the lover's "complaint" in *The Temple of Glass* (before 1420), lines 970–1039. At least the narrator's elaborate preparations for quoting the lover's words (lines 946–63) are filled with echoes and near quotations of *Troilus and Criseyde*. But while the complaint begins with two stanzas of praise and submission that strike a familiar note (*inc.:* "Princess of iouþe, and flour of gentiless") and ends with the kind of closing summation found in the Harley 682 letters, it lacks any characteristic epistolary formulas. Moreover, it is clearly spoken to the lady (lines 966, 976, 983), who responds by blushing (1040–46).[63] Skeat attributed two genuine love epistles to Lydgate, but the attribution was rejected by MacCracken and by most subsequent scholars.[64] Among Lydgate's authentic courtly lyrics, the one that comes nearest to being a verse love epistle is a ballade in praise of a lady (*inc.:* "Fresshe lusty beaute Ioyned with gentylesse"), written for "Sir Othes of Holand."[65] But the only epistolary formula (line

---

[62] Boffey points out that the letters in *Troilus and Criseyde* are set off graphically in several manuscripts: *Manuscripts of Lyrics*, pp. 42 n. 26, and 58. Elsewhere ("Annotation") she observes that the "Litera Troili" and the "Litera Criseydis" are so highlighted in the majority of the manuscripts (nine of sixteen) and that several other epistolary passages are sometimes highlighted – the summary of Troilus' first letter (in six MSS), the summary of Criseyde's reply, and Pandarus' abbreviation of Oënone's letter (in three MSS each). She also notes a lyric that may have been based on the "Litera Troili" but survives only in its incipit/title: "O fresshes flour": *Manuscripts of Lyrics*, p. 73 n. 33. R. H. Robbins singles out the "Litera Troili" as among the most suitable for excerpting of the "lyric clusters" in *Troilus and Criseyde*: "The Lyrics," pp. 382–83.

[63] Ed. John Norton–Smith, *John Lydgate: Poems*, pp. 97–99.

[64] For MacCracken's argument against Lydgate's authorship of "To My Soverain Lady" (*Index* 1309: Ed. W. W. Skeat, *Chaucer*, vol. 7, pp. 281–84) and "A Goodly Balade" (*Index* 2223: Ed. Skeat, *Chaucer*, vol. 7, pp. 405–7), both preserved in Thynne's 1532 edition of Chaucer, see his edition of the *Minor Poems*, part 2, pp. xlviii–xlix. Jack B. Oruch says that Lydgate is "possibly" the author of "To My Soverain Lady": "St. Valentine," p. 559. See also R. H. Robbins, "Court Love Lyric," pp. 213–14, and Henry Ansgar Kelly, *Chaucer and St. Valentine*, p. 145 n. 41.

[65] *Index* 869. Ed. R. H. Robbins, *SL*, pp. 129–30; H. N. MacCracken, *Minor Poems*, part 2, pp. 379–81. The *Supplement* to the *Index of Middle English Verse* compares this

43: "recommaunde me") is in the envoy, and the poem as a whole is no more epistolary than the ballades in Harley 682.

Since both Lydgate and Hoccleve were admirers of Chaucer's work, authors of verse letters, and authors of conventional love lyrics for the enjoyment of aristocratic audiences, it seems significant that neither produced, so far as we know, a "Chaucerian" love letter of the sort found in Harley 682 and Fairfax 16. Perhaps a certain amount of distance was necessary before the possibility of extracting a new form from Chaucer's work (as opposed to imitating a familiar form, such as the complaint) revealed itself. And the fact that this revelation seems first to have come in the second quarter of the fifteenth century and thus to have coincided with a new and unprecedented vogue for writing letters in English goes a long way toward explaining the delay.

---

poem to *Index* 3291 (*inc.:* "That pasaunte Goodnes, the Rote of all vertve"), a verse love epistle, probably because of the thematic resemblance noted by Ethel Seaton, *Sir Richard Roos*, pp. 156–57.

CHAPTER 5

Flowering and Decline

Once the verse love epistle had been detached from Chaucer's narrative and given independent life in the poetry associated with Charles of Orléans it quickly developed into the dominant form of the late Middle English love lyric. Some two dozen manuscripts and printed editions from around 1450 to 1568 contain examples. The peak of the genre's popularity seems to have occurred during the first decades of the sixteenth century, when the largest collections of verse epistles were assembled, if not composed. By ca. 1540, however, the fashion seems to have changed in England, and few verse love epistles are to be found, although the Bannatyne manuscript (1568) attests to the genre's continued vigor in the north.

The stages in the genre's evolution during the century and more during which it flourished are difficult to establish, not only because many links have been lost through accidents of preservation but also because so many of the sources are impossible to date precisely or even in relation to one another. The problem of dating is especially acute for the fifteenth-century texts, most of which are datable only very approximately by virtue of the hand in which they are written. While these texts must therefore be treated more or less as a contemporaneous group, they can profitably be contrasted with those dating from ca. 1500 on, most of which can be more reliably set in chronological sequence. In almost all cases, it should be noted, the date of a manuscript or printed edition represents only a *terminus ante quem* for the composition of the poems that it contains. For this reason, even contrasts between "fifteenth-century" and "sixteenth-century" verse love epistles can only be tentative, unless information about authorship or influences makes more precise dating possible.

5.1. Transmission

Some important conclusions about the history of the genre can be made simply through examining the context of transmission. All the verse love epistles are preserved in one of three contexts, only one of which has not been seen in the period before ca. 1450. *(a)* Three or more verse love epistles may occur in a single manuscript or section of a manuscript, along with other poems, including love poems, of which they are (numerically) a significant or even the dominant type (cf. MS Fairfax 16). To this category belong Lambeth Palace MS 306; Bodleian Library MS Douce 95, MS Rawlinson poet. 36, MS Lat. misc. c.66 (Humfrey Newton; ca. 1500); Cambridge, Trinity College MS R.3.19 (1478–1483); British Library MS Additional 17492 (Devonshire MS, fols. 26r–30r; 1536–1537); Bodleian Library MS Rawlinson C.813 (1527–1535); and National Library of Scotland MS Advocates 1.1.6 ("Bannatyne MS"; 1568). *(b)* One or two verse love epistles are copied together with other poems but are not necessarily or clearly dominant among the love poems (cf. MS Harley 682). The relevant portions of all four manuscript examples in this category date from the last half of the fifteenth century: National Library of Wales MS Porkington 10; Cambridge University Library MS Ff.1.6 ("Findern Anthology"); British Library MS Harley 7578, and MS Cotton Vespasian D.9. Printed examples are in Pynson's *Boke of Fame* (1526) and Thynne's edition of Chaucer (1532). *(c)* Finally, isolated verse love epistles are copied along with unrelated material, often having been added by a hand later than the one that originally wrote the manuscript. Examples include British Library MS Harley 3810, MS Royal 6B.ix; Bodleian Library MS Douce 326 (end of the fifteenth century); British Library MS Harley 541 (end of the fifteenth century); Bodleian Library MS Arch. Selden B.24 (early sixteenth century); University of Glasgow Library MS Hunterian 230 (after 1509); and British Library MS Harley 4011 (first half of the sixteenth century).

While type *(a)* and type *(c)* transmission are about equally represented in the fifteenth and sixteenth centuries, an interesting movement away from type *(b)* is under way around 1500. Before that date, type *(b)* manuscripts are as common as type *(a)* and type *(c)* manuscripts, but after 1500 type *(b)* is represented only in two printed sources, both of which contain mostly fourteenth- and fifteenth-century works. The shift is even more apparent if one compares the type *(a)* manuscripts from the second half of the fifteenth century with those from 1500 on. The earlier sources contain relatively few verse love epistles – three (Douce 95, Rawlinson poet. 36), four (Lambeth 306), and six (TCC R.3.19). By contrast, those from ca. 1500 on contain seven (BL Add. 17492), ten or eleven (Bodleian Lat. misc. c.66), at least sixteen (Advocates 1.1.6), and at least twenty-five (Rawlinson C.813). Simple numbers can be misleading: the epistle is the only type of love lyric represented in Lambeth 306 and Douce 95, and its share of the total number of love lyrics in Rawlinson poet. 36 (three of six) and in TCC R.3.19 (six of twelve) is much greater than in Advocates 1.1.6. However, the sheer quantity of verse love epistles in the sixteenth-century sources must nevertheless be counted as evidence of the genre's steadily increasing popularity. It seems safe to say that the epistle became the dominant form of the English love lyric in the half-century whose midpoint is 1500: if one omits songbooks, there is hardly a manuscript from this period containing love lyrics that does not also contain at least one verse love epistle.

Two additional facts about transmission confirm the impression of a steady growth in popularity that climaxed in the sixteenth century. Only five verse love epistles can be dated with certainty to the first half of the fifteenth century. From manuscripts datable in the second half of the century the number of examples preserved is already twenty-five; while in sources dating from ca. 1500 on, at least sixty-five verse love epistles survive. While this statistic must be weighed against the likelihood that some examples were composed considerably earlier than the date of the manuscript or book in which they were preserved and against the fact that fewer sources containing verse love letters survive from the sixteenth century than from the second half of the fifteenth century (nine versus twelve), it nevertheless gives a rough idea of the course of the genre's reception. Also striking is the fact that none of these poems occurs in more than one copy. Despite a considerable amount of intertextuality – not only the plundering of a common source, such as *Troilus and Criseyde*, but also the borrowing of lines from other verse love epistles – it is even rare to find poems that are simply reworkings of earlier verse epistles.[1] Accidents of preservation may account for some of this lack of duplication, as does the relative brevity of the poems themselves. But the evidence also seems to suggest that a large part of the genre's audience was engaged in producing as well as reading love epistles and that the genre's practitioners, initially limited to a narrow court circle, came to encompass a rather broad section of the educated populace. The verse love epistle was popular in more than one sense of the word.

---

[1] Examples from MS Lambeth 306 (of a letter from MS Fairfax 16) and from MS Advocates 1.1.6 (of a letter from Rawlinson C.813) are discussed below (5.3.2).

5.2. Social Function

A number of historical factors, some of them discussed at the end of chapter 2, doubtless contributed to the genre's rapid growth. But as with any new genre, the verse love epistle's success must have been due in large part to the functions, both literary and social, that it performed. What those functions might have been can be discovered from evidence within the verse epistles themselves as well as from other sources of information about the "game of love" as it was played in the late Middle Ages. Letters had figured in medieval love narratives from the twelfth century on, for practical and rather obvious reasons. This practical, communicative function, the same one that has always driven real lovers to exchange letters, is still dominant in a work such as *Troilus and Criseyde*. But in the fifteenth century the lover's behavior is increasingly ritualized into a game, whose components are isolated, elaborated, repeated, and apparently savored for their own sake. In many, if not most of the post-Chaucerian love narratives one has the impression of a series of discrete, conventional poses and gestures rather than a coherent action. The "story" does not move toward a resolution but rather seeks to prolong itself indefinitely, through repetition and variation. Indeed, most of the longer love poems of the fifteenth and sixteenth centuries read like reworkings of the same poem.[2] As Huizinga and others have shown, the same period saw a growing tendency among courtiers to act out the ritual, to identify the ideal courtier with the ideal lover found in literature.[3] Though the existence of actual "courts of love" such as the celebrated one associated with Charles VI of France (1400) is open to dispute, there seems little doubt that courtiers, and an increasingly growing number of the gentry and the bourgeoisie, came to regard the behavior and particularly the language of the literary lover as an essential constituent of polite society.[4]

---

[2] Ethel Seaton went so far as to attribute most of the corpus to a single poet: Sir Richard Roos (ca. 1410–1482).

[3] *Waning*, especially chapters 8 and 9. John Stevens used the phrase "the game of love" to describe this ritual, and his remains the fullest study of the relationship between courtly behavior and courtly literature in England from the late fourteenth to the early sixteenth centuries: *Music and Poetry*, pp. 145–229. A more recent treatment that adds some new material and perspectives is Richard F. Green, *Poets and Princepleasers*, chapter 4 (especially pp. 109–27).

[4] On the importance of proper speech, see the studies cited in the previous note, and Larry D. Benson, "Courtly Love," pp. 241–49. Stephan Kohl explores the relationship between the ideal behavior of lovers recorded in "cultural" documents and the

Those who desired to act like lovers in public naturally took their instruction from love literature, particularly, we may presume, those who did not have the opportunity to observe court life firsthand. That interest in love as social decorum seems in turn to have affected the way that love poetry was written. For all its beauty and authority, *Troilus and Criseyde* is too dense, too circumstantial, even too philosophical to serve as a reference manual. The succeeding generations either boiled it down to a series of rules, gestures, and emotions, or chopped it up and reassembled it into readily usable pieces. Even where a narrative is retained, the lovers are stripped of any particularizing features that might block the reader's ability to project their actions and words onto his own situation.[5] At a further stage of reduction, many love narratives from the period supply a set of commandments of love, a practice found earlier in French and Latin but not in English love poetry.

What is not new in the fifteenth-century poems is the emphasis on language as the key to success in the game of love. The perfect courtier must be a master of flirtatious conversation, both the more spontaneous sort that must have been common at social gatherings but that has obviously gone unrecorded, and the more calculated sort recorded in the hundreds of courtly love poems that have been preserved. Indeed, proficiency in the language of love was already appreciated and presumably cultivated by Englishmen of Chaucer's generation. Gawain's arrival at Hautdesert creates a sensation because his fame as a lover leads Bercilak's courtiers to expect to learn the latest refinements of "luf talkyng" (*Sir Gawain and the Green Knight*, lines 915–27). And once Pandarus has persuaded Criseyde at least not to reject Troilus out of hand, her first question is, significantly, "Kan he wel speke of love?" (*T&C*, II, 503). Perhaps the most basic function of the verse love epistle should be sought in this context: it provided a new vehicle for demonstrating one's mastery of the terms of love. And its chances of becoming fashionable can only have been helped by the presence of love letters in *Troilus and Criseyde*, for fifteenth- and sixteenth-century English versifiers the canonical authority on the language of love.

A poem from the Devonshire Manuscript (1532–1541) illustrates this

---

contrasting "non-cultural" (i.e., real-life) attitudes toward marriage, using examples from the Paston, Cely, and Stonor letter collections, in "Private Letters," pp. 124–28. The same material is found in Kohl's book, *Das englische Spätmittelalter*, pp. 105–12.

[5] On this feature of medieval love poetry, see especially Judson B. Allen, "Lyric Ego," pp. 199–226, and Raymond Oliver, *Poems without Names*.

most basic function of the genre very well. Complaining about his lady's "disdayn," the unhappy lover recalls his confessions of love:

> Offt haue I shoyd my lovyng hert
> With wordes vnfayned and eke by letter,
> By message all so sent on my part,
> And all to cause her love the gretter[6]

Here the letter is put neatly and explicitly into the set of possible ways to address the lady – direct speech, speech by written proxy, and speech by a living messenger. Again it may be no coincidence that all three methods are employed in Troilus' courtship of Criseyde.

If the love epistle's sole function were to communicate the usual themes of lovers' conversation – chiefly praise of the lady and complaints about the lover's suffering for love of her – it would be difficult to account for its remarkable success. Why should the letter have been singled out as a new vehicle for conventional themes? Some factors external to the game of love have already been cited in partial explanation: the medieval letter had a distinctive, immediately recognizable form; interest in letter writing in English was particularly high during the first half of the fifteenth century. A literary system so thematically closed as courtly love poetry also needed to be revitalized periodically through the introduction of novel forms, though the need for novelty does not in itself explain why the letter, as opposed to, say, the dawn song or the messenger's speech, was the form selected. Ideally, one would like to find an explanation based on a feature unique to or at least primary in the letter.

In fact, late medieval English love poets were aware of a way in which the letter differed from the other two varieties of discourse identified in the poem quoted above: only in letters is the lover's discourse converted into a physical object. This awareness is nothing new. Chaucer, as we have seen, exploited the letter's physicality: it is a receptacle for the lover's tears, themselves physical evidence of his sincere emotions (*T&C*, II, 1027, 1086–88; V, 1335–37); it enjoys an intimacy with the lady that the lover himself is denied (*T&C*, II, 1089–92, 1155; "The Merchant's Tale," 1944); and it can even suffer an ignominious fate ("The Merchant's Tale," 1952–54).[7] By virtue of its existence as a physical object, the letter acquired a second function in the game of love: it could function as a love token, a keepsake, or a gift. Thus, letters are listed

---

[6] Ed. Kenneth Muir, "Unpublished Poems," p. 274.

[7] The anonymous author of the (epistolary?) "compleynt" appended to two copies of Lydgate's *Temple of Glass* (*Index* 147) begs his lady at least to give his verses "a

132

among other suitable gifts to send one's lady, in the thirteenth of Love's twenty statutes in *The Court of Love* (lines 393–99):

> The thirteenth statut, Whylom is to thinke,
> What thing may best thy lady lyke and plese,
> And in thyn hertes botom let it sinke:
> Som thing devise, and take [it] for thyn ese,
> And send it her, that may her herte apese:
> Some hert, or ring, or lettre, or device,
> Or precious stone; but spare not for no price.[8]

Even more emphatic on the letter's double function as synecdochic substitute for the lover and as gift is the discussion of the seven tokens whereby carnal love may be distinguished from physical love, in the treatise called *Disce mori,* compiled in the 1450s, probably at Syon Abbey: "The v'the' tokene of flesshly love is þat þat oon lovere sendeth to þat oþer lettres of love, tokenes and yiftes, which be worshipped, kissed, used and kept as reliques."[9]

Evidence within some of the surviving verse love epistles suggests that such poems were composed for occasions when the exchanging of gifts was traditional or especially appropriate, notably New Year's Day,[10] Saint Valentine's Day,[11] and the departure or return of a loved one.[12] By

---

goode looke" before vengefully consigning them to be "casten fully in þe fyr" (605–9). But if his "litell quarell"

> shal be al to-tore,
> With-outen mercy, and to-rent,
> I preye yowe with my best entent,
> þat with youre owen handes sofft
> þat ye reende and brek it offt:
> For youre touche, I dare wel seyne,
> Wel þe lasse shal ben his peyne,   (610–15)

Ed. J. Schick, *Lydgate's Temple of Glas*, p. 67. In one poem, from MS Porkington 10 (second half, fifteenth century), a lover even vows to wear a "letter" around his head until his fickle lady consents to remove it personally. Ed. Auvo Kurvinen, "MS. Porkington 10," p. 55 (#30, lines 51–54).

[8] Ed. W. W. Skeat, *Chaucer,* vol. 7, p. 420. Cf. also Skelton's *Phyllyp Sparowe*, lines 680–93: ed. Scattergood, *John Skelton*, pp. 88–89.

[9] Ed. Lee Patterson, in *Negotiating the Past*, p. 126; see also p. 142 n. 68.

[10] See *Index* 1789 (from Lambeth 306), and J. Stevens, *Music and Poetry*, pp. 183–84.

[11] For example, the letter by Margery Brews. But it should be noted that the fashion for Saint Valentine's Day poems seems to have ended around the mid fifteenth century, just when the verse love epistle was developing into a distinct genre. See H. A. Kelly, *Chaucer and Saint Valentine,* especially pp. 128–58.

[12] For an example of a welcoming letter, see the first in a series of four love epistles (*Index* 3878) from Cambridge University Library Ff.1.6. A farewell epistle by Humfrey Newton presents itself as (or is accompanied by?) a "tokyn" to be kept in "remenbrance" of the sender (*Index* 768, lines 18–19). The "farewell" poem, perhaps as a spinoff from the love epistle (see 5.4.2. below), and the constant pleas for

the sixteenth century the association between love letters and gifts is so firmly established that one even finds love letters from fathers to daughters.[13] Any poem could of course be written down and sent, either as a message or as a gift, thus performing the same function as a letter.[14] What distinguished the verse epistle per se is that the text itself foregrounded the epistolary function, drawing attention to the physicality of the medium. Considering how popular the "giving" of poems was, the "objectifying" of the love message may help account for the verse love epistle's popularity, even though most such poems would, in any case, have been read publicly.[15] At the same time, the priority of function over form gradually caused the dilution of the specifically epistolary features in many late verse love epistles (e.g., those in BL Add. 17492) or the elaboration of a single part of the letter (usually the farewell) to the point where it becomes the whole poem.

5.3.   Genre Awareness
5.3.1. Terminology

The consequent blurring of the boundary between poems that are epistolary in function only and those that are epistolary in both form and function means that many poems whose authors or recipients would have considered them to be verse love epistles will be overlooked in this study. Even without considering the lost poems, the present corpus is skewed to

---

"remembrance" in the surviving love epistles also suggest that the genre may have been especially closely tied to a specific situation that involved physical separation.

[13] The first letters of each line in one of Humfrey Newton's briefer love epistles (*Index* 2217) spell out "Margeret," the name of one of his daughters. *Index* 1768 concludes with a formula ("Crystes dere blessyng & myne": line 55) that is employed almost exclusively when parents write to their children. Its use is made clear in a humorous verse epistle from the same manuscript (Rawlinson C.813):

Commende me to Raffe, whych my father ys,
And pray hym to send me Godes blessing and hys.
(*Supplement* 2827.5, lines 17–18)

Norman Davis collects many examples of the formula in "Note on *Pearl*."

[14] See, e.g., Lydgate's "A Lover's New Year's Gift," ed. H. N. MacCracken, *Minor Poems*, part 2, pp. 424–27. Many examples of ballades sent as New Year's gifts/greetings can be found among the works of fourteenth- and fifteenth-century French poets, such as Deschamps and Christine de Pisan.

[15] See J. Stevens, *Music and Poetry*, pp. 159–64, and R. F. Green, *Poets and Princepleasers*, pp. 117–19, 126–27. A good example of the thin line between written and spoken discourse in the "game of love" is the "bill" that a lover apparently reads aloud in his lady's presence in *The Court of Love*: ed. W. W. Skeat, *Chaucer*, vol. 7, pp. 431–33. The "bill" itself (lines 841–89) could pass as a verse love epistle, though it lacks any epistolary formulas.

the extent that it probably overrepresents examples in which generic self-consciousness, either through the use of labels or characteristic language, is especially strong. The limitation must be accepted, however, since without some sort of marker one cannot begin to make distinctions between epistolary and non-epistolary love poems. And a corpus of nearly one-hundred poems more or less clearly identified as love epistles from the period ca. 1400 to 1568 certainly constitutes a large and diverse enough group to permit the drawing of reasonably accurate conclusions about the characteristics and the history of the genre.

In fact, especially during the half-century following the genre's beginning, in aristocratic imitations of Chaucer's "Litera Troili," there is considerable evidence of genre awareness among practitioners of the love letter. The most obvious evidence of such awareness is the use of genre labels within the poems themselves. As in the earlier epistles, the preferred terms continue to be "letter(s)" and "bill(et)." A few sixteenth-century poems expand the normal term to "letters of love," but this more precise label seems never to have stabilized into a *terminus technicus* on the level of *salut d'amour*.[16] Other terms that are used occasionally, often alongside and apparently synonymously with the usual "letter" or "bill," include "byble" (*Index* 1329), "wryttyng" (*Index* 2421, *Supplement* 3785.5), "queare" (*Index* 2547), "scedule" (*Index* 2821), and "treytes" (*Supplement* 3917.8), to cite only examples from the anthology of twenty-five love epistles in Rawlinson C.813 (1527–1535).

Less often one finds scribal labels that perform the same function. The most notable example is the set of seventeen poems that Humfrey Newton copied in his own hand on three leaves of his commonplace book (Bodleian Library MS Lat. misc. c.66, fols. 92–94). Ten of these he has provided with a label that clearly identifies them as letters, at least in function if not in form – "Bilet" (*Index* 735), "Littera amandi" (*Index* 2217, 737, 481), and "Mittitur" (*Index* 2281, 1344, 2597, 926, 556, 2263). Only one "epistolary" poem, significantly a borderline case (*Index* 768), has not been given such a label. Newton's care in identifying the genre of his modest compositions is exceptional, though isolated examples can be found in other manuscripts.[17] Elsewhere the context of transmission suggests that sharp genre distinctions are being observed. In MS Porkington 10, for example, there are four love poems in direct

---

[16] See *Index* 1344, line 6 (from Bodleian Lat. misc. c.66); *Index* 3804, line 4, and *Supplement* 2560.5, line 4 (both from MS Rawlinson C.813).

[17] See also *Supplement* 3917.8, from MS Rawlinson C.813: "A lettre of love in the prease of þe bewtye of his love, with þe discription of hur qualiteȝ."

address (items 29, 30, 36, and 37), only one of which (item 36) calls itself a letter and contains epistolary formulas. That same piece (*Index* 1241) stands out among the love poems in being written in octosyllabic couplets, the normal verse form of the *salut d'amour*, rather than in the "Monk's Tale" octaves of the other three.[18] The tendency to group love letters together in anthologies such as Humfrey Newton's, Rawlinson C.813, and the Bannatyne MS is still better evidence for a strong sense of genre.

Despite a tendency toward experimentation during the sixteenth century (see 5.4. below), most love epistles continue to employ to some degree the clusters of formulas at beginning and end, the "I recommend me" and the "I write no more at this time," that characterize the earliest examples of the genre and indeed medieval letters in general. From every period in the genre's history and in nearly every collection of verse love epistles there are poems in which the epistolary conventions are observed painstakingly.[19] Indeed, such elements are the constants that make it possible to speak of a continuous tradition, representatives of which are found as late as 1568, among the "ballattis of luve" in the Bannatyne MS.[20]

5.3.2. Intertextuality

Two additional signs of genre awareness – intertextuality and parody – deserve special attention. Though the practice of reusing material lifted from poems by famous authors, especially Chaucer, or less famous contemporaries is far from unusual among fifteenth- and sixteenth-century versifiers, it is suggestive that most such "borrowing" in verse love epistles comes either from other verse love epistles or from poems that

---

[18] Manuscript context can also suggest that poems without clear signs of genre be included in the corpus. Thus *Index* 3291 occurs together with three similar poems that are more clearly love letters (in Lambeth 306). More extreme examples are a poem from the Devonshire MS ("Who hath more cawse": Muir, #11) and another from the "Findern Anthology" (*Index* 3878, part 4). Though neither is epistolary in form, indeed neither goes so far as to employ direct address, both are probably epistolary in function, given their position within well-defined series of poems that are more clearly love epistles.

[19] From the second half of the fifteenth century, see *Index* 754, 1238, 1241, 2247, 3785; from the turn of the sixteenth century, *Index* 2281; from the first half of the sixteenth century, *Index* 2421, 2821, 3804, 4190, *Supplement* 2560.5.

[20] See, for example, "My dullit corss"; ed. W. T. Ritchie, III, pp. 322–23. A glance at the index of first lines in Appendix I.B. shows the tendency for *poetic* formulas to evolve within the genre as well – for example, the one beginning "Right ...," which comes from the "Litera Troili" (see *Index* 2821–2824).

contain love epistles, chiefly Chaucer's *Troilus and Criseyde* and Stephen Hawes's *The Pastime of Pleasure* (first printed edition 1509).[21] Occasionally this intertextuality produces what could be called variant versions of the same poem. For instance, one of the verse love epistles in Lambeth 306 (*Index* 2247), a collection that may be as early as the 1460s, recasts one of the three letters from Fairfax 16 (*Index* 2182) by changing its three rime royal stanzas to "Monk's Tale" octaves and adding a four-line envoy.[22] More typical is the kind of intertextuality illustrated by Margery Brews's Saint Valentine's Day letter, in which as little as one line or as much as a stanza or two is taken over, with or without modification.[23] Finally, there are the cases where a new poem is constructed almost entirely, *cento*-like, from excerpts from a longer poem or from several poems.[24]

The use made of Stephen Hawes's *The Pastime of Pleasure* in the poems of MS Rawlinson C.813 is important testimony to genre awareness, as well as to the fluid boundary between the love document and the love letter. Hawes's poem contains one letter (lines 3951–4086), written

---

[21] On the practice of borrowing, especially from Chaucer, in fifteenth- and sixteenth-century courtly lyrics, see Ethel Seaton, "'Devonshire Manuscript,'" pp. 55–56; J. Stevens, *Music and Poetry,* pp. 213–14 (using the example of the "Litera Troili"); and R. H. Robbins, "Lyrics," pp. 382–83 (also citing the "Litera Troili" as a "lyric cluster" rich in potential for excerpting). M. B. Parkes and Richard Beadle find evidence that some of the texts in MS Gg.4.27 were used "as a quarry for writing verses or for elegant phrases to be incorporated in highly personal letters": *Facsimile of CUL MS Gg.4.27,* vol. 3, p. 65. Boffey suggests that the Lydgate anthology in MS Sloane 1212 may also have been quarried for personal letters (*Manuscripts of Lyrics,* p. 14 n. 23) and later discusses several examples of intertextuality involving verse love epistles (pp. 90–91). For an Old French verse love epistle in the form of a *cento,* see the poem constructed by the otherwise unknown Simon (second half, thirteenth century) from lyric passages, chiefly Kahedin's farewell letter, in the romance *Tristan* (E. Ruhe, *De Amasio,* pp. 201–3).

[22] Cf. also *Index* 767 (Rawlinson C.813), a "farewell" poem whose first three stanzas are nearly identical with the last three stanzas of poem #268 (ed. W. T. Ritchie, III, pp. 284–85) in the Bannatyne MS. Besides each having one stanza that the other lacks, the two poems also differ in dialect. They are printed side-by-side, in W. Bolle, "Zur Lyrik," pp. 297–98.

[23] For example, cf. *Index* 752, lines 1–2 (from Douce 95) and *Index* 2421, lines 1–2 (from Rawlinson C.813).

[24] Examples include *Supplement* 1926.5 (*Troilus and Criseyde:* see Bolle's parallel-text edition, in "Zur Lyrik," pp. 284–87); *Index* 2510 (*Troilus and Criseyde; The Craft of Lovers;* Lydgate's *Court of Sapience); Index* 2532 (Hawes's *The Pastime of Pleasure* and *The Comfort of Lovers); Supplement* 2532.5 (*Pastime of Pleasure),* the last stanza of which (*Pastime of Pleasure,* 2542–48) also occurs independently, in MS Hunterian 230, to form a *billet doux: Index* 2318; *Index* 2822 and *Supplement* 3917.8 (both from *Pastime of Pleasure).* With the exception of *Index* 2510 (Trinity College Cambridge R.3.19), all these examples come from Rawlinson C.813.

for Venus by Sapience, in response to the Lover's "Supplycacyon" (lines 3804–3908), and carried to La Belle Pucelle by Cupid.[25] This surrogate love letter is excerpted in three of the four Rawlinson verse love epistles that are composed of extracts from the *Pastime*. One of the three (*Index* 2822) is, in fact, little more than a revised version of Hawes's letter, taking only one stanza (lines 50–56) from a different source and omitting only the final ten lines.[26] Another (*Index* 2532) concludes with precisely those final two stanzas omitted from the poem just discussed.[27] The third example (*Supplement* 3917.8) is less striking, in that the material borrowed is not used at the beginning or end of the letter in a way that emphasizes the epistolary character of the source.[28] But even in the Rawlinson MS, with its very high concentration of love epistles, non-epistolary poems can also serve as sources for love epistles. Nor are love epistles unique in borrowing from longer poems.

5.3.3. Parody

More significant and more interesting signs of genre consciousness are the complementary practices of parodying the verse love epistle or employing it for sacred subjects. Both practices are best exemplified in poems from manuscripts dated in the late fifteenth century. The poems in question are especially good indicators of the features that practitioners of the genre perceived as dominant or genre-defining, since the deliberate movement away from the normal function is largely dependent on recognition of the form for its effect. In other words, one expects that such poems will be self-consciously typical, even to the point of exaggerating some conventions, in order to give sharper focus to the discrepancy between expectation and fulfillment on which their effect largely depends. This gap is greater in the broad, often crude satirical inversion than in the more subtle contrafacture, but some of the same conventions are emphasized in both.

---

[25] Ed. William E. Mead, *Pastime of Pleasure*, pp. 149–54.

[26] *Index* 2822, lines 1–49, 57–133 = *Pastime*, lines 3951–99, 4000–4075.

[27] *Index* 2532, lines 155–68 = *Pastime*, lines 4077–90. The Rawlinson adapter has modified *Pastime*, lines 4087–90, in order to make them part of the epistle: in the original they belong to the narrative.

[28] *Supplement* 3917.8, lines 183–217 = *Pastime*, lines 3952–78, 3993–99, 4014–20, 4021–27. The modifications of Hawes's text are also more significant in this poem than in the previous two. For detailed accounts of the borrowing from Hawes's work in the poems of Rawlinson C.813, see Kathleen H. Power, "Edition of Lyrics," pp. 174–75. She does not mention that another verse love epistle from the same manuscript (*Supplement* 1017.5) clearly echoes in its opening lines the first stanza of Hawes's letter.

In one important sense the two parodic love letters in MS Rawlinson poet. 36 (*Index* 3832, 2437) are not typical of the Middle English genre, for they form a paired letter and response. Such pairs, typical in letter collections of the *dictatores,* are represented in Middle English verse only by the macaronic letters discussed in chapter 2.10. and, with qualifications, by the "Litera Troili" and the "Litera Criseydis." Moreover, where such pairs occur, the typical pattern is for the man to write first and for the woman to respond. Perhaps in keeping with the parodic inversion, and certainly in order to give the man the last word, the Rawlinson poems reverse the traditional order. Also deliberate is the man's closer adherence to epistolary conventions governing the opening and closing of the letter. Like the man's reply, the woman's letter opens with a *suprascriptio* that stresses her partner's fickleness:

> To my trew loue and able –
> As the wedyr cok he is stable –
> Thys letter to hym be deliueryd.

But the letter proper opens with only the most perfunctory of salutations before launching into the satirical *effictio* that is its main content:

> Vnto you, most froward, þis lettre I write,
> Whych hath causyd me so longe in dyspayre;

While the man's *suprascriptio* sounds the same note as hers –

> To you, dere herte, variant and mutable,
> lyke to Carybdis whych is vnstable.

– he follows it with an ironic version of the orthodox "floral greeting":

> O Fresch floure, most plesant of pryse,
> fragrant as fedyrfoy to mannys inspeccion,

The same can be said of the *conclusio:* both letters end with brief, ironic "mottoes," parodying a practice not uncommon in contemporary verse love epistles.[29] But again, in the woman's letter the motto follows immediately after the last stanza of vilification, whereas in the man's reply there is a full stanza of satirical *conclusio* (lines 50–56), in which all the conventions of closing identified in the "classic" verse love epistles of Fairfax 16 are systematically inverted:

---

[29] Cf., for example, *Index* 868, 1789, 2247, *Supplement* 2308.8, *Index* 2311, 2529, etc.

Adew, dere herte, for now I make an ende
Vnto suche tyme that I haue better space.
The pyp and þe pose to you I recomend,
And god of hys mercy graunte you so mykyl grace
In paradyse onys to haue a restyng place,
Vp by the nauel, fast by the water gate,
To loke after passage whan it cometh late.

youre owne loue, trusty and trewe,
you haue forsake cause of a newe.

That the woman's neglect of the usual formulas is part of the satire is evident from remarks in the man's reply. Taking advantage of his unusual role as respondent, he does not limit himself to mock *effictio,* as the woman did, but also adopts the role of literary critic:

To me ye haue sent a lettre of derusion,
Endyghted ful freshly with many coryous I-clause.
* * *
The ynglysch of Chaucere was nat in youre mynd,
Ne tullyus termys wyth so gret elloquence,
But ye, as vncurtes and Crabbed of kynde,
Rolled hem on a hepe, it semyth by the sentence;

(lines 5–6, 8–11)

His criticism further recalls the conventional apology for one's poor writing found already in the "Litera Troili" and repeated in many of its successors, particularly in letters by or purporting to be by women.[30]

Since both lovers devote the bulk of their letters to anatomizing the ugliness of their partners, it is tempting to conclude that the wit that doubtless composed both poems regarded praise rather than complaint as particularly appropriate in the love letter. However, it must be noted that the association between praise and blame has a long tradition rooted in classical epideictic rhetoric and that the poet consequently had access to much greater resources for mock praise than for mock complaint.[31]

---

[30] Letters written in the personae of women frequently contain apologies for style, even where no stylistic inadequacy is evident. Cf. *Index* 2547, lines 19–22, and *Index* 754, lines 50–52. However, the apology is conventional in love letters from men as well, and occurs, for example, in the "Litera Troili." See also E. Ruhe, *De Amasio,* p. 90 and p. 388 n. 67.

[31] The rhetorical context receives special emphasis in Jan Ziolkowski, "Avatars of Ugliness," pp. 1–20. Also relevant are Ruhe's remarks on the affinity between the paired letters and responses of the *dictatores'* letter collections and the genre of the *altercatio* (*De Amasio,* pp. 69–71). Stevens, *Music and Poetry,* pp. 220–23, observes that a broad range of satire is integral to the "game of love." Ziolkowski traces the long hisory of the ironic *effictio,* which extends as far back as the fifth-century poet

Furthermore, both correspondents do in fact make at least passing reference to the theme of suffering for love, when they curse anyone who would undergo hardships for the sake of the sorry lover whom they address (*Index* 3832, lines 31–35; *Index* 2437, lines 40–42). The man's concluding motto, announcing that he has forsaken the lady for whose love he is not suffering, extends the "inverted complaint" a step further. A third verse love epistle in the same manuscript (*Index* 1510), set in the same rime royal stanzas as the parodies but copied by a different hand, sheds no light on the issue of dominant themes. Its equally conventional message is neither praise nor complaint but predominantly the pledging of service and fidelity to the lady.

5.3.4. Religious Adaptation

The satirical love epistles from Rawlinson poet. 36 are unique within the corpus.[32] One encounters verse epistles from disillusioned lovers, but rather than parodies these are complaints in which the lover's patience has finally given way to bitter irony or even the resolution to look elsewhere for a kinder lady.[33] The kindest lady of all, whose beauty, purity, and unfailing mercy merit the highest praise and whose servants never have cause to complain, is the Blessed Virgin. And once the verse

---

Sidonius, and discusses eight fifteenth- and sixteenth-century English lyrics that employ the technique (pp. 10–16), including the pair from MS Rawlinson poet. 36. Mitchell (*Thomas Hoccleve,* pp. 52–54) comments briefly on its English phase, and Francis Lee Utley lists many examples of "satirical panegyrics" from medieval and early Renaissance English literature in *Crooked Rib*, p. 45. Also see Theo Stemmler, "'My Fair Lady,'" pp. 205–13. Other (non-epistolary) satirical love poems, not all of them employing extended descriptions, are listed by Robbins, in *SL,* pp. 289–90, and "Satiric Epistles," pp. 418–20. The chiding poem in MS Rawlinson C.813 (*Supplement* 3785.5) might also be added.

[32] Two poems by Skelton, both composed probably in the mid 1490s and printed ca. 1527, may supply additional examples. Stanley Fish compares the first (*Supplement* 3302.5, from *Dyvers Balettys and Dyties Solacyous*) to the woman's letter from Rawlinson poet. 36 (*Index* 3832), in that both observe the form of the compliment while replacing its substance with insult: *Skelton's Poetry,* pp. 46–49 (on the verse compliment, see also below, n. 55). Aside from its use of direct address and its reference to the act of writing (line 4), Skelton's poem has no distinctive epistolary features. The second Skelton poem (*Supplement* 4217.3, from *Skelton Laureat Agaynste a Comely Coystrowne*) is even less epistolary in form than the inverted compliment: only the final couplet, an envoy addressing it to "mastres Anne," suggests that it may have been intended as a letter. Fish argues persuasively for reading it as a dialogue or flyting (p. 40). The most recent edition is John Scattergood, ed., *John Skelton,* pp. 42–43, 40–41.

[33] See, e.g., *Supplement* 3785.5; Bannatyne, #336 (ed. W. T. Ritchie, IV, 19–22).

love epistle developed into a conventional vehicle for courtly discourse, it was highly likely that love letters to the Blessed Virgin would appear.[34] It is difficult to be certain how widespread Marian verse love epistles were in the Middle English tradition, partly because the boundaries between epistolary and non-epistolary greetings to the Virgin could be vague and partly because the clues within a given text are not always sufficient to rule out the possibility of its being addressed to an earthly lover. Since the epistolary nature of such poems was simply one conventional pose among several options, the problem of delivering the text to Heaven never arose.

A poem preserved in MS Douce 326 (*Index* 927) illustrates nicely the ambiguities that make the assignment of genre so difficult. Indeed, its editors agreed neither on its form nor on its addressee: Carleton Brown hedges on the form but confidently groups it with poems addressed to the Blessed Virgin, while R. T. Davies labels it "A love letter" and seems to consider it a secular poem.[35] In verse form (six stanzas, rime royal) and in theme (offer of service, accompanied by praise) the poem is comparable to the classic verse love epistle, but the strongest evidence is its opening stanza of greeting:

> Goe, lytyll byll, & doe me recommende
> Vn-to my lady with godely countynaunce,
> ffor, trusty messanger, I the sende.
> Pray her that sche make puruyaunce;
> ffor my love, thurgh her sufferaunce,
> In her Bosome desyreth to reste,
> ssyth off all women I loue here beste.

Though this stanza resembles an envoy, its placement at the head of the poem is strong evidence of epistolary intent. Noteworthy too is the use of the common genre label "byll" (repeated in line 14), the presence of the "me recommende" formula, and the emphasis on the text's being sent as a "messanger" into the lady's presence.

---

[34] Two centuries earlier, in France, the *salut d'amour* had flourished alongside the *salut Nostre Dame,* though the latter genre was not epistolary but rather a vernacular adaptation of the *Ave Maria:* E. Ruhe, *De Amasio,* pp. 232–33. See also H. F. Williams, "French Valentine," pp. 292–95. *Le livre d'Enanchet* (first half, thirteenth century), on the other hand, contains an authentic "remaking" (*Kontrafaktur*) of a (prose) secular love letter into a letter to the Blessed Virgin: E. Ruhe, *De Amasio,* pp. 181–84.

[35] In *Lyrics of Fifteenth Century,* Brown titles it "A Love Message to My Lady" (ed., pp. 75–76), and in the *Index,* "An Envoy Addressed to Our Lady." Davies's edition is in *Medieval English Lyrics,* pp. 201–2.

Whether the lady is to be understood as the celestial Blessed Virgin or as an hyperbolized earthly lady is more difficult to decide. None of the praise offered her would be out of place in a secular love poem of the more idealized sort, though some elements fit the Blessed Virgin especially well. The epithets "lylly off redolence" and "rose off conffydence" (lines 8, 10) may simply draw on a venerable convention of love poetry, but the repetition of the lily comparison (line 33: "Her flauour excedith the fflowr-delyce") strengthens the Marian connection. Praise of the lady's beauty is general and abstract, while her virtues, especially her "grace" (lines 21, 37), receive more than usual emphasis. And, most important, the overall concern of the poem is more with the lady's ability to give comfort than with the lover's sufferings, which earn him the right to expect the lady's "mercy." The letter bespeaks a tranquil confidence that its message will be favorably received, an impression that is not seriously undercut by the conventional petition in the final stanza:

> Hyr I beseche, seth I not feyne
> Butt only putt me in hur grace,
> That off me she not dysdeyne,
> Takyng regarde at old trespace;   (lines 36–39)

However, it is above all the fourth stanza that points toward the Blessed Virgin as the lady addressed: without it there would be little incentive to question the poem's secularity, whatever the poet's intention:

> The cause þerfor, yf she wyll wytt,
> Wyll I presume on sych a flowre
> ssay, off hyr, for yt ys I-wrytt,
> she is þe feyrest paramour
> And to man in ych langour
> Most souerayne medyatryce.
> Ther-ffor I loue þat flowre of pryce.   (lines 22–28)

The reference to the lady as "medyatryce," an epithet almost exclusively reserved for the Blessed Virgin, is the least ambiguous signal of its devotional theme. That the scribe who copied the poem regarded it as religious is suggested by his identifying the source ("yt ys I-wrytt") of the epithet "feyrest paramour," as the "Pulcherrima mulierum" of *Canticles*.[36] Along with the Church, the Blessed Virgin was the most common allegorical referent for the bride in medieval interpretations of *Canticles*.

---

[36] See Brown's note to line 25.

Brown prints another epistolary poem, from MS Royal 6B.ix, among the "Songs and Prayers to the Blessed Virgin."[37] A single "Monk's Tale" octave of greeting, the poem may originally have been the first stanza of a longer verse love epistle, but the signature at the end ("Quod H. Bowesper") indicates that the scribe thought it complete. Unlike the previous example, there is nothing in this brief poem to indicate anything but a conventional secular theme:

> Ryht godely, fressh flour of womanhode,
> My lyues Ioy, myn hertes plesance,
> Example of trouth and rote of godelyhode,
> And verayly my lyues sustenance –
> And, with al þe hool, feythful obeisance
> That seruant can thenk or deuyse,
> To you þat haue myn herte in gouernance,
> Me recomande in all my best wyse.[38]

Although the poem occurs in a manuscript of religious works, it is scrawled on the flyleaf in a hand later than that of the other contents.

While no other clear examples of verse love epistles to the Blessed Virgin survive, a few secular epistles in which elements of Marian poems are incorporated suggest that the border may have been crossed more often than the single surviving contrafacture might otherwise indicate.[39] One of the verse love letters in Trinity College Cambridge MS R.3.19 (*Index* 1838) begins by addressing the Virgin and then shifts to addressing an earthly lady. The lover does no more than invoke Mary's aid in the difficult task of appealing to his lady love:

> Lady of pite, for þy sorowes þat þou haddest
> ffor Iesu þy son, in tyme of hys passion,
> haue revthe of me that ys most maddest
> In love to wryte and shew myn entencion
> To her that hath my lyfe in correccion.
> Both lyfe and dethe, all ys at her wyll.
> Now helpe me, lady, and let me nat spyll.[40]

---

[37] *Lyrics of Fifteenth Century*, p. 72. In the *Index* (2824) Brown labels it "To the B.V."

[38] I have corrected Brown's misreadings "gvuernance" (7) and "recemande" (8) from the manuscript.

[39] The *Index* (3498) also calls a verse love epistle from the Bannatyne MS (#252; ed. W. T. Ritchie, III, pp. 263–64) "A secular treatment of a Hymn to the Heavenly Mistress," but without indicating whether a specific hymn is being imitated or whether the description is merely conjectural.

[40] Ed. R. H. Robbins, "Love Epistle by 'Chaucer,'" p. 290.

The very next poem in the manuscript, also a love letter (*Index* 2510), begins in a similar fashion, with an appeal to the "King of kinges, and father of pitee" comprising four stanzas (out of thirteen) taken from Lydgate's *Court of Sapience*.[41] The borrowed stanzas form a preamble on the subject of mercy to what is a rather clumsily organized epistle. A third verse love epistle preserved only in Thynne's 1532 edition of Chaucer (*Index* 2223), opens by addressing the lady in terms that may have been borrowed from a poem to Mary:

> Moder of norture, best beloved of al,
> And fresshest flour, to whom good thrift god sende.
> Your child, if it list you me so to cal,
> Al be I unable my-self so to pretende,
> To your discrecioun I recommende
> Myn herte and al,[42]

But this poem is no more addressed to the Blessed Virgin than is another verse love epistle that owes its preservation to Thynne (*Index* 1309), who mistakenly printed it as the ending of Lydgate's "Balade in Commendation of Our Lady."[43] The couplet ending stanza 12 –

> "*Salve, regina!*" singing laste of al,
> To be our helpe, whan we to thee cal!   (lines 83–84)

– (and perhaps the stanza following it) apparently misled Thynne into ignoring the predominantly secular quality of the poem as a whole.

5.4. Formal Experimentation and Innovation

An increased self-consciousness about the genre, its functions, and the formal rules governing it had other results besides the parodies and adaptations just discussed. As time went on, and particularly as the genre reached the height of its fashion in the sixteenth century, there was an

---

[41] Stanza 9 is also borrowed, from *The Craft of Lovers* (stanza 19), which occurs earlier in the manuscript. The only printed editions are in Stow's *Chaucer* (1561) and Alexander Chalmers, ed., *English Poets*, vol. 1, pp. 562–63. Chalmers's edition is based on the text in Stow, which omits the stanza from *The Craft of Lovers*. For a modern edition of *The Craft of Lovers*, see Erik Kooper, "Slack Water Poetry," pp. 473–89.

[42] Ed. W. W. Skeat, *Chaucer*, vol. 7, p. 405.

[43] Ed. W. W. Skeat, ibid., pp. 281–84. On the manuscript evidence proving that the Marian poem (*Index* 99) is separate from the love letter, see Skeat, ibid., pp. xlvi-xlvii.

increased tendency toward experimentation and departure from the classic form. Two results of this experimentation – the progressive reduction of restrictive epistolary formulas, and the elaborating of a part of the letter to the point where it broke off to form a separate subgenre – probably contributed directly to the genre's rapid demise in the middle of the century.

5.4.1. Verse Form and Length

In what can be termed its "external form" – stanza, meter, and total number of lines – the verse love epistle was always "open," particularly by comparison with the fixed forms (with one of which, the ballade, it could and did overlap). Poems as long as 273 lines and as short as four lines have equally good claims for inclusion in the corpus. This lack of stability, together with a fairly restricted set of distinctive themes, always made the genre susceptible to loss of identity. Indeed, the set form of the sonnet must have been partly responsible for its success in taking over the functions previously performed by the love epistle during the latter half of the sixteenth century. Yet it is possible to trace a "classic form" of the verse epistle – three to six rime royal or "Monk's Tale" stanzas (21–48 lines) – all the way from the circle of Charles of Orléans to the Bannatyne MS. The fact that four of the first five verse love epistles take this form is all the more significant in that their direct model, Chaucer's "Litera Troili," is so much longer (fifteen rime royal stanzas). This discrepancy may help to explain why the "classic" stanza forms, especially rime royal, are more often retained in the later development of the genre than is the "classic" length, and why epistles longer than forty-eight lines are more common than epistles shorter than twenty-one lines. The strength of the norm is evident in the twenty-three verse love epistles preserved in ten manuscripts from the second half of the fifteenth century.[44] Eighteen of these poems are written in one of the approved stanzas, and eleven of those fall within the "classic" length.[45] Even the five exceptions to the approved stanza point up the strength of the convention. The three verse

---

[44] Lambeth 306, Douce 95, Harley 3810, Cotton Vespasian D.9, Porkington 10, Rawlinson poet. 36, Trinity College Cambridge R.3.19, Harley 7578, Douce 326, Royal 6B.ix. I have included neither the two poems from the Findern Anthology (due to their uncertain date) nor the poem from Harley 541 (which is probably in rhymed prose).

[45] The exceptions range from eight lines (one "Monk's Tale" stanza) to 222 lines (thirty-two rime royal stanzas, with two lines missing), though half of them are between fifty-two and sixty lines long.

love epistles in Douce 95 are truly anomalous: one is the only macaronic example from the period (*Index* 724: nine quatrains; 36 lines), another is longer than all but one other example from the period (*Index* 752: thirty-four quatrains; 136 lines), while the third employs a stanza never again seen in the genre's history (*Index* 754: six ten-line stanzas [abababcccb, stanza 1 lacks a line]; 59 lines). Only one verse epistle from Trinity College Cambridge R.3.19 does not employ an approved stanza (*Index* 2311: thirteen quatrains; 52 lines); but this manuscript also supplies five of the seven poems that exceed the "classic" length, including what is by far the longest example from this period (*Supplement* 2478.5). The love epistle in Porkington 10 (*Index* 1241), on the other hand, probably conforms to an older norm: in length and verse form (twelve octosyllabic couplets) it resembles nothing so much as the late fourteenth-century Anglo-Norman *salut d'amour* from MS Harley 3988 (eleven octosyllabic couplets).[46]

At first sight, the restrictions in both length and stanza seem to have loosened a great deal during the period from ca. 1500 to 1537. Of the forty-nine examples preserved in sources dated to this time span,[47] twenty-one to twenty-three, that is, if one counts two ambiguous cases,[48] slightly less than half are in one of the two approved stanzas. Taking the higher number, eight of those twenty-three have the "classic" length of twenty-one to forty-eight lines. In reality, the loosening of the stanza requirement is probably less significant than it appears to be. By far the most popular "new" stanza is the quatrain, which may well have been viewed as a simple (and increasingly preferred) variation on the "Monk's Tale" octave, accomplished by the dropping of a single requirement (ababbcbc becomes abab / cdcd). One can observe this perceptual shift actually occurring in several of the poems in question. In one of Humfrey Newton's poems, which he sets in octaves, the "Monk's Tale" pattern is observed in the first and third stanzas, while the second is rhymed as two quatrains (*Index* 768). The same occurs in a poem from Rawlinson C.813, but with the proportions reversed: the first five stanzas are set as octaves, even though only the first is held together by the continuing b-rhyme (*Index* 1329). Moreover, the final eight lines, which are not set as an

---

[46] See chapter 2.8.

[47] Bodleian Lat. misc. c.66, Rawlinson C.813, BL Add. 17492, Arch. Selden B.24, Hunterian 230, Harley 4011, Pynson (1526), Thynne (1532).

[48] *Index* 1329 is discussed below. *Index* 2421 employs an artful twelve-line stanza, the basis for which is a rime royal stanza (with alliteration), to which a five-line "bob-and-wheel" has been attached.

octave, are couplet-rhymed. A second poem in the same manuscript shows that the converse could also happen: even though all but the last twelve of its sixty-eight lines fit the "Monk's Tale" pattern, which is further underscored by the refrain at the end of each octave, the scribe has set the entire poem as quatrains (*Supplement* 2560.5).[49] If the verse love epistles in quatrains are treated as variations of the octave, then the adherence to approved stanza forms is very high indeed – forty-five of forty-nine, of which seventeen are in rime royal, twenty-two in quatrains, and six in "Monk's Tale" octaves.[50]

Even with the poems in quatrains included, the proportion of verse love epistles that exhibit "classic" length as well as stanza (eighteen of forty-nine) is still somewhat lower than among those from the previous century. Longer poems, in particular, claim a much larger share of the corpus. Of the twenty-five love epistles in Rawlinson C.813, only nine fall within what had been the normal range, while thirteen are longer than forty-eight lines. The only collection that seems to favor the "classic" dimensions is the series of seven from the Devonshire MS (BL Add. 17492). In fact, if the lower limit is dropped to twenty lines, all but one sixteen-line poem fit within the lower end of the scale, the longest poems extending only to twenty-eight lines.[51] Humfrey Newton's is the only collection that exhibits some interest in the shorter "billet doux": four of eleven letters are four to eight lines long, and only one is longer than

---

[49] The final three "quatrains" probably form a looser octave, without refrain and with assonance rather than rhyme providing the link, and a pair of couplets. On this poem see especially K. H. Power, "Edition of Lyrics," pp. 128–30. One of Humfrey Newton's love letters has a similar structure, only inverted (*Index* 2281). The first three "quatrains," containing the formulas of greeting, are linked together by rhyme (abab / acac / caca), the second and third forming a "Monk's Tale" octave. The first line of stanza 4 is then taken up as a refrain that ends every second stanza for the remainder of the poem, creating a series of five octaves, a few of which are further linked through the "Monk's Tale" rhyme scheme.

[50] The relative absence of couplets, the normal form for the *salut d'amour*, is notable. Aside from two poems by Humfrey Newton (*Index* 926: eleven couplets; *Index* 1344: one quatrain, then eleven couplets), the only example is "The Letter of Dydo to Eneas" printed by Pynson (*Supplement* 811.5: 121 couplets; plus an envoy of two rime royal stanzas and "the prologue of the translatour" of nine rime royal stanzas), where the choice of the heroic couplets doubtless was determined by the use of decasyllabic couplets in the immediate source, Octovien de Saint-Gelais' French translation of *Heroides, vii.*

[51] The shorter poem (ed. K. Muir, "Unpublished Poems," p. 264, #11) is also the only one in the group that lacks any epistolary features: the speaker refers to his lady in the third person throughout and employs no formal greeting or farewell. It is only the poem's position within a series of epistles that earns it a (rather insecure) place in the corpus.

148

forty-eight lines (*Index* 2281: 68 lines). Only one other verse love epistle shorter than twelve lines survives from this period, and that is a stanza from Hawes's *Pastime of Pleasure*, copied as a separate poem (*Index* 2318).

Despite the shift toward the quatrain as the preferred stanza and the increased preference for longer poems, some sense of the "classic form" seems to have endured, at least in the north. Though older by some thirty years than the latest of the sources just surveyed, the Bannatyne MS (Advocates 1.1.6) is remarkably conservative. Of the sixteen love poems that can with some assurance be called epistles, fourteen are set in rime royal or "Monk's Tale" stanzas, and none in quatrains.[52] Especially striking is the fact that seven of those fourteen employ the octave, which had been losing popularity in favor of the quatrain since ca. 1500. The conservatism is just as evident as regards length: twelve of the fourteen poems in approved stanzas are also between twenty-one and forty-eight lines long.[53] More than a century after the genre's "invention," such remarkable orthodoxy is difficult to explain. It is not, for example, a simple matter of conservatism regarding verse forms within the collection as a whole. The quatrain and other, less common forms are well represented among the "Ballattis of Luve." Nor can they all be regarded as earlier compositions that happened to be preserved in a late manuscript, since Bannatyne ascribes several of them to his contemporaries Steill and Scott and even incorporates his own anagram at the end of another.

5.4.2. Number, Position, and Proportion of Parts

The Bannatyne letters are also conservative in the degree to which most of them continue to begin with formal greetings and end with formal leave-takings, the clearest signs of epistolary form. However, since the presence of such elements is in the case of the Bannatyne collection the chief means of determining which poems belong to the genre, one risks arguing in circles by pressing the point. There are certainly some and perhaps quite a few poems in the manuscript that lack such distinguishing features but were nonetheless composed or regarded as love epistles.[54] Still, the fact that such conventions are still being observed in 1568 is notable, given their absence from many earlier verse love epistles. None

---

[52] The two anomalies employ stanzas of nine lines (aabaabbab) and five lines (aabab).

[53] The exceptions are both longer – seventy-four and eighty lines.

[54] See the entry for Advocates 1.1.6. in Appendix I.A.24. for some examples.

of the seven letters in the Devonshire MS employs a formal greeting, for example, though all but two employ the farewell. And Humfrey Newton dispenses with both greeting and farewell in more than half of the love poems that he marks as letters, especially in those that form acronyms of the names of family members and friends.[55] Besides the tendency to drop (or attenuate) the greeting or leave-taking or both, producing a poem that may be but cannot be proved to be an epistle, two different developments affecting the distinctive "internal form" of the epistle characterize the later history of the genre: *(1)* the greeting is moved away from its normal position at the letter's beginning, or *(2)* one of the formal dominants, greeting or farewell, becomes detached (and often elaborated) to make up the entire message.

"Letters" that end rather than begin with the formal greeting are already familiar from the prehistory of the genre. The envoy of the ballade, in particular, encouraged this deviation from traditional epistolary form. Love letters on this pattern are still found a century after Gower wrote his *Cinkante Balades*,[56] but more common is the use of both formal greeting at the beginning and an envoy repeating the greeting, often by addressing the letter itself ("Go, little bill") and instructing it to greet the

---

[55] I.e., *Index* 735, 2217, 737, and 481 (*Index* 556 and 2263 also lack greeting and farewell). John Skelton uses the first letter of each stanza to spell out the name "Kateryn," in a praise poem that may be an epistle but, like the acronyms of Newton, lacks any characteristic epistolary features: *Supplement* 1829.8; ed. V. J. Scattergood, *John Skelton*, pp. 43–45. A few of Skelton's verse compliments from the *Garlande or Chapelet of Laurell* (1523) have traces of the formulas found in the verse love epistles. See especially the opening stanzas of "To the ryght noble Countes of Surrey" and "To mastres Margaret Tylney." The whole set of compliments that Skelton addressed to his patroness and her ladies-in-waiting occupies pp. 335–43 of Scattergood's edition (the poems in question are on pp. 335–36 and 338–39). The verse compliment, a form with obvious affinities to the love letter, achieved considerable popularity in the sixteenth century. As Fish points out, Skelton undercuts the conventions that he pretends to follow: *Skelton's Poetry*, pp. 228–30. For more straightforward examples, compare those by Nicholas Grimald in *Tottel's Miscellany*: ed. Hyder E. Rollins, vol. 1, #139, 140, 142–47, and one by Fulke Greville printed by E. K. Chambers, in *Sixteenth-Century Verse*, p. 201 (#122). The letters presented to the Queen in John Lyly's *Entertainments* (1592) are mainly of this type: ed. R. W. Bond, *Complete Works*, vol. 1, pp. 467–70 and 486–89. An exception is the satirical letter sent from a soldier to "Lady Squemish" (pp. 487–88), which was apparently inserted for comic relief.

[56] For example, *Index* 231, four "Monk's Tale" octaves labeled "Balade" in the manuscript (Harley 7578; late fifteenth century). Cf. also *Index* 3291 (from Lambeth 306; 1460s), where the lover calls himself "newe troiles" in the seventh (and final) rime royal stanza; *Index* 1180 (from Rawlinson C.813; 1527–1535); and "O cupid king" (from Advocates 1.1.6; 1568), ed. W. T. Ritchie, III, pp. 282–83.

lady.[57] A similar technique is to replace the usual formulas of farewell by repeating the "I me (re)commend" formula at the letter's end.[58] Two poems from the Bannatyne MS, both in "Monk's Tale" octaves, further refine the technique by making the "I me commend" formula part of the refrain that ends each of their three stanzas.[59] Other letters open with several stanzas of praise, complaint, or protestation of devotion, before getting around to the formal greeting, a technique that can, at its best, heighten the poem's emotional intensity without seriously compromising its epistolary character.[60] Beginning in the last quarter of the fifteenth century, one encounters love epistles that defer the greeting by opening with a stanza or two of reflection on the theme of the message that follows,[61] or, more frequently, of invocation addressed to the god of love, the Blessed Virgin, or some other intercessor.[62] In one extreme example, the "prologue" extends to 105 lines, beginning with a 35-line retelling of the Judgment of Paris. After so elaborate an introduction, it is no wonder

---

[57] An especially good example is *Index* 2223, originally a triple ballade (from which the third stanza of the second ballade has been lost) composed of nine rime royal stanzas with a "Monk's Tale" octave as envoy (from Thynne's 1532 *Chaucer*). The envoy formula "Go, little bill" can also be incorporated into a conventional greeting at the letter's beginning, as it is in *Index* 927 (from Douce 326; late fifteenth century).

[58] An example is *Index* 751/*Supplement* 2308.8 (from Cotton Vespasian D.9; second half, fifteenth century), which may combine parts of two or more verse love epistles, but which the scribe clearly meant to represent a single letter. The formulas of greeting occur in the first two stanzas and again in the penultimate stanza. The repetition of the opening formulas, though without the omission of the closing ones, is already found in the "Litera Troili."

[59] *Index* 2517 (in which the refrain is also the first line of the first stanza), and "Lanterne of lufe" (ed. W. T. Ritchie, III, pp. 312–13). Cf. also *Index* 926 (in couplets), where the opening formula "command me hertely / Vnto her" (lines 1–2) is repeated in the last line (22).

[60] See *Index* 1510, where the formal greeting and the formal farewell share the third and final stanza (from Rawlinson poet. 36; second half, fifteenth century), and *Supplement* 2384.8, where a very full set of greeting formulas occurs in stanzas 5 and 6 of an eight-stanza poem (from Trinity College Cambridge R.3.19; 1478–1483).

[61] E.g., the fickleness of women, in a letter from a disillusioned lover to his lady (from Advocates 1.1.6; 1568), ed. W. T. Ritchie, IV, pp. 19–22; or unrequited love, in *Index* 1329 (from Rawlinson C.813; 1527–1535). See also *Supplement* 2245.1, also from Rawlinson C.813.

[62] See *Index* 1838 (Blessed Virgin) and 2510 (God, the "father of pitee") (both from Trinity College Cambridge R.3.19; 1478–1483); "O cupid king" (from Advocates 1.1.6; 1568), ed. W. T. Ritchie, III, pp. 282–83. Similar invocations are sometimes embedded within the text: see, for example, the apostrophes to "Seint Valentyne" and to "Cupide" in the second and third stanzas of *Index* 231 (from Harley 7578; late fifteenth century).

151

that the letter itself goes on for another 168 lines.[63] The case is rather different with the fifteenth-century *Parliament of Love (Index* 2383; from CUL Ff.1.6), in which a love epistle of three rime royal stanzas is "framed" by the eighty-seven lines of narrative, mostly in octosyllabic couplets,[64] that precede it. The technique recalls Chaucer's framing of "Complaints" in *Anelida and Arcite, The Complaint unto Pity,* and *The Complaint of Mars.*[65]

Common to all the poems just discussed is the shifting of the formal dominant – the polite, often formulaic greeting – from its normal, expected position at the head of the letter. This disappointing of expectation can often increase the prominence of the greeting, as when a poem in which the absent lover is evoked in the third person is abruptly transformed into direct discourse – a letter – in the final stanza.[66] More obvious testimony to the greeting's dominant role within the genre's morphology is the existence of verse epistles that consist of nothing else. In most cases, such letters are shorter than normal. Some, consisting of a single stanza, may well have been extracted from a longer epistle, the rest of which has been lost.[67] A somewhat longer, extremely aureate piece, either in rather inept alliterative verse or, more likely, in rhymed prose, provides a good example of a love letter that is all greeting:[68]

> O desiderabull dyamunt distinit with diuersificacion,
> Ditate with deité and yndesynent dileccion,

---

[63] *Supplement* 3917.8 (from Rawlinson C.813; 1527–1535). It is worth noting that two more love letters in the same manuscript, like this one in rime royal stanzas (but without prologues), are also exactly 168 lines long (*Index* 2496, 2532).

[64] Lines 25–31 form a rime royal stanza.

[65] Lydgate's *The Temple of Glass (Index* 851), lines 970–1039, provides another good example, which, were it not explicitly said to have been spoken in the lady's presence (1041), might pass for a verse love epistle. The same is true of the "bill" from *The Court of Love* (lines 841–89; see above, n. 15).

[66] Rawlinson C.813 has some especially good specimens of this type: see *Supplement* 733.1, *Index* 1768.

[67] For example, *Index* 2824 (from Royal 6B.ix; late fifteenth century?). The one-stanza salutation from Hunterian 230 (*Index* 2318), is in fact extracted from a larger work, Hawes's *Pastime of Pleasure* (lines 2542–48). The first four lines of a fragmentary song in MS Douce 381 (first half, fifteenth century) may also have come from a love epistle (*Index* 4199).

[68] *Supplement* 2412.5, from MS Harley 541, fol. 208r (end of the fifteenth century). Apparently this letter has never been printed. For other love letters that contain little besides greeting, see *Index* 1510, *Supplement* 2497.5, and "Lanterne of lufe" (ed. W. T. Ritchie, III, pp. 312–13). None of these is so pure an example as the text from Harley 541.

The whych splendiferus clarité is deserens defeccion,
Youre lucyble uertue hesite, replete with discrecion,
Youre mellifluus suauyté and aureall decoracion,
The famous facundité diserte yn all dyffynycion,
Youre potent probyté ympassyble of deieccion
And micant strenuyté without any decepcion,
Youre radicaunt vertues withoute tenebrosyté
          Me to love and magnyfye behovith, sapient with
                    speciosité.
To youre yndyssoluble, cordyall connexion
I me Recomende with most perfite dyleccion,
Which is so radycaunt yn myne amerous affeccion
That youre personall absens and corporall dissession
May neuer reserate youre dulcyfluus desideracion
Fro my meret intencion
                  of your absens
                  and joying of your presence.

After the greeting, the often equally formulaic leave-taking is the most distinctive formal element of an epistle. But one indication of the greeting's preeminence is the difficulty of deciding whether a poem that consists entirely of farewells constitutes a genuine letter. In part this is because the formulas of leave-taking are less fixed than those of greeting and often depend on there being a text to precede them. One can hardly begin by announcing "I write no more for lack of space." Only rarely can one be sure that the formulas in a farewell poem are epistolary formulas.[69] Moreover, there are non-epistolary precedents for the Middle English poems in which a lover bids his mistress farewell.

The most popular type of lover's farewell poem, consisting of an unspecified number of lines beginning "Farewell," followed by flattering epithets or some other form of praise, seems to be based on French models.[70] Although the anaphoric farewell poem probably existed independently at first, by the second half of the fifteenth century it was associated with the verse love epistle, if not annexed to it. That the form

---

[69] Four of the verse love epistles from Rawlinson C.813 employ a concluding formula emphasizing confidentiality:

> Froo whens ytt cummethe ytt hathe no name,
> but frome hym þat ys nameles;
> & whyder ytt shall, ytt sayethe the same,
> by-cause they shulde be blameles.

(*Supplement* 1349.5, lines 45–48. Cf. *Supplement* 2271.6, lines 29–32; *Index* 1329, lines 43–44; *Supplement* 2560.5, lines 65–68). The formula occurs in no other surviving examples of the genre.

[70] For examples by Deschamps, see G. Raynaud, ed., *Oeuvres complètes*, pt. 3 (1882), pp. 347, 348.

may have been regarded, at least by some people, as a variety of the love epistle is suggested by the fact that most of the surviving examples are found in manuscripts that also contain love epistles. In fact, the three richest collections of verse love epistles (Bodleian Lat. misc. c.66, Rawlinson C.813, Advocates 1.1.6) each contain at least one example of the anaphoric lover's farewell.[71] More important, in each of these manuscripts, as well as in the earlier MS Douce 95 (second half, fifteenth century), occurs a farewell poem that is clearly a love letter and that, in all but one case, employs precisely such a series of anaphoric farewells. The earliest example, *Index* 752, is also the most impressive. After two quatrains of greeting, followed by eighteen of praise and complaint, the lover announces that his already long epistle is at last approaching an end:

> But sith it stant in suche degre
> and may non-other-wyse trende,
> of ffarewell myn ende shall be
> To you-ward wher-euere ye wende: (lines 81–84)

The promised conclusion consists of no fewer than thirteen quatrains of anaphoric farewells. Less mechanical is the poem from Rawlinson C.813 (*Index* 4210), which incorporates a shorter and more varied anaphoric string (lines 50–61) into a fairly complex leave-taking (lines 43–77). In the remaining two examples (*Index* 768, *Supplement* 765.3), the convention is still further integrated: in each the explicit "farewells" occur only in the first stanza of a short letter whose theme is parting and whose final stanza contains additional formulas of leave-taking. Here we approach the equivalent of the letter that is all greeting, and as if in recognition of that fact, the poem from the Bannatyne MS (*Supplement* 765.3) is followed immediately by another poem of four stanzas, the first a lament on the sorrows of parting and the remaining three anaphoric farewells.[72] This, and the fairly numerous poems like it, may well have constituted an important subgenre of the verse love epistle.

At their worst, the experiments with the form of the love epistle produced clumsy hybrids or poems barely recognizable as belonging to the genre. Less often there occurs a happy innovation that suggests

---

[71] Robbins prints two relatively short specimens that are not preserved with epistles: *SL,* p. 207.

[72] Ed. W. T. Ritchie, III, pp. 284–85. Another version of this poem, without the opening lament but with a fourth stanza of anaphoric farewells, is found in Rawlinson C.813 (*Index* 767). The refrain from these poems occurs once (line 16) in a longer farewell poem in the same verse form (seven "Monk's Tale" octaves) from Humfrey Newton's commonplace book (*Index* 137).

productive new directions for the genre but that invariably remains an isolated inspiration without issue. A good example is a poem from Rawlinson C.813 (*Index* 2421) that draws on techniques more familiar in poetry of the fourteenth century to revitalize the conventional love epistle.[73] Its external form is basically the "classic" six rime royal stanzas, but elaborated by the addition of fairly systematic alliteration and above all a 5-line bob-and-wheel. The epistolary formulas are scrupulously observed but are less obtrusive in this artful and vigorous stanza. The effect can best be judged from the first and last stanzas, where the concentration of epistolary elements is, as usual, the highest:

> O excelent suffereigne, most semely to see,
> bothe prudent & pure lyke a perle of prise,
> also fair of fygure & oreant of bewtye,
> bothe cumlye & gentyll, & goodly to aduertyse,
> your brethe ys swetter then balme, suger, or lycoresse.
> I am bolde on yow, thoughe I be nott able
> to wrytte to your goodly person, whyche ys so ameable,
>> by reason
>> for ye be bothe fair & free,
>> therto wysse & womanly,
>> trew as turtyll on a tree,
>> with-owt any treason.
>>   * * *
>
> Thys, at thys tyme, thys byll shalbe concludyd,
> the more breuely for to make an ende.
> I trust verely I shall nott be illusyde
> of yow to whome thys symple letter I sende.
> With loue to contynue thys I entende,
> & soo I trust þat ye wyll the same.
> Cryste kepe vs bothe from bodely hurte & shame
>> all-wey.
>> A-dew! fare-well! my swete;
>> tyll efte that we mete
>> my harte ye haue to kepe,
>> by God that made thys day.   (lines 1–12, 61–72)

5.5. Themes

The period of the genre's maturity brought few thematic innovations to set alongside the formal experiments just discussed. The key themes of

---

[73] George Kane, who dates the poem in "the high fifteenth century," compares its stanza to the highly elaborate one of *Somer Sunday* (*Index* 3838) and describes its style as a mixture of "aureate terms and Harley lyric images": "Short Essay," p. 116 n. 2.

love epistles continued to be those of love poetry in general – praise and complaint. As a group, the epistles are especially likely to include complaint about the suffering caused by separation from the beloved, but that theme is by no means their exclusive property.[74] The most distinctive theme continues to be the act of writing itself, and the explicit recognition of the letter as a physical object that will traverse the distance separating the lovers, often accompanied by a gift or love token.[75] Perhaps the most significant thematic innovations are the parodies and contrafactures discussed earlier. One might also add a handful of letters from "disillusioned" lovers, who presumably having complained for years about their unrewarded devotion, finally break forth with antifeminist spleen.[76]

Though not, strictly speaking, new, the love letter written from the woman's point of view clearly gained an unprecedented popularity during the late fifteenth and early sixteenth centuries. In most cases it is difficult to tell whether the letter was actually composed by a woman or was written by a man adopting a female persona, in the manner of Chaucer's "Litera Criseydis" and Gower's *Cinkante Balades,* #44. The latter is clearly true of the woman's letters in the macaronic pair from Cambridge University Library Gg.4.27 (*Index* 19) and the satirical pair from Rawlinson poet. 36 (*Index* 3832). Presumably, the same applies to the two love letters from women to men that Humfrey Newton wrote into his commonplace book.[77] On the other hand, there is no doubt that Margery Brews wrote the Saint Valentine's Day letter discussed earlier, and it is quite possible that the series of four thirteen-line love epistles addressed to an absent (male) lover are the original compositions of the lady who added them to the "Findern Anthology" (*Index* 3878).[78] The remaining examples are anonymous and in some cases barely distinguishable in the sentiments that they express from those by men. Indeed,

---

[74] It is interesting that a motif associated with this theme, namely, the dream of erotic fulfillment from which the lover awakens to renewed frustration, is well represented in love epistles. P. J. Frankis knew of nine Middle English and Scots lyrics in which the motif occurs, of which at least four are love epistles (*Index* 366, 2517, 2532, 3291), and another three come from manuscripts that contain a large number of verse epistles (Rawlinson C.813, Advocates 1.1.6): "Erotic Dream," pp. 228–37.

[75] E.g., *Index* 768, 1789.

[76] See *Supplement* 3785.5 (Rawlinson C.813), and "In all this warld no man may wit" (Advocates 1.1.6; ed. Ritchie, IV, pp. 19–22).

[77] *Index* 481, 768. *Supplement* 2267.5, addressed to a man but written entirely in the hand of John Paston III, is probably a letter of friendship rather than a love letter.

[78] If the series of seven verse epistles from the Devonshire MS are in fact the prison correspondence of Lord Thomas Howard and Lady Margaret Douglas, then the sixth poem in the series (Muir, #12) is also a woman's composition.

the editor of one of them (*Index* 754) changed the sex of the writer merely by emending "as she" to "ass he" (line 11) and "manhede" to "maiden-hede" (line 32).[79]

Whoever compiled the anthology of lyrics in Rawlinson C.813 was a connoisseur not only of the verse love epistle but also of this particular variety. Four of the twenty-five love epistles in the collection are by women, all of them grouped within the final third of the anthology (#36, 37, 41*, 51). The first two differ little in their contents from the other verse epistles, though the rhyme scheme of one is exceptionally inept.[80] The woman who writes the third letter (*Supplement* 733.1) is apparently married, a familiar predicament but one that serves to distinguish hers from the usual epistolary complaint:

> for to on I have my troweth i-plyght
> & a-noder hathe my harte yn holde.
>
> (lines 3–4 = #41, lines 39–40)

The very last poem in the collection (*Index* 2821), however, is perceptibly different from the usual fare, not only because of its theme and the restraint of its language but also because of its superior quality as a poem. The woman might be writing in response to virtually any of the epistolary complaints that fill the manuscript's pages, for she cites all the commonplaces of unrequited love as she takes up in turn each point of her suitor's letter of complaint.[81] However, her attitude is more reasonable, realistic, and, apparently, sincere. She is careful to temper her gentle mockery of his hyperbolic protestations (lines 15–42) with touching assurances of her continued good faith despite adversity, which recall the letter of Margery Brews. Since the poem is too long to quote in full, and since parts of it are borrowed from Hawes, a few stanzas from the beginning and end will have to suffice by way of illustrating its merits:

> Right best beloved & most in assurance
> of my trewe harte, I me recommende
> hartely vnto yow with-owten vareance;
> & haue receyved þe whiche ye to me did send,
> wherby I perceyve your louing harte & minde;
> desiring yow in the same soo to continewe,
> & then for your grett paynes comfforte may insuye.

---

[79] Ed. R. H. Robbins, *SL*, pp. 202–4.

[80] *Supplement* 1017.5: rhymed ababxacxxxdcxdd. The poem that follows, *Index* 2547, calls itself a "letter of translatyon / owt of Frenche" near the end (lines 19–20); but the final two stanzas (lines 15–22) are lifted from the final stanza of Lydgate's *The Churl and the Bird*. See W. Bolle, "Zur Lyrik," p. 289.

[81] For other "reasoned replies" from women, see E. Ruhe, *De Amasio*, pp. 235–37.

Thanking me for my kindnes in times paste,
your desire is I shuld kepe in mynde
the purpose I was in when ye spake with me laste.
Truly, vnconstant you shall me neuer fynde,
but euer to be trewe, feithfull & kinde,
& to yow beire my trew harte withouten vareance,
desiring you to make me noo dyssemblance.

Also, wher you saye þat my bewtye soo sore
shuld you inflame with persing violence,
þat with extreme love of me you shuld be caught in snare,
I mervell therof gretly without douttance
that itt shuld haue suche might or puisance,
for I knowe right well I was neuer soo bewtiouse
that I shuld you constren to be soo amorous.

* * *

Butt I wylbe trewe though I shuld continewe
all my hole lyffe in payne & heuynesse;
I wyll neuer change you for any other newe.
Yow be my joye, my comfforte & gladnes,
whome I shall serve with all dilligence.
Exyle me neuer from your harte soo dere,
whiche vnto my harte haue sett you most nere.

(lines 1–21, 50–56)

Perhaps evidence that at least some of the letters that take the woman's
point of view were actually written by female participants in the "game of
love" is the nearly complete neglect in England of the more artificial
"women's letters," the translations and imitations of Ovid's *Heroides* that
became fashionable in France during the last few decades of the fifteenth
century and that produced a new genre of heroical epistle, the *épître
amoureuse*, which was equally popular during the first few decades of the
sixteenth century.[82] The key work in the *Heroides* revival, Octovien de
Saint-Gelais' first complete verse translation *Les XXI Epistres d'Ovides*
(ca. 1492; twenty printed editions before the mid sixteenth century), was
known to at least some Englishmen, but has left only a single trace in the
history of the Middle English verse love epistle. *The Letter of Dydo to
Eneas (Supplement* 811.5), included by Richard Pynson in the second
part of his Chaucer edition (1526), seems to make use of Octovien de
Saint-Gelais' translation. Indeed, "the prologue of the translatour" (nine
rime royal stanzas), which precedes the letter proper (121 heroic cou-

---

[82] The *épître amoureuse* gave rise in turn to the love elegy. See especially C. M.
Scollen, *Birth of Elegy*, and E. Ruhe, *De Amasio*, pp. 286–89.

158

plets, plus an envoy of two rime royal stanzas), explicitly states that the poem is translated from French. However, since the correspondence only extends through the first half of the English version, the translator may have worked from an intermediary French version of the letter rather than from Octovien's translation itself.[83] Other than this isolated example, the *Heroides* play no part in the history of the Middle English love epistle, unless one counts their possible influence on Chaucer's "Litera Troili" and "Litera Criseydis."[84] Both Chaucer and Gower translated excerpts from several of the *Heroides,* in *The Legend of Good Women* and the *Confessio Amantis,* respectively, but never with the purpose of constructing a complete love epistle. Like the verse love epistle itself, the *Heroides* revival came to England long after it had swept through France. The first full English translation, by George Turberville, appeared in 1567, and imitations, such as Michael Drayton's *Englands Heroicall Epistles* (1597–1599), only near the end of the sixteenth century.[85] Thus, while the *Heroides* revival marked a decisive break from the already long-decadent medieval verse love epistle in France,[86] in England the medieval tradition continued unbroken; indeed it flourished as never before, at least through the first third of the sixteenth century, and even longer in Scotland.[87]

5.6. The End of the Tradition

As in France a century before, the medieval verse love epistle had been on the wane in England for some time before new varieties of verse love epistle, chiefly heroical, arrived on the scene. Its demise is probably due

---

[83] Götz Schmitz, *Frauenklage*, pp. 27–32, and Julia Boffey, "Letter of Dido," pp. 339–53. Appendix II, below, is the first modern edition of the poem.

[84] A minor exception is a love epistle from Rawlinson C.813 (*Supplement* 3917.8), whose author is fond of displaying his knowledge of classical authors such as Ovid and Tibullus, especially in the long prologue preceding the letter. Twice within the letter itself he paraphrases the same well-known line from the *Heroides* (lines 160–61, 254–55; cf. *Her.,* iv, 10).

[85] For a list of the English imitators of the *Heroides* in the late sixteenth century, see H. Dörrie, *Der heroische Brief,* pp. 158–59. Schmitz, *Frauenklage,* treats many of the later "heroical epistles" by Drayton, Daniel, and others, as well as the earlier use of the *Heroides* in the works of Gower and Chaucer.

[86] See E. Ruhe, *De Amasio,* pp. 20–21, 287–88, 292–93.

[87] Claudio Guillén notices a markedly increased awareness of and interest in the letter as a literary form throughout Europe, beginning around the turn of the sixteenth century. His examples confirm that in most aspects of this general "epistolary revival," and not only in the *Heroides* revival, England's participation lagged a half-century or more behind the continent. "Renaissance Letter," pp. 70–101.

to a combination of factors, not the least of them the natural tendency for literary fashions to change. The existence of parodies indicates that the form was already becoming predictable in the second half of the fifteenth century, and the increased experimentation evident by around 1500 was surely an attempt to revitalize the genre, to free it from restrictions that had begun to feel oppressive. But that freedom came with a price. With few distinctive themes and no distinctive external form, the verse epistle was able to safeguard its identity chiefly by means of those set formulas and the simple internal structure of greeting-message-farewell with which the sixteenth-century innovators tampered or even dispensed altogether. Even the experiments with length caused trouble. Epistles shorter than the "classic" minimum (twenty-one lines) had room for nothing but the formalities, while every increase in the epistle's length beyond the "classic" maximum (forty-eight lines) made those same genre-determining formalities correspondingly less salient. The short verse epistles in the Devonshire MS (1536–1537) delete the formal dominant, the salutation, to make room for the message, while the long verse epistles in Rawlinson C.813 (1527–1535) lack the compression and formal cohesion of their fifteenth-century predecessors. It is in no small part due to the conservatism about verse form and length evident in the Bannatyne MS (1568), that the genre held its own longer in Scotland than in the south.

Even if the experiments of the early sixteenth century had not exacerbated the inherent weaknesses of the verse love epistle, other forces were threatening its position atop the hierarchy of the love lyric. Already in the first decades of the century, in court circles, the function that the love epistle performed in the "game of love" was increasingly being performed by shorter, more purely "lyrical" songs, often accompanied in the manuscripts by music. The competition was intensified by the growing influence of poetry imported from Italy and especially of verse forms such as the sonnet. Such poems could be sent just as if they were verse epistles, and they had the additional advantages of novelty, prestige, and a definite verse form. Had they been longer, they might have absorbed the form of the verse epistle along with its function, as the ballade did in fourteenth-century France. But a glance at the "songs and sonnets" gathered in a typical collection such as *Tottel's Miscellany* (1557) shows how completely the distinctively medieval verse love epistle had passed out of fashion by mid century. In none of these poems is there any trace of the epistolary formalities that were so common in the love lyrics written a generation earlier.

160

The poems of Sir Thomas Wyatt, both those included in *Tottel's Miscellany* and those preserved in manuscript, demonstrate that the shift is not due to a simple change in the conventional formulas of epistolography. When Wyatt wishes to write a verse epistle, as in the poem beginning "Greting to you bothe yn hertye wyse," he uses the same familiar phrases of salutation and conclusion as his fifteenth-century predecessors did.[88] If he does not use them in his love poems in direct address,[89] that fact suggests at the very least that he had little interest in whether his readers recognized those poems as epistles. A special case is the poem, possibly written in a female persona, which begins "Lyke as the Swanne towardis her dethe" (#LXX). Both the opening quatrain, which echoes the first lines of Dido's lament in *Heroides,* vii, and the paranomasic repetition of the word "note" firmly establish its epistolary character. Yet the formal characteristics of verse letters are here, as elsewhere, entirely lacking.

Eventually the changes in epistolography that had been carried through on the continent and that had affected the shape of literary as well as non-literary letters found their way to England. The second half of the sixteenth century brought the first letter-writing handbooks in English, William Fulwood's *The Enimie of Idlenesse* (1568), Abraham Fleming's *A Panoplie of Epistles* (1576), and Angel Day's *The English Secretorie* (1586), all of them drawing heavily on continental treatises in French or Latin.[90] Fulwood's is in fact largely a translation of a French work, *Le stile et manière de composer, dicter, et escrire toute sorte d'epistres, ou lettres missiues, tant par réponse que autrement, auec epitome de la poinctuation françoise* (Lyons, 1555?).[91] But the English treatise differs from its source in setting aside a final chapter devoted entirely to model love letters. Moreover, half of the twelve love letters are in verse, a treatment accorded no other type of model letter in the collection. Fulwood continued to be interested in the love letter, adding another verse example and three more prose examples to the third edition of the *Enimie*

---

[88] Ed. Kenneth Muir and Patricia Thomson, *Collected Poems*, pp. 225–26. All references to Wyatt's poems are to Muir and Thomson's edition and are given in the text.

[89] E.g., #XXXIV, LVII, LXXII, LXXIII, LXXVIII, LXXXV, CLI, CLII, CLIV, CLVIII, CLXXXVI, CCI, CCII, CCXV, and CCLI. Among the poems of Wyatt's younger contemporary and disciple Henry Howard, Earl of Surrey, there is only one piece that could with reason be called a love letter (*Tottel,* #262). Later in the century, however, George Gascoigne included several verse love letters in his *Posies* (1575): ed. John Cunliffe, *Complete Works,* vol. 1, pp. 131, 331, 462, etc.

[90] Concerning these works see Katherine Gee Hornbeak, *Complete Letter Writer,* pp. 1–29, and Jean Robertson, *Art of Letter Writing,* pp. 9–24.

[91] R. B. McKerrow so dates the first edition in his "Retrospective Review" of Fulwood's *Enimie of Idlenesse,* p. 391.

(1578). A French source for all but one of the nine prose letters can be identified, but the seven verse love epistles may well be Fulwood's own compositions.[92] Though hardly great poetry, Fulwood's love epistles clearly belong to a different age than those that have been the subject of this study, including the ones that George Bannatyne copied among his "Ballattis of Luve" in the very same year that the *Enimie of Idlenesse* was first published. But no description will show as clearly the distance traversed as a single example from Fulwood's hand:[93]

> A louer pearst with Cupides bowe,
> thinks long till he be rid from woe.
>
> When sturdy storms and whirling windes
> the waters wan do tosse,
> The seely Ship is troubled sore,
> in daunger of his losse.
> So in like wise when *Cupide* hath,
> wyth dynting Dart in hand,
> Pierst through the harts of louers true
> as all agast they stand,
> Before his godhed forced straight,
> downe for to fall and yeld:
> No strugling strength may him withstand
> no buckler nor no shield.
> This *Cupide* he this cruell god,
> with fyry flaming Dart,
> Hath wounded me in euery vayne,
> but chiefly at the heart.

---

[92] Five of the six prose letters in the first edition are translated from *Le stile et manière*. The three prose letters added to the third edition all come from the popular romance *Amadis of Gaul*, probably translated with the assistance of Thomas Paynell's *florilegium* of that romance, which was published in the same year and with the same printer as the first edition of Fulwood's *Enimie: The moste excellent and pleasaunt Booke, entituled: The treasurie of Amadis of Fraunce: Conteyning eloquente orations, pythie Epistles, learned Letters, and feruent Complayntes, seruing for sundrie purposes . . . Translated out of French into English* (London: by Henry Bynneman, for Thomas Hacket, 1568), pp. 258–60. Both Paynell and Fulwood worked from the French translation of the Spanish *Amadis* begun by Nicholas de Herberay in 1540. See also John J. O'Connor, *"Amadis de Gaule,"* p. 132.

[93] The second verse love epistle from the first edition (1568), pp. 138v–139v. In the title I have corrected an inverted *u* (louer) and an inverted *e* (he). Otherwise I alter the text of the 1568 edition only by silently expanding abbreviations. The remaining five verse love epistles, and five of the prose ones, from this edition are printed by Paul Wolter, in the Appendix to his *William Fulwood*, pp. 67–68. The two letters that he does not print (including the one quoted here) and the four added to the third edition are printed in M. Camargo, "Love Letter," pp. 273–77.

162

There doeth the sting abyde and stay,
there doeth the shaft remaine:
All remedie is past I know,
to ease me of this payne.
Except that thou to whome I write,
true comfort to me show:
For thou art onely she that may,
release me of this woe.
Thou onely arte (and none but thou)
myne onely ioy, or griefe:
My happy state, or great decay,
send therefore some reliefe.
Destroy not him, whom well thou maist
without thy losse preserue:
Shew faithfull constancie to him,
that myndeth not to swerue.
He nought desyres but loue for loue,
and faith for faith againe:
That both together in great ioy
and comfort may remaine.
Detract no tyme, consider well,
when paine doth men oppresse,
Eche houre think they to be twayne,
till they haue found redresse.
And thus bicause my griefs encrease,
I say my deere adieu:
and pray thee to haue mynde on him,
that vnto thee is true.

FINIS

CHAPTER 6:
Conclusion

Compared with other Middle English lyric genres, the verse love epistle is in some respects typical and in others exceptional. Like most Middle English lyrics, the majority of the verse love epistles are brief, conventional in theme, and thoroughly anonymous. Given the vagaries of transmission and the imprecision of dating by handwriting alone, it is impossible even to establish with certainty the chronological order in which they were composed. They are also typical in being firmly bound up with specific occasions or social functions that can be recovered only imperfectly and with great difficulty. One is always left feeling that what can be directly observed in the surviving texts is somehow not what constitutes their essential identity.

Perhaps what is most exceptional about the verse love epistle is the solid empirical evidence of its existence as a genre and its popularity. The consistent use of the term "letter" and its synonyms discloses a continuity that might otherwise have been missed, since the outward form of the poems is far from uniform over the genre's long history. How many other Middle English lyric genres remain invisible because they never acquired a consistent label, or at least one that can now be recognized as such? Also unusual is the fact that the verse love epistle defined itself in relation to two distinct kinds of discourse: other contemporary varieties of the love lyric, and the medieval letter, a type of discourse that had a clear formal and functional identity. The general characteristics of medieval letters, particularly the formulas of greeting and farewell, make it possible to recognize as love epistles poems that lack identifying labels, while the frequent use of identifying labels helps reveal the degree to which verse love epistles were permitted to circumvent the rules governing normal letters. Even applied conservatively, these criteria yield a corpus of nearly a hundred verse love epistles preserved in sources dating from around 1400 to 1568, the period during which it is also proper to speak of the love letter as a distinct lyric genre.

Although the love letter was a recognized form in twelfth-century Provençal poetry (*salutz*) and in thirteenth-century French poetry (*salut d'amour*), there is little evidence of a tradition in England before the last quarter of the fourteenth century. The few earlier examples that survive are widely scattered in time and language (Latin, Anglo-Norman, English) and in several cases form part of a larger narrative. Signs of a growing awareness of the letter's potential for independent lyric development are clearer in the last few decades of the fourteenth century, though chiefly among Anglo-Norman writers. After "balade," "lettre" is the term that John Gower most frequently employs to describe the poems in his *Cinkante Balades*. Though Gower seems to consider his poems as letters more in a functional than in a formal sense, a few contemporary poems also make a point of employing epistolary form in a way that recalls the Old French *salut d'amour*.

The key text in English from this period, Geoffrey Chaucer's *Troilus and Criseyde*, contains both the fullest account of the love letter's function and the most authoritative model for its form. Chaucer actually reduced from three to two the number of love letters found in his source, Boccaccio's *Il Filostrato*, by paraphrasing rather than quoting in full the first letters exchanged by Troilus and Criseyde. However, in greatly expanding and complicating the courtship narrative Chaucer elaborated the letter's clear and important function in the ritual of courtly love. As a physical object that not only speaks for the lover but also metonymically stands for him (it contains his own words, written by his own hand, and even stained with his own tears), the letter takes its place within a controlled sequence of ever closer approaches to the lady. It comes after the go-between has reported the lover's words and after the lady has exchanged looks with the lover but before a direct exchange of words or physical contact has occurred. Despite much in it that concerns the specific details of Troilus' relationship with Criseyde, the "Litera Troili" provided an equally influential model for the form and themes that characterized the verse love epistle. Given the prestige of *Troilus and Criseyde* during the century and a half following Chaucer's death, it is not surprising that it generated the new genre of the verse love epistle, even though neither in this work nor elsewhere did Chaucer cultivate the love letter as an autonomous form.

It apparently took a generation or more for the seed planted by Chaucer to germinate, since the emergence of the verse love epistle as an independent genre in English can be traced only as far back as the second quarter of the fifteenth century, in two collections of lyrics associated with Charles of Orléans and the English nobility of his acquaintance. The two verse love epistles from MS Harley 682 and the three from MS

166

Fairfax 16 are important not only because they are the earliest examples of the genre in its mature form, but also because the other contents of the manuscripts in which they are preserved make clear the position of the new genre within the contemporary system of love lyrics. In Harley 682, the love letters are formally distinguished from the fixed-form poems, many of which nonetheless function in a way similar to the letters. As flexible-form poems that draw attention to their own physicality and their missive function, the love letters resemble the love documents, from which they are in turn distinguished by their personal style, befitting the direct address to the lady as opposed to the quasi-official address to a personification or a mythological figure. The love letters in Fairfax 16 are juxtaposed most directly with poems called "complaints," from which they differ to some degree in their emphasis on their status as physical objects and on the theme of separation but more radically in their studied use of the language and structure characteristic of medieval letters in general. Each of them incorporates the highly conventional varieties of greeting and leave-taking found already in the "Litera Troili."

The subsequent history of the genre during the century of its flowering and decline is characterized by increasing instability. While the use of genre terms, together with such practices as intertextuality, parody, and contrafacture, indicate a continuous tradition, the rules of the genre became less and less restrictive. The external form of the love epistle was never fixed, but during the fifteenth century there was a definite preference for either rime royal stanzas or "Monk's Tale" octaves (later replaced by quatrains) and for a length ranging between twenty-one and forty-eight lines. By around 1500, when the genre seems to have reached the height of its popularity, much longer love epistles are common, and much shorter ones occur occasionally as well. There are formal inconsistencies: many of the later examples omit the characteristic formulas of greeting or farewell; others shift the greeting from its customary position or, alternatively, expand either the greeting or the leave-taking until it comprises the entire poem.

Since its form was so unstable and its themes amenable to treatment in other genres such as the complaint and the praise poem, the verse love epistle's generic integrity probably depended above all on its social function. At the most essential level, the letter existed as a material object that physically carried the lover's greeting, literally traversing the distance that separated lover from beloved. However, since virtually any love poem, once it was written down, had the potential to be used as a letter in this purely functional sense, the verse love letter's important role within the courtly "game of love" was not sufficient to guarantee its continued existence as an autonomous genre without the added support of distinctive language, structure, or themes. Although the genre's demise was therefore inevitable, it seems to have been precipitated by the new vogue for the sonnet and other verse forms imported from Italy. After 1540, the only unambiguous examples of the Middle English verse love epistle are those in the Bannatyne MS (1568). When verse love epistles are once again written by English poets, beginning just before 1600, they are modeled not on Chaucer's "Litera Troili" but on Ovid's *Heroides*, and they belong not to a medieval but to a Renaissance genre.

Although the primary goal of this study has been to trace the origins and development of the verse love epistle, it should be obvious from the foregoing summary that genre history always implies genre theory. The book offers itself not only as a chapter in the history of medieval love poetry but also as a practical exercise in defining a lyric genre in general and a medieval lyric genre in particular. A genre such as the verse love epistle exists on many different levels. The directly observable features of specific poems – language, theme, verse form – are organized on a deeper level by a more essential form, which is often realized only partially in the surface of the text; by a network of overlappings and contrasts with neighboring genres; and by the social function or functions appropriate to the genre, the use to which the poems will be put by their authors and intended audience. Nor are the intersections among these various levels always and everywhere the same. Thus, while generic categories are indispensable, they can never be neatly and exhaustively formulated: no matter how carefully it is done, the portrait of a genre will always, inevitably leave something out.

Zusammenfassung

"Liebesgedichte in Briefform" sind innerhalb der verschiedenen Gattungen der mittelenglischen Lyrik gekennzeichnet durch die häufige Verwendung des Begriffs "lettre" und seiner Synonyme, mit deren Hilfe bestimmte Liebesgedichte beschrieben werden. Sobald man aber versucht, die "Liebesgedichte in Briefform" zu definieren, um ihre Entstehung und Entwicklung aufzuzeigen, stellt sich heraus, daß es schwierig ist, Gemeinsamkeiten innerhalb der Gruppe, die von ihren Verfassern "lettres" genannt werden, zu erkennen sowie Unterschiede zu anderen Gruppen zeitgenössischer Liebeslyrik festzustellen. Die Gattung der "lettres" hat nie eine ihr eigene charakteristische Versform oder eigene Themen entwickelt. Die einzigen sichtbaren Merkmale, die als verlässlicher Indikator für eine Gattungszugehörigkeit dienen können, sind die Begrüßungs- und Abschiedsformeln, die mittelalterliche Briefe insgesamt charakterisieren; aber solche Merkmale fehlen oft völlig bei Gedichten, die trotzdem klar als Briefe gekennzeichnet sind. Um die Gattung in ihrem historischen Kontext zu rekonstruieren, ist es deshalb nötig, (1) die sich ständig verschiebenden Grenzen zwischen den "Liebesgedichten in Briefform" und den verschiedenen Formen der Liebeslyrik, die eng damit verwandt sind, darzustellen und (2) den Gebrauch dieser "Liebesgedichte in Briefform" durch Autoren und intendierte Leser so exakt wie möglich zu bestimmen. Der durch diese Gattung evozierte Erwartungshorizont steht in Verbindung mit ihrem "Sitz in der Literatur" und mit ihrem "Sitz im Leben".

Die historische Entwicklung der mittelenglischen "Liebesgedichte in Briefform" gliedert sich in drei Stufen: (1) eine frühe Phase, bis zum Ende des 14. Jahrhunderts, (2) eine Entwicklungsstufe, die die erste Hälfte des 15. Jahrhunderts umfaßt, und (3) eine Blütezeit, von der Mitte des 15. bis zur Mitte des 16. Jahrhunderts. Eine doch recht beachtliche Anzahl anglo-normannischer "Liebesgedichte in Briefform" stammt aus den letzten Jahrzehnten des 14. Jahrhunderts; besonders erwähnenswert sind die in Gowers *Cinkante Balades*. Der wichtigste Text aus der ersten Periode ist aber Chaucers *Troilus and Criseyde*, wo sich sowohl eine detaillierte Beschreibung der sozialen Funktion der Briefe innerhalb des höfischen "game of love" als auch ein Modell-Liebesbrief findet, der viele Möglichkeiten zur Nachahmung bot.

Die ersten voll entwickelten Beispiele autonomer "Liebesgedichte in Briefform" in Englisch sind in zwei wichtigen Sammlungen (MS Harley 682 und MS Fairfax 16) von Liebesgedichten erhalten, die mit Charles d'Orléans in Verbindung gebracht werden. Die Liebesbriefe überschneiden sich teilweise von der Form (Liebesurkunde), vom Thema (Klagelied) und von der Funktion (Ballade) her mit anderen Arten von Liebesgedichten in diesen gut gegliederten Sammlungen. Die ihnen gemeinsamen Gegensätze zu diesen benachbarten Lyrikformen sind demnach entscheidend für die Definition der neuen Gattung.

Die letzte Phase der Entwicklung der "Liebesgedichte in Briefform" ist gekennzeichnet durch eine stetig wachsende Popularität (mehr als 90 Zeugnisse sind aus dieser Periode erhalten) und durch eine wachsende Tendenz zum Experimentieren mit Formen, bis hin zum Verzicht auf alle erkennbaren Elemente der Briefform. In dem Maße, in dem die "Liebesgedichte in Briefform" immer stärker durch ihre Funktion bestimmt werden, hören sie auf, sich von anderen Liebesgedichten zu unterscheiden, die genauso gut hätten niedergeschrieben und verschickt werden können. Der Niedergang der Gattung wurde daher durch die Vorliebe für neue Formen lyrischer Dichtung um die Mitte des 16. Jahrhunderts zwar nicht verursacht, aber doch beschleunigt.

English Verse Love Epistles, ca. 1400–1568

The purpose of this appendix is to provide a concise overview of the entire corpus that can serve both as a reference on questions of transmission and as an index. In Part A, all manuscripts containing verse love epistles are listed, as much as possible in chronological order. For each manuscript information is supplied regarding date and provenance (where known), especially of the relevant contents, together with the most important bibliography, other than Julia Boffey, *Manuscripts of Lyrics*, the standard guide to all these manuscripts. The verse love epistles are listed in the order of their occurrence in the manuscript, by their number in the *Index of Middle English Verse* or the *Supplement* to that *Index* if they have one, by first line if they do not. Also included is the publication information for the edition cited in the main text (the *Index* and *Supplement* may be consulted for other editions). At the end of each manuscript entry, the context of transmission will also be discussed briefly, along with any new information about date, provenance, or authorship. Any poems that have been identified as love letters by previous scholars but are here rejected will be mentioned in this section, along with the reason for their exclusion from the corpus. Part B lists all genuine verse love epistles in alphabetical order by first line, providing *Index* or *Supplement* number where possible, the source manuscript or printed edition, and the verse form.

Part A

1. Cambridge University Library MS Gg.4.27
   Early fifteenth century; East Anglia

   M. B. Parkes and Richard Beadle, eds., "Commentary," *Facsimile of CUL MS Gg.4.27,* vol. 3 (1980).

   Index 16: fols. 10v–11r.
   Ed. E. K. Chambers and F. Sidgwick, *Early English Lyrics*, pp. 15–17.

   Index 19: fol. 11r-v.
   Ibid., pp. 18–19.

Macaronic pair, titled "De amico ad amicam" and "Responcio" in the manuscript. The final poems in a series of six lyrics, the first three by Chaucer, the fourth a macaronic parliament of fowls (*Index* 1506). Rossell H. Robbins, "Satiric Epistles," p. 420, dates the love letters in the late fourteenth century; R. T. Davies, *Medieval English Lyrics*, p. 159, dates them in the early fifteenth century.

London, BL, MS Harley 3362 (second half, fifteenth century) also contains the full text of *Index* 16 (fols. 90v–91r) and the first fifteen lines of *Index* 19 (fol. 91r). Most of the other contents of the manuscript are in Latin.

Index 147: fols. 509v–516v.
Ed. J. Schick, *Lydgate's Temple of Glas*, pp. 59–67.

Treated as a continuation of the *Temple of Glass* in MS Gg.4.27 and in BL, MS Additional 16165, fols. 231r–241v (a fragment also occurs in MS Sloane 1212, fol. 4r-v), this poem of 314 octosyllabic couplets is a boundary case. It is called a "compleynt" in the headings to both copies, as well as in the text itself (line 599), and it lacks both epistolary formulas and structure. But the abundant references to the separation of the lovers, to the act of writing and sending the poem, and to the lady's handling it with her "owen handes sofft" (613) suggest that it functioned as a letter.

2. London, British Library MS Harley 682
   Mid fifteenth century

Robert Steele, ed., *English Poems of Charles of Orléans,* vol. 1.

Index 2184: fols. 131r–133r.
Ed. Steele, *English Poems*, vol. 1, pp. 191–93.

Index 4192: fols. 139v–140v.
Ibid., pp. 206–7.

If the poems were composed in English by Charles, they must predate his return to France in 1440. Many of the fixed-form poems in the collection also resemble love epistles.

3. Oxford, Bodleian Library MS Fairfax 16
   Ca. 1450; probably for John Stanley, Esq. (1400-?1469)

Henry N. MacCracken, "English Friend," pp. 142–80.
John Norton-Smith, ed., "Introduction," *Bodleian Library MS Fairfax 16*.
Johannes P. M. Jansen, ed., *'Suffolk' Poems*.

Index 2823: fol. 320r-v.
Ed. Jansen, *'Suffolk' Poems*, p. 84.

Index 2182: fols. 323v–324r.
Ibid., p. 92.

Index 2230: fols. 324v–325r.
Ibid., p. 95.

The three "Lettyrs" occur in the second of the two collections of love lyrics comprising the last of five separate booklets making up the manuscript.

4. London, Lambeth Palace Library MS 306
   Second half, fifteenth century; London

M. R. James and Claude Jenkins, *Catalogue of Manuscripts in Lambeth Palace*, pp. 421–26.
J. P. M. Jansen, *'Suffolk' Poems*, pp. 5–7.

Index 1789: fol. 136v.
Ed. F. J. Furnivall, *Political, Religious, and Love Poems,* pp. 38–39.

Index 2247: fol. 137r.
Ibid., p. 40.

Index 3291: fols. 137v–138r.
Ibid., pp. 43–44.

Index 868: fol. 138r-v.
Ibid., pp. 41–42.

In part a commonplace book, in part what Boffey calls a "hold-all collection" (*Manuscripts of Lyrics*, pp. 20–23), the manuscript is written in three fifteenth-century hands, with many additions, most of them in a variety of sixteenth-century hands. It contains several romances, poems both secular and religious, medical recipes, heraldic materials, chronicles of England, and saints' lives, among other things. The love epistles are items 4–7 in the group of eight items copied by the second fifteenth-century hand (B). They are preceded (fols. 134r–136r) by two poems in praise of Edward IV (ed. Furnivall, *Political, Religious, and Love Poems*, pp. 1–5), separated by a satirical poem about women, and are followed by a description of Edward III's retinue at the siege of Calais (1346). Although James dates the original hands "Cent. XV late," there is good reason to believe that a large portion of the contents was assembled in the 1460s. *(1)* The first item in hand A, a collection of historical materials from several sources, arranged as annals and titled "Cronycullys of Englonde" (fols. 1r–46r), breaks off with the entry for 1465 (ed. James Gairdner, *Three Chronicles,* pp. 1–80). *(2)* The first poem in the section copied by scribe B praises King Edward IV and Richard Earl of Warwick (the Kingmaker), together with their fathers, as saviors of England. Since Edward is already king and Warwick is still alive, the poem must have been composed between 1461 and 1471. Rossell H. Robbins dates it 1461 or, at least, "long before the defection of Warwick in 1467": *Historical Poems*, p. 379. The second poem in praise of Edward, which immediately precedes the four love epistles, must also date from the same period, since the king is still a "virgin knight" (Robbins, *Historical Poems*, p. 381). Edward's marriage, in May 1464, was first made public in October of that year. On these two poems see also V. J. Scattergood, *Politics and Poetry*, pp. 191–93. *(3)* On fol. 132r, a fifteenth-century hand, different from the major ones, has inserted a partial description of Edward IV's reception at Bristol in 1461 (ed. Gairdner, *Three Chronicles*, pp. 85–86). James dates this item 1469, but cites Gairdner, who dates it 1461, as his authority. *(4)* Finally, the notes on the lining leaves at the front of the volume include a description of the lists at Smithfield, in 1467. The fact that the second love epistle (*Index* 2247) is a reworking of a love epistle from

Fairfax 16 (*Index* 2182), also supports a date of composition early rather than late in the second half of the century.

5. Oxford, Bodleian Library MS Douce 95
Second half, fifteenth century

Falconer Madan et al., *Summary Catalogue,* vol. 4 (1897), pp. 519–20 (#21669).

Index 752: fols. 1r–3r.
Ed. Robbins, *SL,* pp. 209–14.

Index 754: fol. 3v.
Ibid., pp. 202–4.

Index 724: fol. 6r.
Ibid., pp. 160–62.

The verse epistles, together with an alliterative poem of advice to the king (fols. 4r–6r; *Index* 605), are treated by the scribe as a coherent group. Most of the remaining contents of the manuscript are in Latin. According to A. I. Doyle, this miscellany was "compiled not before 1419": "The Manuscripts," p. 99.

6. London, British Library MS Harley 3810, Part 1
Second half, fifteenth century

Richard Jordan, "Kleinere Dichtungen," pp. 253–66.

Index 3785: fol. 16r–v.
Ed. Robbins, *SL,* pp. 198–200. Also in Jordan, "Kleinere Dichtungen", pp. 265–66.

The love letter is preceded by *Sir Orfeo* and three religious poems, all in the same hand.

7. London, British Library MS Cotton, Vespasian D.9, Part 7
Second half, fifteenth century

H. L. D. Ward, *Catalogue of Romances,* vol. 2 (1893), p. 539.

Index 751: fol. 188r–v.
Supplement 2308.8: fols. 188v–189r.
Ed. (as a single poem) Robbins, *SL,* pp. 200–202.

The love epistle(s) is/are written as a single passage of prose. Several stanzas are defective, and the whole appears to have been pieced together from two or even three different verse epistles. It is followed by an incomplete love poem in the same hand (*Index* 2491) and is preceded by a 260-line fragment of "The Stacyons of Rome" (fols. 183r–188r; *Index* 1172), a poem also found in MS Lambeth 306 (fols. 152v–165r). Robbins' edition requires correction at lines 21 ("schaming"> "schaung" [i.e., change]) and 38 ("Reserthe"> "Resorthe").

8. Aberystwyth, National Library of Wales MS Porkington 10
Second half, fifteenth century (1453–1500)

174

Auvo Kurvinen, "MS. Porkington 10," pp. 33–67.

Index 1241: fol. 154r-v.
Ed. Kurvinen, "MS. Porkington 10," pp. 56–57.

The love letter is the thirty-sixth of fifty-five items in a codex that resembles, in the diversity of its contents, collections such as Lambeth 306 and Douce 95. Other love lyrics are items 29, 30, and 37.

9. Oxford, Bodleian Library MS Rawlinson poet. 36
   Second half, fifteenth century

F. Madan et al., *Summary Catalogue,* vol. 3 (1895), p. 292 (#14530).
Rose Cords, "Fünf me. Gedichte," pp. 292–93.

Index 3832: fols. 3v–4r.
Ed. Robbins, *SL,* pp. 219–20.

Index 2437: fols. 4r–5r.
Ibid., pp. 220–22.

Index 1510: fol. 5v.
Ibid., pp. 193–94.

The manuscript is a slender volume of nine English poems (the last, a translation, alternates Latin prose and English verse), in what appear to be three contemporary hands. The pair of satirical love letters are the last of five poems in hand A: they are followed by three brief love poems in hand B, of which the remaining love letter is the last.

10. Cambridge, Trinity College MS R.3.19
    1478–1483; London (belonged to John Stow)

M. R. James, *Manuscripts in Trinity College,* vol. 2 (1901), pp. 69–74.
Bradford Y. Fletcher, ed., *MS Trinity R.3.19,* pp. xv-xxxi.

Supplement 2384.8: fol. 2r-v.
Ed. Kenneth G. Wilson, "Unpublished Love Poems," pp. 402–4.

Supplement 2478.5: fols. 4r–6v.
Ibid., pp. 407–15.

Index 2311: fol. 157r-v.
Ed. Robbins, *SL,* pp. 139–41.

Index 1238: fol. 159v.
Ibid., pp. 192–93.

Index 1838: fol. 160va-vb.
Ed. Rossell H. Robbins, "Love Epistle by 'Chaucer,'" pp. 290–92. Also in Henry A. Person, ed., *Cambridge Middle English Lyrics,* pp. 14–16, and Wilson, "Unpublished Love Poems," pp. 415–18 (with several errors).

Index 2510: fol. 161ra-vb.
Ed. John Stow, *Chaucer* (1561); reprinted in Alexander Chalmers, ed., *Works of English Poets,* vol. 1, pp. 562–63 (both Stow and Chalmers omit stanza 9, and alter the spelling and even some readings of the manuscript).

The manuscript is a miscellany, mainly containing verse in English. All six verse love epistles belong to an anthology of eighteen English works, twelve of them love poems, copied in a single hand. The anthology fills two gatherings of eight leaves each (fols. 1–8, 154–161), which were separated during binding: the break occurs in the middle of item 8.

11. London, British Library MS Harley 7578
    Late fifteenth century

    Eleanor P. Hammond, *Chaucer*, pp. 330–31.

    Index 231: fol. 15r.
    Ed. Walter W. Skeat, *Complete Works of Chaucer,* vol. 4 (1894), pp. xxvii-xxviii.

    The love epistle is a borderline case, labeled "Balade" in the manuscript. Fols. 2–20 contain fifteen poems, including some by Chaucer and Lydgate, written in a single hand that Hammond dates "late XV century (or later)."

12. Oxford, Bodleian Library MS Douce 326
    Late fifteenth century (manuscript proper, fifteenth century)

    Summary Catalogue, vol. 4 (1897), p. 596 (#21900).

    Index 927: fol. 14r-v.
    Ed. Carleton Brown, *Lyrics of Fifteenth Century*, pp. 75–76.

    The love letter was added in the late fifteenth century to a manuscript of the "Vita de Amys & Amylion." Above it a different hand has written "Jhus" (i.e., "Jesus").

13. London, British Library MS Royal 6B.ix
    Late fifteenth century (?)

    George F. Warner and Julius P. Gilson, *Catalogue of Manuscripts in Royal and King's Collections,* vol. 1, p. 137.

    Index 2824: fol. 198r.
    Ed. Brown, *Lyrics of Fifteenth Century,* p. 72.

    The one-stanza love epistle was added, in a later hand, on the flyleaf of a large fifteenth-century collection of religious materials, probably for the use of a preacher. Nothing is known of the "H. Bowesper" (scribe? author?) whose name appears below the poem.

14. London, British Library MS Harley 541, Part 13.
    End of fifteenth century

    Richard L. Greene, *Early English Carols,* p. 301.

    Supplement 2412.5: fol. 208r.
    Ed. in chapter 5.4.2.

    The manuscript contains a wide variety of material, in hands from the fifteenth to the seventeenth centuries. The love letter is either an inept attempt at four-stress, alliterative, monorhymed "verse," or an aureate exercise in rhymed prose, using alliteration as an additional ornament. Supporting the latter view is the fact that the monorhyme is broken only twice, at the end of each grammatical period.

15. Cambridge University Library MS Ff.1.6
Mid fifteenth-mid sixteenth centuries; southern Derbyshire

Rossell H. Robbins, "Findern Anthology," pp. 610–42.
Richard Beadle and A. E. B. Owen, eds., "Introduction," *Cambridge University Library MS. Ff.1.6.*
Kate Harris, "Origins and Make-up," pp. 299–333.

Index 2383 (lines 88–108): fols. 51r–53r (fol. 53r).
Ed. F. J. Furnivall, *Political, Religious, and Love Poems*, pp. 48–51 (pp. 50–51).

Index 3878: fols. 135r–136r.
Ed. Robbins, "Findern Anthology," pp. 634–35.

The anthology, which originally belonged to a well-to-do south Derbyshire family, contains sixty-two items – the majority by Gower, Chaucer, Hoccleve, and Lydgate, but some probably composed by local amateurs – copied in some forty different fifteenth- and sixteenth-century hands. *The Parliament of Love* (*Index* 2383), in a fifteenth-century hand, concludes with a verse love epistle. *Index* 3878, the only item copied in one of the hands that Harris describes as "clearly quite late in appearance" ("Origins and Make-up," pp. 317, 318), is a set of four poems, identical in verse form (Robbins, "Findern Anthology," p. 615, calls them "A Love Cycle"), addressed by a lady to her absent lover.

16. Oxford, Bodleian Library MS Lat. misc. c.66 (Capesthorne MS)
Ca. 1500; Cheshire

Rossell H. Robbins, "Poems of Humfrey Newton," pp. 249–81.

Index 2281: fol. 92va-vb.
Ed. Robbins, "Poems of Humfrey Newton," pp. 260–62.

Index 735: fol. 92vb.
Ibid., p. 262.

Index 2217: fol. 93va.
Ibid., pp. 266–67.

Index 737: fol. 93va.
Ibid., p. 267.

Index 481: fol. 93va.
Ibid.

Index 768: fol. 93vb.
Ibid., p. 268.

Index 1344: fol. 93vb-va.
Ibid., pp. 268–69.

Index 2597: fol. 94ra.
Ibid., pp. 269–70.

Index 926: fol. 94rb.
Ibid., p. 271.

Index 556: fol. 94rb.
Ibid., pp. 271–72.

Index 2263: fol. 94vb.
Ibid., p. 274.

The love letters are part of a group of seventeen poems that Newton copied in his own hand on three leaves of his commonplace book. Most of the poems, including all the love epistles, were his own compositions. The crowded, careless presentation (and the low quality of the verse?) lead Boffey to conclude that these are merely drafts for more polished reading versions (*Manuscripts of Lyrics,* pp. 23–24). Most of the love letters are provided with an identifying label: "Bilet" (*Index* 735), "Littera amandi" (*Index* 2217, 737, 481), or "Mittitur" (*Index* 2281, 1344, 2597, 926, 556, 2263). The exception (*Index* 768) is a "farewell" poem that has more epistolary markers than the other example of this form in the same group (*Index* 137). Another poem (*Index* 855) classified as a "love epistle" in the *Index* (p. 753) has no epistolary characteristics.

17. Oxford, Bodleian Library MS Arch. Selden B.24
    Early sixteenth century (manuscript proper, 1488); Scotland.

    E. P. Hammond, *Chaucer,* pp. 341–43.
    J. Norton-Smith and I. Pravda, eds., *Quare of Jelusy,* pp. 10–14.

    Index 2478: fols. 231r, 230r.
    Ed. Robbins, *SL,* pp. 197–98.

    The love letter, "written as continuous prose in a 16th-century cursive hand" (Norton-Smith and Pravda, p. 11), is the last of twenty-two items in the manuscript. It is copied on two leaves, bound in reverse order, that serve as extra flyleaves. Portions of the text have been lost due to deterioration of the leaves. *The Lufaris Complaynt* (*Index* 564; fols. 219r–221v), which is part of the original collection compiled in 1488, has also been classified as a verse love epistle (see *Supplement,* p. 534). The poem has no epistolary features and is not even addressed directly to the lady; only the last two lines of its prologue indicate any connection with the genre:

    > Bot furth my letter as I can It write
    > I will proceid thareof to the endite

    For an edition of this "borderline case," see Kenneth G. Wilson, "*Lay of Sorrow* and *Lufaris Complaynt,*" pp. 719–23.

18. London, British Library MS Harley 4011
    First half, sixteenth century (manuscript proper, second half, fifteenth century)

Julia Boffey, "Unnoticed Love-Lyrics," p. 20.

Not indexed ("my owne dere hart I grete you well"): fol. 163v.
Ed. Boffey, "Unnoticed Love-Lyrics," p. 20.

The love epistle is a late addition to a manuscript whose contents are mainly works by Lydgate.

19. Glasgow, University Library MS Hunterian 230
    After 1509 (manuscript proper, first half, fifteenth century)

John Young and P. Henderson Aitken, *Catalogue of Manuscripts in Hunterian Museum*, pp. 174–75.

Index 2318: fol. 246v.
Ed. Robbins, *SL,* p. 152.

The brief love letter, a stanza from Hawes's *Pastime of Pleasure* (first printing 1509) with an introductory couplet, was added to the manuscript in the first half of the sixteenth century.

20. Richard Pynson, *The Boke of Fame*
    London, 1526

Hammond, *Chaucer*, pp. 114–15.
Götz Schmitz, *Die Frauenklage*, p. 336.
Julia Boffey, "Book of Fame and Letter of Dido," pp. 339–53.

Supplement 811.5: f3va-f5rb.
Ed. in Appendix II.

Each of the three parts of the British Library's unique copy of Pynson's edition is treated as a separate unit. The second carries the title "Here begynneth the boke of Fame made by Geffray Chaucer: with dyvers other of his workes." It contains *The House of Fame, The Parliament of Fowls,* "La bell dame sauns mercy," *Truth,* "Morall prouerbes of Christyne" (Anthony Woodville's translation of Christine de Pisan's *Prouerbes Moraux),* "The complaynt of Mary Magdaleyne," "The Letter of Dydo to Eneas" (*Supplement* 811.5), and "Prouerbes of Lydgate" (i.e., the *Consulo Quisquis Eris).*

21. William Thynne, ed., *The Workes of Geffray Chaucer newly printed with dyvers workes whiche were neuer in print before.*
    London, 1532.

Hammond, *Chaucer*, pp. 116–18.
Derek S. Brewer, ed., "Introduction," *Geoffrey Chaucer: The Works, 1532.*

Index 2223: fol. 234v.
Ed. Skeat, *Chaucer,* vol. 7 (1897), pp. 405–7.

Index 1309: fols. 374vb–375va.
Ibid., pp. 281–84.

The first love letter, entitled "A goodly balade of Chaucer," is printed immediately after *The Legend of Good Women.* The second is printed, as in

Stow (1561), as the conclusion of Lydgate's "A balade in commendation of our Lady" (*Index* 99). For the manuscript evidence proving that *Index* 1309 is a separate poem, see Skeat, *Chaucer*, vol. 7 (1897), pp. xlvi-xlvii.

22. Oxford, Bodleian Library MS Rawlinson C.813
    1527–1535.

Frederick M. Padelford and Allen R. Benham, "Songs in Rawlinson C.813," pp. 309–97.
Wilhelm Bolle, "Zur Lyrik," pp. 273–307.
F. M. Padelford, "Rawlinson C.813 Again," pp. 178–86.
Kathleen H. Power, "Edition of English Lyrics." (This edition and Bolle's article, pp. 300–307, contain numerous corrections and emendations of Padelford and Benham's text.)
Sharon L. Jansen Jaech, "English Political Prophecy," pp. 141–50.

Supplement 1349.5: fols. 2r–3r.
Ed. Padelford and Benham, "Songs in Rawlinson C.813," pp. 313–15 (#3).

Index 1768: fols. 3r–4r.
Ibid., pp. 315–16 (#4).

Supplement 2271.6: fol. 4r-v.
Ibid., pp. 316–17 (#5).

Index 2532: fols. 14v–18r.
Ibid., pp. 328–33 (#13).

Supplement 2532.5: fols. 18r–21v.
Ibid., pp. 333–38 (#14).

Index 2822: fols. 21v–24r.
Ibid., pp. 338–41 (#15).

Index 2496: fols. 24v–27v.
Ibid., pp. 341–46 (#16).

Index 3804: fol. 33r.
Ibid., p. 354 (#22).

Index 4210: fols. 43v–44v.
Ibid., pp. 354–56 (#23).

Index 1180: fols. 44v–45r.
Ibid., pp. 356–57 (#24).

Index 1329: fols. 45r–46r.
Ibid., pp. 357–58 (#25).

Index 2529: fol. 46r-v.
Ibid., pp. 358–59 (#26).

Supplement 1926.5: fols. 48v–49v.
Ibid., pp. 362–63 (#30).

Index 2421: fols. 50v–51v.
Ibid., pp. 365–67 (#32).

Index 729: fol. 52r-v.
Ibid., pp. 368–69 (#34).

Supplement 1017.5: fol. 53v.
Ibid., p. 370 (#36).

Index 2547: fols. 53v–54r.
Ibid., pp. 370–71 (#37).

Index 366: fols. 54r–55r.
Ibid., pp. 371–72 (#38).

Supplement 2560.5: fols. 55r–56r.
Ibid., pp. 372–74 (#39).

Supplement 2245.1: fols. 57v–58r.
Ibid., pp. 376–77 (#41).

Supplement 733.1: fol. 58v.
Ibid., p. 377 (as last four stanzas of #41).

Supplement 3785.5: fol. 62r-v.
Ibid., pp. 382–84 (#45).

Index 4190: fol. 63r-v.
Ibid., pp. 384–85 (#47).

Supplement 3917.8: fols. 64r–69v.
Ibid., pp. 385–93 (#48). (Heading, line 1: "lire" should read "lettre"; line 270: "here" should read "lettre")

Index 2821: fols. 71r–72v.
Ibid., pp. 395–97 (#51).

Many of the poems in this anthology were probably collected, if not composed, in the early 1520s, but the political prophesies that accompany them suggest a date nearer to 1535 (and definitely after 1527) for the copying of the manuscript. Several possibly epistolary poems have not been listed above because of insufficient evidence. The *Supplement* (p. 534) calls #46 and #50 (*Supplement* 3228.5, 2439.5) "love epistles," but they are no more epistolary than several other love poems in direct address, such as #11 and #33 (*Supplement* 159.8, *Index* 2498). A special case is the anaphoric "farewell" poem (#35; *Index* 767), a form that certainly had an affinity with the verse epistle. Bolle ("Zur Lyrik," p. 283) ascribes a large number of the poems in the anthology, including all but five of the love epistles (Padelford's #34, 36, 38, 45, 47), to a single anonymous composer/compiler, and Power ("Edition of English Lyrics," pp. lxxxv-lxxxvii) also comments on the large amount of shared material in many of the same poems. Power concludes that the anthology belonged to a member of "the new rising bourgeois class" (p. lxxxix), while John Stevens assigns its poetry to the "below-stairs" variety as opposed to that of the court circle: *Music and Poetry*, p. 224.

23. London, British Library MS Additional 17492 (Devonshire MS)
    1536–1537 (manuscript as a whole, 1532–1541)

Raymond Southall, "Devonshire Manuscript," pp. 142–50.

Not indexed ("Now may I morne as one off late"): fol. 26r.
Ed. Kenneth Muir, "Unpublished Poems," pp. 261–62.

Supplement 4201.6: fol. 26v.
Ibid., p. 262.

Not indexed ("What thyng shold cawse me to be sad?"): fol. 27r.
Ibid., pp. 262–63.

Not indexed ("Alas that men be so vngent"): fol. 27v.
Ibid., p. 263.

Not indexed ("Who hath more cawse for to complayne"): fol. 28r.
Ibid., p. 264.

Not indexed ("I may well say with joyfull harte"): fol. 28v.
Ibid., p. 264.

Not indexed ("To your gentyll letters an answere to resyte"): fol. 29r.
Ibid., p. 265.

The letters are copied, one to a page, in the same hand. Both Muir and Southall identify them as the verse correspondence of Lord Thomas Howard and Lady Margaret Douglas, composed during their imprisonment for their "impolitic" marriage (1536–1537). More questionable is their further hypothesis that the next poem in the manuscript (*Supplement* 2577.5; fols. 29v–30r) belongs to the same series, having been written by Lady Margaret immediately following her husband's death in prison. The piece is actually a complaint stitched together from *Troilus and Criseyde* (see *Supplement*), and differs from the others in presentation (spills over onto a second page, lacks the "finis" that concludes all seven letters) and perhaps in hand as well.

24. Edinburgh, National Library of Scotland MS Advocates 1.1.6 (Bannatyne MS)
1568; Edinburgh.

W. Tod Ritchie, ed., *Bannatyne Manuscript*.
Denton Fox and William A. Ringler, eds., "Introduction," *Advocates' MS. 1.1.6.*

Index 3498: fol. 218r-v.
Ed. Ritchie, *Bannatyne Manuscript*, vol. III, pp. 263–64 (#252).

Not indexed ("To ȝow þat is þe harbre of my Hairt"): fols. 218v–219r.
Ibid., pp. 264–65 (#253).

Not indexed ("ffresche fragrent flour of bewty souerane"): fols. 219v–220r.
Ibid., pp. 266–69 (#255).

Index 2517: fol. 220r-v.
Ibid., p. 269 (#256).

Not indexed ("Ma commendationis w^t humilitie"): fol. 223r-v.
Ibid., pp. 278–80 (#264).

182

Not indexed ("O cupid king quhome to sall I complene"): fols. 224v–225r.
Ibid., pp. 282–83 (#266).

Supplement 765.3: fol. 225r.
Ibid., pp. 283–84 (#267).

Not indexed ("Haif hairt in hairt ȝe hairt of hairtis haill"): fol. 228r.
Ibid., pp. 293–94 (#275).

Not indexed ("No woundir is altho⸍ my hairt be thrall"): fol. 234r-v.
Ibid., pp. 309–11 (#287; by Bannatyne).

Not indexed ("Lanterne of lufe and lady fair of hew"): fol. 235r.
Ibid., pp. 312–13 (#289; by "steill").

Not indexed ("Considdir hairt my trew intent"): fols. 235v–236r.
Ibid., pp. 315–16 (#291; by "Scott": reply to #275).

Not indexed ("Absent I am rycht soir aganis my will"): fol. 237r.
Ibid., p. 319 (#294; by "steill"?).

Not indexed ("Only to ȝow in erd þat I lufe best"): fols. 237v–238r.
Ibid., pp. 321–22 (#296; by "Scott").

Not indexed ("My dullit cors dois hairtly recommend"): fol. 238r-v.
Ibid., pp. 322–23 (#297).

Supplement 2497.5: fol. 238v.
Ibid., pp. 323–24 (#298). Perhaps by Dunbar: see James Kinsley, ed., *Poems of Dunbar*, pp. 137–38, 329.

Not indexed ("In all this warld no man may wit"): fols. 257r–258v.
Ed. Ritchie, *Bannatyne Manuscript*, vol. IV, pp. 19–22 (#336).

This famous collection of poetry was compiled by George Bannatyne, probably at Edinburgh, during a period of plague. The love epistles come from the fourth part of the collection, titled "Ballattis of luve," which comprises 143 poems (#238–380). Besides the sixteen listed above, at least ten more may have been intended or perceived to belong to the genre (see Ritchie, *Bannatyne Manuscript*, vol. III, pp. 272–73, 274, 284–85, 289–90, 292–93, 336–38, 342–43, 344–45, 351, and 353–54).

Part B

"A celuy que pluys eyme en mounde": *Index* 16
CUL Gg.4.27, fols. 10v–11r
Harley 3362, fols. 90v–91r
72 lines: 12 stanzas (aabccb), alternating French, English, Latin

"A soun treschere et special": *Index* 19
CUL Gg.4.27, fol. 11r-v
Harley 3362, fol. 91r (lines 1–15)
54 lines: 9 stanzas, same as *Index* 16

"Absent I am rycht soir aganis my will": not indexed
Advocates 1.1.6, fol. 237r
21 lines: 3 stanzas, rime royal

"Al hoolly youres, withouten otheres part!": *Index* 231
Harley 7578, fol. 15r
32 lines: 4 stanzas, "Monk's Tale" octave

"Alas that men be so vngent": not indexed
BL Add. 17492, fol. 27v
24 lines: 6 quatrains

"As I my-selfe lay thys enderჳ nyght": *Index* 366
Rawlinson C.813, fols. 54r–55r
48 lines: 12 quatrains

"Beaute of you burne in my body abydis": *Index* 481
Bodl. Lat. misc. c.66, fol. 93va.
7 lines: 1 stanza, rime royal (acronym)

"bot on thynge, mastres, greues me ful sore": *Index* 556
Bodl. Lat. misc. c.66, fol. 94rb
32 lines: 8 quatrains

"Considdir hairt my trew intent": not indexed
Advocates 1.1.6, fols. 235v–236r
45 lines: 9 stanzas (aabab)

"En Iesu Roy soueraign": *Index* 724
Douce 95, fol. 6r
36 lines: 9 quatrains, alternating French and English

"Entierly belouyd & most yn my mynde": *Index* 729
Rawlinson C.813, fol. 52r-v
32 lines: 8 quatrains

"Evyn as mery as I make myght": *Supplement* 733.1
Rawlinson C.813, fol. 58v
16 lines: 4 quatrains

"Euerlastynge lof to me I haue tane": *Index* 735
Bodl. Lat. misc. c.66, fol. 92vb
4 lines: 1 quatrain (acronym)

"Euer souereyn swete, swettist in siჳt": *Index* 737
Bodl. Lat. misc. c.66, fol. 93va
4 lines: 1 quatrain (acronym)

"Exemplye sendynge to you, rowte of gentylnes": *Index* 751
Cotton Vespasian D.9, fol. 188r-v
25 lines: 4 stanzas, rime royal (stanza 2 lacks third line; stanza 4 lacks third and fourth lines)

"Excellent soueraine, semely to see": *Index* 752

Douce 95, fols. 1r–3r
136 lines: 34 quatrains

"Ffair fresshest erþly creature": *Index* 754
Douce 95, fol. 3v
59 lines: 6 stanzas (abababcccb) (stanza 1 lacks fifth line)

"Fair weill my Hairt fair weill bayth freind and fo": *Supplement* 765.3
Advocates 1.1.6, fol. 225r
28 lines: 4 stanzas, rime royal

"fair-well, þat was my lef so dere": *Index* 768
Bodl. Lat. misc. c.66, fol. 93vb
24 lines: 3 octaves, 2 of them "Monk's Tale" rhyme scheme

"Folke discomforted bere heuy countenaunce": *Supplement* 811.5
Pynson, *Boke of Fame,* f3va-f5rb
256 lines: 121 heroic couplets, plus envoy of 2 stanzas, rime royal (preceded by
a prologue: 9 stanzas, rime royal)

"Frissche flour of womanly nature": *Index* 868
Lambeth 306, fol. 138r-v
34 lines: 4 stanzas, "Monk's Tale" octave, plus final couplet

"ffresche fragrent flour of bewty souerane": not indexed
Advocates 1.1.6, fols. 219v–220r
72 lines: 8 stanzas (aabaabbab)

"Go, litull bill, & command me hertely": *Index* 926
Bodl. Lat. misc. c.66, fol. 94rb
22 lines: 11 couplets

"Go! little bill, and do me recommende": *Index* 927
Douce 326, fol. 14r-v
42 lines: 6 stanzas, rime royal

"Grene flowryng age of your manly countenance": *Supplement* 1017.5
Rawlinson C.813, fol. 53v
15 lines: erratic rhyme scheme (ababxacxxxdcxdd)

"Haif hairt in hairt ʒe hairt of hairtis haill": not indexed
Advocates 1.1.6, fol. 228r
21 lines: 3 stanzas, rime royal

"Hevy thoughtes & longe depe sykyng": *Index* 1180
Rawlinson C.813, fols. 44v–45r
24 lines: 3 stanzas, "Monk's Tale" octave

"Honour and Ioy, helth and prosperyte": *Index* 1238
T. C. Cambridge R.3.19, fol. 159v
35 lines: 5 stanzas, rime royal

"Honoure witt all mannere of heylle": *Index* 1241
Porkington 10, fol. 154r-v
24 lines: 12 octosyllabic couplets

"I have non English convenient and digne": *Index* 1309
Thynne, 1532 *Chaucer*, fols. 374vb–375va
112 lines: 16 stanzas, rime royal

"I loue on louyd, I wotte nott what loue may be": *Index* 1329
Rawlinson C.813, fols. 45r–46r
48 lines: 5 octaves (traces of "Monk's Tale" rhyme scheme), plus 4 couplets

"I may well say with joyfull harte": not indexed
BL Add. 17492, fol. 28v
24 lines: 6 quatrains

"I Pray you, M, to me be tru": *Index* 1344
Bodl. Lat. misc. c.66, fol. 93vb/a
26 lines: 1 quatrain, then 11 couplets

"I recommende me to yow with harte & mynde": *Supplement* 1349.5
Rawlinson C.813, fols. 2r–3r
52 lines: 13 quatrains

"In all this warld no man may wit": not indexed
Advocates 1.1.6, fols. 257r–258v
80 lines: 10 stanzas, "Monk's Tale" octave (with refrain)

"In my hertt is þer nothyng off remembrauns": *Index* 1510
Rawlinson poet. 36, fol. 5v
21 lines: 3 stanzas, rime royal

"Iesue, þat ys most of myght": *Index* 1768
Rawlinson C.813, fols. 3r–4r
56 lines: 14 quatrains

"Iuellis pricious cane y non fynde to selle": *Index* 1789
Lambeth 306, fol. 136v
30 lines: 4 stanzas, rime royal, plus 1 couplet

"Lady, of pite for þy sorowes þat þou haddest": *Index* 1838
T. C. Cambridge R.3.19, fol. 160va-b
70 lines: 10 stanzas, rime royal

"Lanterne of lufe and lady fair of hew": not indexed
Advocates 1.1.6, fol. 235r
24 lines: 3 stanzas, "Monk's Tale" octave

"Loo he that ys all holly yourȝ soo free": *Supplement* 1926.5
Rawlinson C.813, fols. 48v–49v
63 lines: 9 stanzas, rime royal

"Ma commendationis wᵗ humilitie": not indexed
Advocates 1.1.6, fol. 223r-v
48 lines: 6 stanzas, "Monk's Tale" octave

"Myn hertys joy, and all myn hole plesaunce": *Index* 2182
Fairfax 16, fols. 323v–324r
21 lines: 3 stanzas, rime royal

"Myn only ioy my lady and maystres": *Index* 2184
Harley 682, fols. 131r–133r
96 lines: 12 stanzas, "Monk's Tale" octave

"Most soueren lady, comfort of care": *Index* 2217
Bodl. Lat. misc. c.66, fol. 93va
8 lines: 2 quatrains (acronym)

"Moder of norture, best beloved of al": *Index* 2223
Thynne, 1532 *Chaucer*, fol. 234v
64 lines: Triple balade: 9 stanzas, rime royal, plus 1 stanza envoy, "Monk's
Tale" octave (lacks third stanza of second balade)

"My best bylovyd lady and maistresse": *Index* 2230
Fairfax 16, fols. 324v–325r
28 lines: 4 stanzas, rime royal

"My dullit cors dois hairtly recommend": not indexed
Advocates 1.1.6, fol. 238r-v
32 lines: 4 stanzas, "Monk's Tale" octave

"My harte ys sore, but yett noo forse": *Supplement* 2245.1
Rawlinson C.813, fols. 57v–58r
36 lines: 9 quatrains

"My hertes Ioie all myn hole plesaunce": *Index* 2247
Lambeth 306, fol. 137r
28 lines: 3 stanzas, "Monk's Tale" octave, plus 1 quatrain envoy

"Mi Mornynge, M, greues me sore": *Index* 2263
Bodl. Lat. misc. c.66, fol. 94vb
16 lines: 4 quatrains

"my owne dere hart I grete you well": not indexed
Harley 4011, fol. 163v
32 lines: 8 quatrains

"My swetharte & my lyllye floure": *Supplement* 2271.6
Rawlinson C.813, fol. 4r-v
32 lines: 8 quatrains

"My worshipfful and reuerent lady dere": *Index* 2281
Bodl. Lat. misc. c.66, fol. 92va-b
68 lines: set as 17 quatrains, but has strong traces of "Monk's Tale" rhyme
scheme

"No woundir is altho¹ my hairt be thrall": not indexed
Advocates 1.1.6, fol. 234r-v
74 lines: 9 stanzas, "Monk's Tale" octave, plus 1 couplet (probably lacks
beginning)

"Now fayreste of stature formyd by nature": *Supplement* 2308.8
Cotton Vespasian D.9, fols. 188v–189r
28 lines: 4 stanzas, rime royal

"Now fresshe floure, to me that ys so bryght": *Index* 2311
T. C. Cambridge R.3.19, fol. 157r-v
52 lines: 13 quatrains (with concluding motto)

"Now good swet hart & myn ane good mestrys": *Index* 2318
Hunterian 230, fol. 246v
7 lines: 1 stanza, rime royal

"Now may I morne as one off late": not indexed
BL Add. 17492, fol. 26r
20 lines: 5 quatrains

"O beauteuous braunche, floure of formosyte": *Supplement* 2384.8
T. C. Cambridge R.3.19, fol. 2r-v
56 lines: 8 stanzas, rime royal

"O cupid king quhome to sall I complene": not indexed
Advocates 1.1.6, fols. 224v–225r
42 lines: 6 stanzas, rime royal

"O desiderabull dyamunt distinit with diuersificacion": *Supplement* 2412.5
Harley 541, fol. 208r
18 lines (?): probably rhymed prose

"O excelent suffereigne, most semely to see": *Index* 2421
Rawlinson C.813, fols. 50v–51v
72 lines: 6 stanzas, rime royal plus bob-and-wheel

"O fresch floure, most plesant of prysc": *Index* 2437
Rawlinson poet. 36, fols. 4r–5r
60 lines: 8 stanzas, rime royal, plus an introductory and a concluding couplet

"O Lady, I schall me dress with besy cure": *Index* 2478
Arch. Selden B.24, fols. 231r, 230r
32 lines: 4 stanzas, "Monk's Tale" octave

"O lady myne, to whom thys boke I sende": *Supplement* 2478.5
T. C. Cambridge R.3.19, fols. 4r–6v
222 lines: 32 stanzas, rime royal (stanza 1 lacks seventh line; stanza 6 lacks second line)

"O loue most dere, o loue most nere my harte": *Index* 2496
Rawlinson C.813, fols. 24v–27v
168 lines: 24 stanzas, rime royal

"O lusty flour of ʒowᵗ benyng and bricht": *Supplement* 2497.5
Advocates 1.1.6, fol. 238v
40 lines: 5 stanzas, "Monk's Tale" octave

"O mercifull and O merciable": *Index* 2510
T. C. Cambridge R.3.19, fol. 161ra-vb
91 lines: 13 stanzas, rime royal

"O Maistres myn, till ʒow I me commend!": *Index* 2517

188

Advocates 1.1.6, fol. 220r-v
24 lines: 3 stanzas, "Monk's Tale" octave

"O, my dere harte, the lanterne of lyght": *Index* 2529
Rawlinson C.813, fol. 46r-v
39 lines: 5 stanzas, rime royal, plus 2 couplets

"O my lady dere, bothe regarde & see": *Index* 2532
Rawlinson C.813, fols. 14v–18r
168 lines: 24 stanzas, rime royal

"O my swete lady & exelente goddas": *Supplement* 2532.5
Rawlinson C.813, fols. 18r–21v
175 lines: 25 stanzas, rime royal

"O resplendent floure! prynte þis yn your mynde": *Index* 2547
Rawlinson C.813, fols. 53v–54r
22 lines: 1 couplet, then 5 quatrains

"O souereyn prince of all gentillness": *Index* 2383 (lines 88–108)
CUL Ff.1.6, fol. 53r
21 lines: 3 stanzas, rime royal (introduced by a narrative, in couplets)

"O, swete-harte, dere & most best belouyd": *Supplement* 2560.5
Rawlinson C.813, fols. 55r–56r
68 lines: 8 octaves, the first 7 "Monk's Tale" (with refrain), plus 2 couplets

"O ye my emperice, I your servaunt þis to you I say": *Index* 2597
Bodl. Lat. misc. c.66, fol. 94ra
48 lines: 12 quatrains

"Only to ȝow in erd þat I lufe best": not indexed
Advocates 1.1.6, fols. 237v–238r
42 lines: 6 stanzas, rime royal

"Right best beloved & most in assurance": *Index* 2821
Rawlinson C.813, fols. 71r–72v
63 lines: 9 stanzas, rime royal

"Ryght gentyll harte of greane flouryng age": *Index* 2822
Rawlinson C.813, fols. 21v–24r
133 lines: 19 stanzas, rime royal

"Ryght goodly flour, to whom I owe servyse": *Index* 2823
Fairfax 16, fol. 320r-v
28 lines: 4 stanzas, rime royal

"Ryht godely, fressh flour of womanhode": *Index* 2824
Royal 6.B.ix, fol. 198r
8 lines: 1 stanza, "Monk's Tale" octave

"That pasaunte Goodnes, the Rote of all vertve": *Index* 3291
Lambeth 306, fols. 137v–138r
42 lines: 6 stanzas, rime royal

"The well of vertew and flour of womanheid": *Index* 3498
Advocates 1.1.6, fol. 218r-v
28 lines: 4 stanzas, rime royal

"To ʒou, hie worschip & magnificence": *Index* 3785
Harley 3810, Pt. I, fol. 16r-v
56 lines: 7 stanzas, "Monk's Tale" octave

"To yow, mastres, whyche haue be-longe": *Supplement* 3785.5
Rawlinson C.813, fol. 62r-v
56 lines: 7 stanzas, "Monk's Tale" octave (with refrain)

"To ʒow þat is þe harbre of my Hairt": not indexed
Advocates 1.1.6, fols. 218v–219r
42 lines: 6 stanzas, rime royal

"To your gentyll letters an answere to resyte": not indexed
BL Add. 17492, fol. 29r
28 lines: 4 stanzas, rime royal

"Trew loue, to me yn harte soo dere": *Index* 3804
Rawlinson C.813, fol. 33r
12 lines: 3 quatrains

"Vnto you, most froward, þis lettre I write": *Index* 3832
Rawlinson poet. 36, fols. 3v–4r
40 lines: 5 stanzas, rime royal, plus an introductory triplet and a concluding couplet

"Welcome be ye, my souereine": *Index* 3878
CUL Ff.1.6, fols. 135r–136r
51 lines: probably 4 poems, each with the same form (aabba aab aabba) (the first poem lacks the fifth line)

"What thyng shold cawse me to be sad?": not indexed
BL Add. 17492, fol. 27r
28 lines: 4 stanzas, rime royal

"Whatt tyme as Parys, son of Kyng Priame": *Supplement* 3917.8
Rawlinson C.813, fols. 64r–69v
273 lines: 39 stanzas, rime royal

"Who hath more cawse for to complayne": not indexed
BL Add. 17492, fol. 28r
16 lines: 4 quatrains (monorhymed)

"With greate humylyte I submytt me to your gentylnes": *Index* 4190
Rawlinson C.813, fol. 63r-v
35 lines: 5 stanzas, rime royal

"With hert repentaunt of my gret offence": *Index* 4192
Harley 682, fols. 139v–140v
42 lines: 6 stanzas, rime royal

"Wyth sorowful syghes and wondes smart": *Supplement* 4201.6
BL Add. 17492, fol. 26v
20 lines: 5 quatrains

"With woofull harte plungede yn dystresse": *Index* 4210
Rawlinson C.813, fols. 43v–44v
77 lines: 11 stanzas, rime royal

The following poems, from sources not indexed in Part A, are labeled "love epistles" in the *Index* (see especially p. 753) or the *Supplement* (see especially p. 534), but have been excluded from the corpus either *(1)* because they lack epistolary features or other corroborating evidence, or *(2)* because they are not *verse* epistles or *love* epistles.

Index 303: six lines of verse quoted in Margery Brews's Valentine's letter to John Paston III; even if treated as a separate poem, it is not a verse epistle.

Supplement 763.5: no epistolary features; a complaint with a song-like refrain.

Index 1360: the versified conclusion to a long letter in prose from Pampyng and John Paston to Margaret Paston.

Supplement 2267.5: a borderline case, but probably a letter of friendship addressed by John Paston III to the Earl of Oxford.

Index 3321: Lydgate's "Epistle to Sibille"; not a love poem.

Index 4199: the first quatrain of this fragment could have come from a love epistle, but the four lines of monorhymed refrain and the accompanying music indicate that it functions as a song.

"The Letter of Dydo to Eneas"

Richard Pynson, *The Boke of Fame* (London, 1526), f3va-f5rb

Note: The spelling of Pynson's text has been retained. Abbreviations have been expanded silently, and capitalization and punctuation (in the original, mainly virgules) have been modernized. Insertions in the text are enclosed in pointed brackets < >, interpolations in square brackets [ ]. All other editorial changes are indicated in footnotes.

Thus endeth "The Complaynt of Mary Magdaleyn." And herafter foloweth "The Letter of Dydo to Eneas," and fyrst the prologue of the translatour.

Folke discomforted bere heuy countenaunce:
As ye haue cause, so order your chere.
But yet some folke whiche vse dissemblaunce
Wolde say other meanes moche better were,
That is to say, good countenaunce to bere   5
Whan ye haue cause of thought or heuynesse,
That folke perceyue nat your grefe and distres.

But as for me, me thynke playnnesse is best,
After your chere to shewe your wo.
Shewe outwarde what ye bere within your brest.   10
Sithe ye of force must chuse one of the two,
Eyther among the dissemblers to go
Or els be playne, chose after your lust.
But playnnesse is the waye of parfyte trust.

To purpose, lo, thus wyse it is ment: 15
Bycause that I haue loued very long
And haue no ioye vnto this day present,
Constrayned me to write this rufull songe
Of poore Dydo, forsaken by great wronge
Of false Ene, who causeth my hand to shake   20
For great furye that I ayenst hym take.

[f3vb]
Ah, false vntrouth, vnkinde delyng and double!
My hande quaketh whan I write thy name.

Thou hast brought all true louers in trouble
By thy vntrouthe. Wherfore, o lady Fame,   25
Blowe vp thy trumpe of sclaunder and of shame;
Forthwith to shewe of Ene his false delyte,
Make me your clerke, simply as I can write.

Shall I go to the well of Helycon,
To the Muses, for to pray them of ayde?   30
Nay, nay, alas! for they wepe e",euerychone
For pore Dydo, thus pytously arayde.
And nowe Juno accompteth her dismayde,
For the knot that she trusted shulde last
Is nowe become bothe lose and vnstedfast.   35

What remedy, where shulde I seke socour
Of Niobe, of Myrra, or of Byblis,
Of Medea or Lucrece, the romayne flour?
None of them all may graunt me helpe in this,
Nor yet Uenus, that goddes of loue is: 40
She is parciall, she loueth Enee so.
Wherfore, helpe me, ye cruell Celeno,

For lyke as I, barreyne of eloquence,
Presume to translate, nat worthy to bere
The ynkehorn of them that write in good sentence.   45
For lernyng lacketh and reason is nate clere,
Afore poetes my workes dare nat appere;
Whiche causeth me helpe to requyre
Of Celeno, full of enuyous yre.

Prayeng all them that shall this rede or se   50
To be content at this my poore request,
In this translacion to pardon me
And of my mynde to reporte the best.
To translate Frenche I am nat redyest:
No marueyle is, sithe I was neuer yet   55
In those parties where I might langage gete.

From Troy distroyed full passed yeres seuyn,
Thus Eneas arryued at Carthage,
And at the last, by influence of heuyn,
Mette with his folkes, tossed in the sees rage.   60
Uenus and Juno entended maryage
Bitwene him and Dido; but this vntrue man
Brake that promyse, wherfore thus she began.

Thus endeth the prologe.

Right as the swan, whan her dethe is nye,
Swetely dothe syng her fatall desteny, 65
Lykewise I, Dido, for all my true loue,
Whiche by no prayer can you remoue
Nor hath in you no more hope of lyfe,
Write vnto you my sorowes most pensyfe.
For well knowe I my chaunces be so yll 70
That they shalbe the troublers of my wyll.
But sithe that I haue lost all my renowne,
Whiche that through the worlde dyd sowne,
But a small losse is of the surplusage
As for to lose wordes, writyng or message. 75
Enee, ye take a great iourney in hande,
To forsake poore Dido and all her lande:
So by one wynde shalbe forthe past
Your faithe, promise, your sayle and eke your mast.
Nowe ye delyte to dresse your passage, 80
In hope therby to haue auauntage
And for to seche Italyens groundes,
Whiche be nat yet within your boundes.
Pleaseth nat you this cyte of Cartage
Nor the countre nor lande good for tyllage? 85
The thynges well done and sure ye dispice;
Thynges vncertayne ye sertche and entprise.
But what be they at your aduyse, Enee,
By whom their lande gouerned shalbe
And submyt them to you, a poore stranger? 90
Wyll they to your lawes put them selfe in danger?
Certenly, as by your dedes I perceyue,
Other louers in recompence ye haue.
And if ye haue faithe of another lady,
She shalbe disceyued as well as I. 95
But whan tyme shall come, the day and hour
That ye shall bylde a mighty strong tour
And a cyte, Cartage to resemble,
To the whiche people shall assemble,
That your renowne may be spred ouer all, 100
Holdyng your ceptre in your chere ryall,
Nowe put the case: suche be your desteny
That ye may happe gouerne all Italy,
Yet shall ye neuer haue spouse nor wyfe
Kynder than me. I loue you as my lyfe! 105
I bren as hote, sithe loue made my hert tame,
As brimstone whiche in the fyre dothe flame.
Knowe ye for trouth, whan ye saile in the sees
I shall haue you alway before myn eyes.

195

Yet alway feirs and forgetfull ye be: 110
Of others welthe ye haue enuy, I se.
Well ought I than, were I a symple wight,
Hate his swete wordes and flye fro his sight.
But though that he wyll flye fro me,
I can nat forgete nor hate my swete Ene. 115
I playne ynough of his dealyng vntrue,
But somoch more loue doth my hert subdue.
O Cupido, and ye, Uenus, his moder dere,
Haue some pyte of my soroufull chere,
And lyke as ye with your peersyng darte 120
With loue of false Ene stroke me to the hert,
To th'ende that he in whom I put my trust
Pyte my wepyng and be nat vniust.
Alas, howe moche hath it be my domage
That I trusted to his plesant visage! 125
And to moch, for trouth, deceyued was I the hour
Whan his beaute wan me without socour.
Certes in maners, in swetenesse and in grace
To his mother vnlyke in euery place:
For she is swete and he is vnkynde. 130
A droppe of trouthe in him I can nat finde.
I beleue, than – I thynke it without blame –
Ye were neuer borne of so swete a dame,
But borne in rockes, in thornes or among breers,
Among tygres and wolues, cruell and feers. 135
There were ye borne and lyued without norture,
For without mercy thou arte of thy nature.
Or I may saye surely, without dout,
In the see thy byrth was brought about,
And in the same, where thou haddest thy springing, 140
Thou folowest in nature thy begynning.
[f4va]
But wheder flyest thou, thou false Enee?
In what perill is thy lyfe ordayned to be?
What, seest nat thou,¹ vntrue and frowarde,
The gret troubles, the countre colde and harde, 145
And of the see the water whiche dothe swell,
Whiche for to passe be right depe and cruell?
Seest thou nat also howe force of the wynde
Is ayenst the? Print these thinges in thy minde.
Certainly, the tempest and the rage 150
Is more stedfast than is thy false corage.
And more there is of surete in the see
Than in thy will, which maketh me to blame the.
Alas, I haue nat at the somoch enuy

---

¹ the cod.

196

To wisshe the hurt, though thou thinke contrary,   155
Nor to desyre, for to reuenge myne angre,
To put your lyfe in so pytous daunger.
But ayenst me great hate ye haue conceyued
And moch desyre that I shulde be deceyued,
Sithe that ye wyll suche daunger vndertake   160
But to th'entent that ye may me forsake.
It appereth well ye care nat for to dye,
Sithe ye so sone put your lyfe in ieopardy.
Tary a space, if that it may you please,
Tyll that the see be more calme and at ease,   165
To th'ende that ye, for enuy or for stryfe
Of your goyng, ye do nat lese your lyfe.
Haue ye nat knowen the troublous tempest
Whiche in the see dothe ryse from Est to West?
Thousande dangers hourly there doth encrese: 170
Ought ye nat than of your iorney to cese?
But sithe ye haue dayly great busynesse,
Wherof commeth your froward wylfulnesse
That ye wolde sayle and in payne be moued?
Marueyle nat than, though ye be reproued;   175
For certainly, they be neuer well assured
Which vnto ladyes so ofte be periured,
But tosse and sayle, after their faithe is gone,
Whan they haue lefte their ladyes alone.
Of trouthe, the see dothe oft drowne and receyue   180
Within his wawes folkes which lust deceyue.
Chefely on false louers that dothe befall,
And the reason is this: for fyrst of all
Uenus the goddes, whose seruauntes louers be,
Was engendred of the fome of the see.   185
Alas, what feare my hert distroyeth!
Why doute I to anoy hym that me anoyeth?
Better were to lyue and contynue brethe.
I loue moch more your lyfe than your dethe
[f4vb]
And rather desyre to dye with a good wyll   190
Than ye shulde sayle and be in great peryll.
I pray you nowe, set your hert at rest.
Se howe the sees are troublus with tempest.
In your sayling is many a quicke sande,
Whan ye departe fro me and fro my lande.   195
And if it chaunce ye be drowned at a clappe –
But I pray God kepe you fro suche myshap –
Whan ye and your ship be lyke to perishe,
That ye were here than wyll <ye> often wyshe.
Than, Enee, your false forsweryng   200
first shall come to your vnderstandyng.

197

Than in your mynde Dydo ye shall espy,
Whom by disceit ye haue caused to dye.
Than shall ye se, to make your hert pensyfe,
The colde ymage of your disceyued wife, 205
Heuy, thoghtfull, with heres pulde fro her hed,
Spotted with blode, wounded, nat fully ded.
Whan your lyfe fayleth, than shall ye sigh sore
And say, "I haue deserued this and more."
Ha, my dere frende, gyue a lytell space 210
To the sees rage, which doth you manace.
Tary a whyle; soiourne a space ye may,
Tyll that there come a more goodly day.
And it may be that all these wawes great
Shall well apese and no more the rockes bete. 215
And if ye haue banysshed fro me pety,
Haue ye regarde to your sonne Ascany.
Shall your sonne se my sorowfull trespace,
Whom ye haue kept in many a diuers place?
Saued ye your folke fro fyre of Troy town 220
To th'ende that the gret see shulde them drown?
I am nat the fyrst, I knowe for certayne,
Whom your langage hath caused to complayne.
But ye that were well lerned for to lye
Haue abused me, alas, through my folly. 225
Your pitous wordes whan I herd with myn eres,
My eyes were moued to stande ful of teres.
After, my hert moche enclyned to pyte
Was holly moued to haue your amyte.
That redy wyll and my defaut sodayne 230
Shall nowe be cause of my later payne.
I thynke, for trouth, that God for your vice
In eche place shal you punishe and chastice.
Seuyn yeres without rest, by lande and by see,
Ye were in warres and great aduersyte. 235
At the last, <by> weder driuen ye were hyder.
I was content that we shulde lyue togyder
[f5ra]
And by payne had of your name knowlege.
My body and landes to you I dyd pledge.
Wolde to God that the fame and yll renowne 240
On my synne were vtterly layde downe!
I was to blame to enclyne and reioyce
In the swete wordes of your pitous voice,
Trustyng your true spouse to be;
But the fayntnesse of loue disceyued me. 245
Pardon ye me of that I was so swyfte:
I dyde it nat for golde nor for no gyfte.
One that semed kynde, louyng and honest

Ouercame me to folowe his request.
His noble blode and his[2] swete countenaunce   250
Gaue me good hope and of mynde assuraunce.
I knowe no woman so good nor so wyse
That wolde the loue of suche one dispice;
For in him is no defaut but one:
He lacketh pyte, whiche causeth me to mone.   255
Yf Goddes wyll be that ye shall nedes hens,
I wolde he had forbode you my presens.
Alas, ye se and knowe this without fayle,
That your people be wery of traueyle,
And to haue rest they wolde be very fayne,   260
Tyll that they may be esed of their payne.
Also, your shippes be nat fully prest,
Your sayles broken, your[3] gables yet vnfest.
Yf I of you haue ought deserued
By any thyng wherin I haue you serued   265
And euer wyll serue you, in my best wyse,
For recompence at lest of that seruyce,
I pray you hertely, let this be done:
Purpose your mynde nat to go so sone,
Tyll the tyme that the see and the rage   270
Be well apesed and of his wawes aswage
And tyll that I may suffre with good hert
Your departure, sithe ye wyll nedes depart,
And more easely suffre and endure
Thought, traueyle, payne and displeasure.   275
For in good faithe, I trust of very trothe
That ayenst me ye can nat long be wroth.
Yet I pray you, come regarde the ymage
Of her that wrote to you this langage.
Alas, I write, and to encrease my sorowe,   280
There standeth the swerde that shall kyll me tomorowe.
With my teres this swerd is spotted,
Whiche in my brest in hast shalbe blotted,
And all shalbe in stede of teres on the sworde
Spotted with blode, trust me at a worde.   285
[f5rb]
Ha, the swerde ye lefte me whan ye went,
To my desteny is conuenyent:
Of an vnhappy offryng and gyfte but small
My sepulture is made great therwithall.
This shall nat be the fyrst glayue or darte   290
That hath peersed me to the herte;
For afore this loue, that setteth folke to scole,

---

[2] hir *cod.*
[3] you *cod.*

Wounded me sore – I se I was more fole.
O suster Anne, ye knewe my hert dyd blede
Or I consented vnto this dede.   295
Whan I am deed and brent to asshes colde,
Than shall ye serch and with your handes vnfolde
The pouder of my bones and surely kepe
In your chambre, there as ye vse to slepe.
Fro I be deed, folkes wyll no more call me   300
Chast Dido, somtyme wyfe to Sechee.
On the marble shall stande this scripture,
As an Epitaphe vpon my sepulture:
"Here lyeth Dido, to whom Enee vntrewe
Gaue cause of deth and the swerd that her slewe."   305

Lenuoy of the translatour.

Ye good ladyes whiche be of tender age,
Beware of loue, sithe men be full of crafte.
Though some of them wyll promyse mariage,
Their lust fulfylde, suche promise wylbe laft.
For many of them can wagge a false shaft,   310
As dyd Enee, cause of quene Dydose dethe,
Whose dedes I hate and shall during my brethe.

And if that ye wyll you to loue subdue,
As thus I meane, vnto a good entent,
Se that he be secrete, stedfast and true   315
Or that ye set your mynde on hym feruent.
This is myne aduyse, that ye neuer consent
To do that thing whiche folkes may reproue
You in any thyng that ye haue done for loue.

*Thus endeth "The Letter of Dydo to Eneas." And here foloweth a lytell exortacion
howe folke shulde behaue them selfe in all companyes.*

200

Works Cited

Primary Works

Beadle, Richard, and A. E. B. Owen, eds. *The Findern Manuscript: Cambridge University Library MS. Ff.1.6* (London, 1977).

Benson, Larry T., et al., eds. *The Riverside Chaucer,* 3d ed. (Boston, 1987).

Boffey, Julia. "Two Unnoticed Love-Lyrics from the Early Sixteenth Century," *Notes and Queries,* 226 (1981), 20–21.

Bond, R. W., ed. *The Complete Works of John Lyly,* 3 vols. (Oxford, 1902).

Brewer, Derek S., ed. *Geoffrey Chaucer: The Works, 1532, with Supplementary Material from the Editions of 1542, 1561, 1598, and 1602* (Menston, Yorkshire, 1969; reprinted 1974, 1976).

Brewer, J. S., ed. *Giraldi Cambrensis Opera,* 8 vols., Rerum Britanicarum Medii Aevi Scriptores (Rolls Series), 21 (London, 1861–1891; reprinted Wiesbaden, 1966).

Brook, G. L., ed. *The Harley Lyrics: The Middle English Lyrics of MS. Harley 2253,* 4th ed. (Manchester, 1968).

Brown, Carleton, ed. *Religious Lyrics of the Fifteenth Century* (Oxford, 1939; reprinted 1962).

Bühler, Curt F., ed. *The* Epistle of Othea, *Translated from the French Text of Christine de Pisan by Stephen Scrope,* EETS, o.s. 264 (London, 1970).

Chalmers, Alexander, ed. *The Works of the English Poets, from Chaucer to Cowper,* 21 vols. (London, 1810).

Chambers, E. K., ed. *The Oxford Book of Sixteenth-Century Verse* (Oxford, 1932; reprinted 1939, 1945).

Chambers, E. K., and F. Sidgwick, eds. *Early English Lyrics* (London, 1937).

Champion, Pierre, ed. *Charles d'Orléans: Poésies,* 2 vols., Les classiques français du moyen âge (Paris, 1923–1927; reissued 1971).

Cords, Rose. "Fünf me. Gedichte aus den Hss. Rawlinson Poetry 36 und Rawlinson C.86," *Archiv für das Studium der neueren Sprachen und Literaturen,* 135 (1916), 292–302.

Cunliffe, John W., ed. *The Complete Works of George Gascoigne,* 2 vols. (Cambridge, 1907–1910; reprinted New York, 1969).

Davies, R. T., ed. *Medieval English Lyrics: A Critical Anthology* (London, 1963).

Davis, Norman, ed. *Paston Letters and Papers of the Fifteenth Century,* 2 vols. (Oxford, 1971–1976).

Day, Angel. *The English Secretorie* (London, 1586).

Dobson, E. J., ed. *The English Text of the* Ancrene Riwle, *Edited from B. M. Cotton MS. Cleopatra C.VI,* EETS, o.s. 267 (London, 1972).

Fleming, Abraham. *A Panoplie of Epistles* (London, 1576).

Fletcher, Bradford Y., ed. *MS Trinity R.3.19*, The Facsimile Series of the Works of Geoffrey Chaucer, 5 (Norman, OK, 1987).

Foster, Brian, ed., with the assistance of Ian Short. *The Anglo-Norman Alexander (Le roman de toute chevalerie) by Thomas of Kent*, 2 vols., Anglo-Norman Text Society, 29–31 (London, 1976, for 1971–1973), A-NTS, 32–33 (London, 1977, for 1974–1975).

Fox, Denton, and William A. Ringler, eds. *The Bannatyne Manuscript: National Library of Scotland Advocates' MS. 1.1.6* (London, 1980).

Fulwood, William. *The Enimie of Idlenesse: teaching the maner and stile howe to endite, compose, and write all sorts of Epistles and Letters* (London, 1568; 2d ed. 1578).

Furnivall, F. J., ed. *Political, Religious, and Love Poems,* EETS, o.s. 15 (London, 1866).

Furnivall, F. J., ed. *Hoccleve's Works: I. The Minor Poems,* EETS, e.s. 61 (London, 1892).

Gairdner, James, ed. *Three Fifteenth-Century Chronicles,* The Camden Society, n.s. 28 (London, 1880).

Gollancz, Sir Israel, ed. *Hoccleve's Works: II. The Minor Poems in the Ashburnham Ms. Addit. 133,* EETS, e.s. 73 (London, 1925).

Greene, Richard L., ed. *The Early English Carols,* 2d ed. (Oxford, 1977).

Hammond, Eleanor P., ed. *English Verse between Chaucer and Surrey* (Durham, NC, 1927).

Hilka, Alfons. "Die anglonormannische Kompilation didaktisch-epischen Inhalts der Hs. Bibl. nat. nouv. acq. fr. 7517," *Zeitschrift für französische Sprache und Literatur,* 47 (1925), 423–54.

Jansen, Johannes Petrus Maria, ed. *The 'Suffolk' Poems: An Edition of the Love Lyrics in Fairfax 16 Attributed to William de la Pole* (Groningen, 1989).

Jordan, Richard. "Kleinere Dichtungen der Handschrift Harley 3810," *Englische Studien,* 41 (1910), 253–66.

Kinsley, James, ed. *The Poems of William Dunbar* (Oxford, 1979).

Koch, John. "Anglonormannische Texte im Ms. Arundel 220 des Britischen Museums," *Zeitschrift für romanische Philologie,* 54 (1934), pp. 20–56.

Könsgen, Ewald, ed. *Epistolae duorum amantium: Briefe Abaelards und Heloises?,* Mittellateinische Studien und Texte, 8 (Leiden and Cologne, 1974).

Kooper, Erik. "Slack Water Poetry: An Edition of the *Craft of Lovers*," *English Studies,* 68 (1987), 473–89.

Kühnel, Jürgen, ed. *Du bist min, ih bin din: Die lateinischen Liebes- (und Freundschafts-) Briefe des clm 19411. Abbildungen, Text und Übersetzung,* Litterae, Göppinger Beiträge zur Textgeschichte, 52 (Göppingen, 1977).

Kurvinen, Auvo. "MS. Porkington 10: Description with Extracts," *Neuphilologische Mitteilungen,* 54 (1953), 33–67.

Macaulay, G. C., ed. *The Complete Works of John Gower,* 4 vols. (Oxford, 1899–1902).

MacCracken, Henry N. "An English Friend of Charles of Orléans," *PMLA,* 26 (1911), 142–80.

MacCracken, Henry N., ed. *The Minor Poems of John Lydgate,* 2 vols., EETS, e.s. 107 (London, 1911, for 1910), EETS, o.s. 192 (London, 1934, for 1933).

Mead, William E., ed. *The* Pastime of Pleasure *by Stephen Hawes,* EETS, o.s. 173 (London, 1928, for 1927).

Meyer, Paul. "Mélanges Anglo-normands," *Romania,* 38 (1909), 434–41.

Monfrin, J., ed. *Abélard,* Historia calamitatum, 2d ed. (Paris, 1962).

Muir, Kenneth. "Unpublished Poems in the Devonshire MS.," *Proceedings of the Leeds Philosophical and Literary Society,* Literary and Historical Section, vol. VI (ii), part IV (1947), 253–82.

Muir, Kenneth, and Patricia Thomson, eds. *Collected Poems of Sir Thomas Wyatt* (Liverpool, 1969).

Norton-Smith, John, ed. *John Lydgate: Poems* (Oxford, 1966).

Norton-Smith, John, ed. *Bodleian Library MS Fairfax 16* (London, 1979).

Norton-Smith, John, and I. Pravda, eds. *The Quare of Jelusy* (Heidelberg, 1976).

Padelford, Frederick M., and Allen R. Benham, "Liedersammlungen des XVI. Jahrhunderts, besonders aus der Zeit Heinrichs VIII: IV.7. The Songs in Manuscript Rawlinson C.813," *Anglia,* 31 (1908), 309–97.

Pantin, W. A. "A Medieval Treatise on Letter-Writing, with Examples, from the Rylands Latin MS. 394," *Bulletin of the John Rylands Library,* 13 (1929), 326–82.

Paris, Paulin, ed. *Le* Livre du Voir-dit *de Guillaume de Machaut* (Paris, 1875; reprinted Geneva, 1969).

Parkes, M. B., and Richard Beadle, eds. *Geoffrey Chaucer: Poetical Works. A Facsimile of CUL MS Gg.4.27,* 3 vols. (Cambridge, 1979–1980).

Paynell, Thomas, trans. *The moste excellent and pleasaunt Booke, entituled: The treasurie of Amadis of Fraunce: Conteyning eloquente orations, pythie Epistles, learned Letters, and feruent Complayntes, seruing for sundrie purposes ... Translated out of French into English* (London, 1568).

Peck, Russell A., ed. *Confessio Amantis* (New York, 1968).

Pernicone, Vincenzo, ed. *Giovanni Boccaccio:* Il Filostrato *e* Il Ninfale Fiesolano, Scrittori d'Italia, 163 (Bari, 1937); reprinted, with facing English translation, in *Giovanni Boccaccio,* Il Filostrato, trans. Robert P. ap Roberts and Ann Bruni Seldis (New York, 1986).

Person, Henry A., ed. *Cambridge Middle English Lyrics,* rev. ed. (Seattle, 1962; reprinted New York, 1969).

Power, Kathleen H. "An Edition, with Commentary, of the English Lyrics on Folios 1–72 of the Bodleian MS Rawlinson C.813" (Diss. Univ. of Western Australia 1975).

Purkart, Josef, facs. ed. and trans. *Boncompagno da Signa,* Rota Veneris (Delmar, NY, 1975).

Pynson, Richard, ed. *The Boke of Fame* (London, 1526).

Radice, Betty, trans. *The Letters of Abelard and Heloise* (Harmondsworth, 1974).

Raynaud, Gaston, ed. *Oeuvres complètes de Eustache Deschamps,* 11 vols., SATF, 9 (Paris, 1878–1903).

Richardson, Henry G. "Letters of the Oxford *Dictatores,*" in H. E. Salter, W. A. Pantin, and H. G. Richardson, *Formularies Which Bear on the History of Oxford c. 1204–1420,* 2 vols., Oxford Historical Society, n.s. 4 and 5 (Oxford, 1942), 329–450.

Ritchie, W. Tod, ed. *The Bannatyne Manuscript,* 4 vols., The Scottish Text

Society, n.s. 22–23 (vols. II-III, Edinburgh and London, 1928), n.s. 26 (vol. IV, 1930), and 3d ser. 5 (vol. I, 1934); reprinted New York, 1972.

Robbins, Rossell H. "Two Middle English Satiric Love Epistles," *Modern Language Review*, 37 (1942), 415–21.

Robbins, Rossell H. "The Poems of Humfrey Newton, Esquire, 1466–1536," *PMLA*, 65 (1950), 249–81.

Robbins, Rossell H. "A Love Epistle by 'Chaucer,'" *Modern Language Review*, 49 (1954), 289–92.

Robbins, Rossell H. "The Findern Anthology," *PMLA*, 69 (1954), 610–42.

Robbins, Rossell H., ed. *Secular Lyrics of the Fourteenth and Fifteenth Centuries*, 2d ed. (Oxford, 1955).

Robbins, Rossell H., ed. *Historical Poems of the Fourteenth and Fifteenth Centuries* (New York, 1959).

Rollins, Hyder E., ed. *Tottel's Miscellany*, rev. ed., 2 vols. (Cambridge, MA, 1965).

Rossetti, William Michael. *Chaucer's Troylus and Cryseyde compared with Boccaccio's Filostrato*, Chaucer Society Publications, 21 (London, 1873; reprinted New York, 1967).

Roy, Maurice, ed. *Oeuvres poétiques de Christine de Pisan*, 3 vols., SATF, 22 (Paris, 1886–1896).

Scattergood, John (V. J.), ed. *John Skelton: The Complete English Poems* (New Haven and London, 1983).

Schick, J., ed. *Lydgate's Temple of Glas*, EETS, e.s. 60 (London, 1891).

Showerman, Grant, ed. and trans. *Ovid, Heroides and Amores*, Loeb Classical Library (Cambridge, MA, and London, 1914).

Skeat, Walter W., ed. *The Complete Works of Geoffrey Chaucer*, 7 vols. (Oxford, 1894–1897).

Smithers, G. V., ed. *Kyng Alisaunder*, 2 vols., EETS, o.s. 227 (London, 1952, for 1947), EETS, o.s. 237 (London, 1957, for 1953).

Steele, Robert, ed. *The English Poems of Charles of Orléans*, 2 vols., EETS, o.s. 215 (London, 1941), (with Mabel Day) EETS, o.s. 220 (London, 1946, for 1944).

Stengel, E. "Die ältesten Anleitungsschriften zur Erlernung der französischen Sprache," *Zeitschrift für neufranzösische Sprache und Literatur*, 1 (1879), 1–40.

Le stile et manière de composer, dicter, et escrire toute sorte d'epistres, ou lettres missiues, tant par réponse que autrement, auec epitome de la poinctuation françoise (Lyons, 1555?).

Stow, John, ed. *The Workes of Geffrey Chaucer, Newly Printed* (London, 1561).

Thynne, William, ed. *The Workes of Geffray Chaucer newly printed with dyvers workes whiche were neuer in print before* (London, 1532).

Wilson, Kenneth G. "Five Unpublished Secular Love Poems from MS Trinity College Cambridge 599," *Anglia*, 72 (1954), 400–418.

Wilson, Kenneth G. "*The Lay of Sorrow* and *The Lufaris Complaynt:* An Edition," *Speculum*, 29 (1954), 708–26.

Windeatt, B. A., ed. *Geoffrey Chaucer, Troilus and Criseyde: A New Edition of "The Book of Troilus"* (London and New York, 1984).

Wright, Thomas, and J. O. Halliwell, eds. *Reliquiae Antiquae*, 2 vols. (London, 1841–1843; reprinted New York, 1966).

204

Secondary Works

Alford, John A. "Literature and Law in Medieval England," *PMLA,* 92 (1977), 941–51.

Allen, Judson B. "Grammar, Poetic Form, and the Lyric Ego: A Medieval *a priori,"* in *Vernacular Poetics in the Middle Ages,* ed. Lois Ebin (Kalamazoo, 1984), 199–226.

Arn, Mary-Jo. *"Fortunes Stabilnes:* The English Poems of Charles of Orleans in Their English Context," *Fifteenth-Century Studies,* 7 (1983), 1–18.

Bech, M. "Quellen und Plan der *Legende of Goode Women* und ihr Verhältnis zur *Confessio Amantis," Anglia,* 5 (1882), 313–82.

Bennett, J. A. W. "Gower's 'Honeste Love,'" in *Patterns of Love and Courtesy: Essays in Memory of C. S. Lewis,* ed. John Lawler (Evanston, 1966), 107–21.

Benson, Larry D. "Courtly Love and Chivalry in the Later Middle Ages," in *Fifteenth-Century Studies: Recent Essays,* ed. Robert F. Yeager (Hamden, CT, 1984), 237–57.

Bergner, Heinz. "Mittelenglische Lyrik und die Frage der Gattungen," in *Lyrik des ausgehenden 14. and des 15. Jahrhunderts,* Chloe. Beihefte zum Daphnis, Bd. 1, ed. Franz V. Spechtler (Amsterdam, 1984), 45–65.

Berndt, Rolf. "The Period of the Final Decline of French in Medieval England (Fourteenth and Early Fifteenth Centuries)," *Zeitschrift für Anglistik und Amerikanistik,* 20 (1972), 341–69.

Boffey, Julia. *Manuscripts of English Courtly Love Lyrics in the Later Middle Ages* (Woodbridge, Suffolk, and Dover, NH, 1985).

Boffey, Julia. "Richard Pynson's Book of Fame and the Letter of Dido," *Viator,* 19 (1988), 339–53.

Boffey, Julia. "Annotation in Some MSS of *Troilus and Criseyde"* (unpublished paper), Twenty-fourth International Congress on Medieval Studies, Kalamazoo, May 1989.

Bolle, Wilhelm. "Zur Lyrik der Rawlinson-Hs. C.813," *Anglia,* 34 (1911), 273–307.

Brown, Carleton, and Rossell H. Robbins. *The Index of Middle English Verse* (New York, 1943).

Burrow, J. A. *Medieval Writers and Their Work: Middle English Literature and Its Background, 1100–1500* (Oxford, 1982).

Camargo, Martin. "The Middle English Love Letter and Its Rhetorical Background" (Diss. Illinois 1978).

Camargo, Martin. "The Metamorphosis of Candace and the Earliest English Love Epistle," in *Court and Poet,* ed. Glyn S. Burgess (Liverpool, 1981), 101–11.

Cary, George. *The Medieval Alexander,* ed. D. J. A. Ross (Cambridge, 1956).

Clanchy, Michael T. *From Memory to Written Record: England, 1066–1307* (London, 1979).

Clark, Cecily. "Charles d'Orléans: Some English Perspectives," *Medium Aevum,* 40 (1971), 254–61.

Clark, Cecily. "Postscript," *Medium Aevum,* 45 (1976), 230–31.

Cohen, Helen L. *The Ballade* (New York, 1915).

Constable, Giles. *Letters and Letter-Collections,* Typologie des sources du moyen âge occidental, 17 (Turnhout, 1976).

Constable, Giles. "The Structure of Medieval Society According to the *Dictatores* of the Twelfth Century," in *Law, Church, and Society: Essays in Honor of Stephan Kuttner,* ed. Kenneth Pennington and Robert Somerville (Philadelphia, 1977), 253–67.

Crow, Martin. "John of Angoulême and His Chaucer Manuscript," *Speculum,* 17 (1942), 86–99.

Cummings, Hubertis M. *The Indebtedness of Chaucer's Works to the Italian Works of Boccaccio (A Review and Summary)* (Menasha, WI, 1916).

D'Alfonso, Rossella. "Fra retorica e teologia: il sistema dei generi letterari nel basso medioevo," *Lingua e stile,* 17 (1982), 269–93.

Dahood, Roger. "*Ancrene Wisse,* the Katherine Group, and the *Wohunge* Group," in *Middle English Prose: A Critical Guide to Major Authors and Genres,* ed. A. S. G. Edwards (New Brunswick, 1984), 1–33.

Davenport, W. A. *Chaucer: Complaint and Narrative* (Cambridge, 1988).

Davis, Norman. "The *Litera Troili* and English Letters," *Review of English Studies,* n.s. 16 (1965), 233–44.

Davis, Norman. "A Note on *Pearl,*" *Review of English Studies,* n.s. 17 (1966), 403–5; reprinted with an Appendix, in *The Middle English* Pearl: *Critical Essays,* ed. John Conley (Notre Dame, 1970), 325–34.

Davis, Norman. "Style and Stereotype in Early English Letters," *Leeds Studies in English,* 1 (1967), 7–17.

Dean, Nancy. "Chaucer's *Complaint:* A Genre Descended from the *Heroides,*" *Comparative Literature,* 19 (1967), 1–27.

Dodd, William G. *Courtly Love in Chaucer and Gower,* Harvard Studies in English, 1 (Cambridge, MA, 1913; reprinted Gloucester, MA, 1959).

Doyle, A. I. "The Manuscripts," in *Middle English Alliterative Poetry and Its Literary Background,* ed. David Lawton (Cambridge, 1982), 88–100.

Dörrie, Heinrich. *Der heroische Brief. Bestandaufnahme, Kritik einer humanistisch-barocken Literaturgattung* (Berlin, 1968).

Dronke, Peter. *Medieval Latin and the Rise of European Love-Lyric,* 2 vols. (Oxford, 1965–1966; 2d ed., 1968).

Fichte, Jörg O. "*Womanly Noblesse* and *To Rosemound:* Point and Counterpoint of Chaucerian Love Lyrics," in *Reconstructing Chaucer: Selected Essays from the 1984 NCS Congress,* ed. D. Pearsall, F. Ridley, and P. Strohm (Norman, OK, 1985), 181–94.

Fish, Stanley. *John Skelton's Poetry* (New Haven and London, 1965).

Fisher, John H. *John Gower: Moral Philosopher and Friend of Chaucer* (New York, 1964).

Fleming, John V. "Hoccleve's 'Letter of Cupid' and the 'Quarrel' over the *Roman de la Rose,*" *Medium Aevum,* 40 (1971), 21–40.

Fowler, Alastair. *Kinds of Literature: An Introduction to the Theory of Genres and Modes* (Oxford, 1982).

Frankis, P. J. "The Erotic Dream in Medieval English Lyrics," *Neuphilologische Mitteilungen,* 57 (1956), 228–37.

Friedman, Albert B. "The Late Mediaeval Ballade and the Origin of Broadside Balladry," *Medium Aevum,* 27 (1958), 95–110.

Fyler, John M. *Chaucer and Ovid* (New Haven and London, 1979).

Gardiner, F. C. *The Pilgrimage of Desire: A Study of Theme and Genre in Medieval Literature* (Leiden, 1971).

Goodrich, Norma L. *Charles of Orléans: A Study of Themes in His French and in His English Poetry* (Geneva, 1967).

Green, Richard F. *Poets and Princepleasers: Literature and the English Court in the Late Middle Ages* (Toronto, 1980).

Greene, Richard L. "Carols," in *A Manual of the Writings in Middle English, 1050–1500*, ed. Albert E. Hartung, vol. 6, part XIV (New Haven, 1980), 1743–52, 1940–2018.

Guillén, Claudio. "Notes toward the Study of the Renaissance Letter," in *Renaissance Genres: Essays on Theory, History, and Interpretation,* Harvard English Studies, 14, ed. Barbara K. Lewalski (Cambridge, MA, 1986), 70–101.

Hagman, Lynn W. "A Study of Gower's *Cinkante Balades*" (Diss. Detroit 1968).

Hammond, Eleanor P. *Chaucer: A Bibliographical Manual* (New York, 1908; reprinted 1933).

Harris, Kate. "The Origins and Make-up of Cambridge University Library MS Ff.1.6," *Transactions of the Cambridge Bibliographical Society*, 8 (1983), 299–333.

Harvey, Carol J. "Macaronic Techniques in Anglo-Norman Verse," *L'Ésprit Créateur*, 18 (1978), 70–81.

Hempfer, K. W. *Gattungstheorie* (Munich, 1973).

Hornbeak, Katherine Gee. *The Complete Letter Writer in English, 1568–1800,* Smith College Studies in Modern Languages, vol. 15, nos. 3–4 (Northampton, MA, 1934).

Huizinga, Johan. *The Waning of the Middle Ages,* trans. F. Hopman (London, 1924).

Ingenschay, Dieter. *Alltagswelt und Selbsterfahrung. Ballade und Testament bei Deschamps und Villon,* Theorie und Geschichte der Literatur und der schönen Künste, 73 (Munich, 1986).

Jaech, Sharon L. Jansen. "English Political Prophecy and the Dating of MS Rawlinson C.813," *Manuscripta*, 25 (1981), 141–50.

James, Montague R. *The Western Manuscripts in the Library of Trinity College, Cambridge,* 4 vols. (Cambridge, 1900–1904).

James, Montague R., and Claude Jenkins. *A Descriptive Catalogue of the Manuscripts in the Library of Lambeth Palace: The Mediaeval Manuscripts* (Cambridge, 1932).

Jansen, Johannes P. M. "Charles d'Orléans and the Fairfax Poems," *English Studies*, 70 (1989), 206–24.

Jauss, Hans Robert. "Theory of Genres and Medieval Literature," in *Toward an Aesthetic of Reception,* trans. Timothy Bahti (Minneapolis, 1982), 76–109: originally published in *Grundriss der romanischen Literaturen des Mittelalters,* vol. 6 (1972).

Kane, George. "A Short Essay on the Middle English Secular Lyric," *Neuphilologische Mitteilungen,* 73 (1972), 110–21.

Kany, Charles E. *The Beginnings of the Epistolary Novel in France, Italy, and Spain,* University of California Publications in Modern Philology, 21, 1 (Berkeley and Los Angeles, 1937).

Kelly, Douglas. *Medieval Imagination: Rhetoric and the Poetry of Courtly Love* (Madison, 1978).

Kelly, Henry Ansgar. *Chaucer and the Cult of Saint Valentine,* Davis Medieval Texts and Studies, 5 (Leiden, 1986).

Kingsford, Charles L. "English Letters and the Intellectual Ferment," in *Prejudice and Promise in Fifteenth-Century England* (Oxford, 1925), 22–47.

Kirby, Thomas A. *Chaucer's 'Troilus': A Study in Courtly Love* (University, LA, 1940).

Kiser, Lisa J. *Telling Classical Tales: Chaucer and* The Legend of Good Women (Ithaca and London, 1983).

Kohl, Stephan. "Private Letters in Fifteenth-Century England and the Problem of Late Medieval Culture," *Fifteenth-Century Studies,* 5 (1982), 117–37.

Kohl, Stephan. *Das englische Spätmittelalter: kulturelle Normen, Lebenspraxis, Texte* (Tübingen, 1986).

Leach, Eleanor Winsor. "A Study in the Sources and Rhetoric of Chaucer's *Legend of Good Women* and Ovid's *Heroides*" (Diss. Yale 1963).

Leclercq, Jean. "L'Amitié dans les lettres au Moyen Age," *Revue du Moyen Age Latin,* 1 (1945), 391–410.

Legge, M. Dominica. *Anglo-Norman Literature and Its Background* (Oxford, 1963).

Leube, Christiane. "Salut d'amor," *Grundriss der romanischen Literaturen des Mittelalters,* vol. 2: *Les Genres Lyriques,* tome 1, fasc. 5 (Heidelberg, 1979), 77–87.

Lewis, C. S. "What Chaucer Really Did to *Il Filostrato,*" in *Selected Literary Essays,* ed. Walter Hooper (Cambridge, 1969; essay originally published in 1932), 27–44.

Madan, Falconer, et al. *A Summary Catalogue of Western Manuscripts in the Bodleian Library at Oxford,* 7 vols. (Oxford, 1895–1953).

Margolin, Uri. "The Concept of Genre as Historical Category" (Diss. Cornell 1972).

McAlpine, Monica E. *The Genre of* Troilus and Criseyde (Ithaca and London, 1978).

McKerrow, R. B. "Retrospective Review" of William Fulwood, *The Enimie of Idlenesse, The Gentleman's Magazine,* 300 (1906), 390–403.

McKinnell, John. "Letters as a Type of the Formal Level in *Troilus and Criseyde,*" in *Essays on* Troilus and Criseyde, ed. Mary Salu (Cambridge, 1979), 73–89.

McLeod, Enid. *Charles of Orleans: Prince and Poet* (London, 1969).

Meech, Sanford B. "Chaucer and an Italian Translation of the *Heroides,*" *PMLA,* 45 (1930), 110–28.

Meech, Sanford B. *Design in Chaucer's Troilus* (Syracuse, 1959).

Minnis, A. J. *Medieval Theory of Authorship: Scholastic Literary Attitudes in the Later Middle Ages,* 2d ed. (Philadelphia, 1988).

Minnis, A. J., A. B. Scott, and David Wallace. *Medieval Literary Theory and Criticism c. 1100–c. 1375* (Oxford, 1988).

Mitchell, Jerome. *Thomas Hoccleve: A Study in Early Fifteenth-Century Poetic* (Urbana, 1968).

Moore, Arthur K. "Middle English Verse Epistles," *Modern Language Review*, 44 (1949), 86–87.

Moore, Arthur K. *The Secular Lyric in Middle English* (Lexington, KY, 1951).

Murphy, James J. *Rhetoric in the Middle Ages* (Berkeley and Los Angeles, 1974).

Murphy, James J. *Medieval Rhetoric: A Select Bibliography,* 2d ed. (Toronto, 1988).

Müller, Günther. "Bemerkungen zur Gattungspoetik," *Philosophischer Anzeiger,* 3 (1928–1929), 129–47.

Naunin, Traugott. "Der Einfluss der mittelalterlichen Rhetorik auf Chaucers Dichtung" (Diss. Bonn 1929).

Neilson, William Allan. *The Origins and Sources of* The Court of Love, Harvard Studies and Notes in Philology and Literature, 6 (Cambridge, MA, 1899; reissued New York, 1967).

Nolan, Charles J., Jr. "Structural Sophistication in 'The Complaint unto Pity,'" *Chaucer Review,* 13 (1979), 363–72.

Norton-Smith, John. "Chaucer's Epistolary Style," in *Essays on Style and Language,* ed. Roger Fowler (London, 1966), pp. 157–65.

O'Connor, John J. *"Amadis de Gaule" and Its Influence on Elizabethan Literature* (New Brunswick, 1970).

Oliver, Raymond. *Poems without Names: The English Lyric, 1200–1500* (Berkeley and Los Angeles, 1970).

Oruch, Jack B. "St. Valentine, Chaucer, and Spring in February," *Speculum,* 56 (1981), 534–65.

Padelford, Frederick M. "MS. Rawlinson C.813 Again," *Anglia,* 35 (1912), 178–86.

Patt, William D. "The Early *Ars dictaminis* as Response to a Changing Society," *Viator,* 9 (1978), 133–55.

Patterson, Lee. *Negotiating the Past: The Historical Understanding of Medieval Literature* (Madison, 1987).

Poirion, Daniel. "Création poétique et composition romanesque dans les premiers poèmes de Charles d'Orléans," *Revue des Sciences Humaines,* n.s. 90 (1958), 185–211.

Poirion, Daniel. *Le Poète et le prince: l'Évolution du lyrisme courtois de Machaut à Charles d'Orléans,* Université de Grenoble Publications de la Faculté des lettres et sciences humaines, 35 (Paris, 1965).

Poirion, Daniel. "Charles d'Orléans et l'Angleterre: Un secret désir," in *Marche romane. Mélanges de philologie et de Littératures romanes offerts à Jeanne Wathelet-Willem,* ed. Jacques de Caluwé (Liège, 1978), 505–27.

Pratt, Robert A. "Chaucer and *Le roman de Troyle et de Criseida,*" *Studies in Philology,* 53 (1956), 509–39.

Quadlbauer, Franz. *Die antike Theorie der* genera dicendi *im lateinischen Mittelalter* (Vienna, 1962).

Richardson, Malcolm. "The *Dictamen* and Its Influence on Fifteenth-Century English Prose," *Rhetorica,* 2 (1984), 207–26.

Rieger, Dietmar. "Einleitung – Das Trobadoreske Gattungssystem und sein Sitz im Leben," *Grundriss der romanischen Literaturen des Mittelalters,* vol. 2: *Les Genres Lyriques,* tome 1, fasc. 3 (Heidelberg, 1987), 15–28.

Robbins, Rossell H. "The Lyrics," in *Companion to Chaucer Studies,* rev. ed., ed. Beryl Rowland (New York and London, 1979), 380–402.

Robbins, Rossell H. "The Structure of Longer Middle English Court Poems," in *Chaucerian Problems and Perspectives: Essays Presented to Paul E. Beichner, C.S.C.,* ed. Edward Vasta and Zacharias P. Thundy (Notre Dame, 1979), 244–64.

Robbins, Rossell H. "The Middle English Court Love Lyric," in *The Interpretation of Medieval Lyric Poetry,* ed. W. T. H. Jackson (New York, 1980), 205–32.

Robbins, Rossell H., and John L. Cutler. *Supplement to the Index of Middle English Verse* (Lexington, KY, 1965).

Robertson, Jean. *The Art of Letter Writing: An Essay on the Handbooks Published in England during the Sixteenth and Seventeenth Centuries* (Liverpool and London, 1942).

Ross, Thomas W. *Chaucer's Bawdy* (New York, 1972).

Ruhe, Ernstpeter. *De Amasio ad Amasiam: Zur Gattungsgeschichte des mittelalterlichen Liebesbriefes,* Beiträge zur romanischen Philologie des Mittelalters, 10 (Munich, 1975).

Scattergood, V. J. *Politics and Poetry in the Fifteenth Century* (New York, 1972).

Scattergood, V. J. "Literary Culture at the Court of Richard II," in *English Court Culture in the Later Middle Ages,* ed. V. J. Scattergood and J. W. Sherborne (New York, 1983), 29–43.

Schaller, Dieter. "Probleme der Überlieferung und Verfasserschaft lateinischer Liebesbriefe des hohen Mittelalters," *Mittellateinisches Jahrbuch,* 3 (1966), 25–36.

Schaller, Dieter. Review of Ernstpeter Ruhe, *De Amasio ad Amasiam, Arcadia,* 12 (1977), 307–13.

Schaller, Hans Martin. "Dichtungslehren und Briefsteller," in *Die Renaissance der Wissenschaften im 12. Jahrhundert,* ed. Peter Weimar (Zurich, 1981), 249–71.

Schirmer, W. F. "Boccaccios Werke als Quelle G. Chaucers," *Germanisch-romanische Monatsschrift,* 12 (1924), 288–305.

Schmitz, Götz. *Die Frauenklage: Studien zur elegischen Verserzählung in der englischen Literatur des Spätmittelalters und der Renaissance* (Tübingen, 1984).

Scollen, Christine M. *The Birth of the Elegy in France, 1500–1550,* Travaux d'Humanisme et Renaissance, 95 (Geneva, 1967).

Seaton, Ethel. "'The Devonshire Manuscript' and Its Medieval Fragments," *Review of English Studies,* n.s. 7 (1956), 55–56.

Seaton, Ethel. *Sir Richard Roos: Lancastrian Poet* (London, 1961).

Shannon, Edgar Finley. *Chaucer and the Roman Poets* (Cambridge, MA, 1929).

Southall, Raymond. "The Devonshire Manuscript Collection of Early Tudor Poetry, 1532–41," *Review of English Studies,* n.s. 15 (1964), 142–50.

Spitzer, Leo. "Emendations Proposed to *De Amico ad Amicam* and *Responcio,*" *Modern Language Notes,* 67 (1952), 150–55.

Stemmler, Theo. *Die englischen Liebesgedichte des MS. Harley 2253* (Bonn, 1962).

Stemmler, Theo. "Zur Verfasserfrage der Charles d'Orléans zugeschriebenen englischen Gedichte," *Anglia*, 82 (1964), 458–73.

Stemmler, Theo. "'My Fair Lady': Parody in Fifteenth-Century English Lyrics," in *Medieval Studies Conference Aachen 1983: Language and Literature*, Bamberger Beiträge zur englischen Sprachwissenschaft, 15, ed. Wolf-Dietrich Bald and Horst Weinstock (Frankfurt, 1984), 205–13.

Stevens, John. *Music and Poetry in the Early Tudor Court* (London, 1961).

Tatlock, J. S. P. "The Epilog of Chaucer's *Troilus*," *Modern Philology*, 18 (1920–1921), 625–59.

Taylor, Davis. "The Terms of Love: A Study of Troilus's Style," *Speculum*, 51 (1976), 69–90.

Taylor, John. "Letters and Letter Collections in England, 1300–1420," *Nottingham Medieval Studies*, 24 (1980), 57–70.

Utley, Francis Lee. *The Crooked Rib: An Analytical Index to the Argument about Women in English and Scots Literature to the End of the Year 1568* (Columbus, 1944).

Viëtor, Karl. "Die Geschichte literarischer Gattungen," in *Geist und Form: Aufsätze zur deutschen Literaturgeschichte* (Bern, 1952), 292–309, 365–67: originally published as "Probleme der literarischen Gattungsgeschichte," *Deutsche Vierteljahrschrift für Literaturwissenschaft und Geistesgeschichte*, 9 (1931), 425–47.

Vising, Johan. *Anglo-Norman Language and Literature* (London, 1923).

Walker, Ian C. "Chaucer and *Il Filostrato*," *English Studies*, 49 (1968), 318–26.

Wallace, David. *Chaucer and the Early Writings of Boccaccio* (Woodbridge, Suffolk, and Dover, NH, 1985).

Walther, Hans. "*Quot-tot*, Mittelalterliche Liebesgrüsse und Verwandtes," *Zeitschrift für deutsches Altertum and Literatur*, 65 (1928), 257–89.

Waltz, Matthias. "Zum Problem der Gattungsgeschichte im Mittelalter. Am Beispiel des Mirakels," *Zeitschrift für romanische Philologie*, 86 (1970), 22–39.

Ward, H. L. D., and J. A. Herbert. *Catalogue of Romances in the Department of Manuscripts in the British Museum*, 3 vols. (London, 1883–1910; reprinted 1961–1962).

Warner, George F., and Julius P. Gilson. *Catalogue of Western Manuscripts in the Old Royal and King's Collections in the British Museum*, 4 vols. (London, 1921).

Wetherbee, Winthrop. *Chaucer and the Poets: An Essay on* Troilus and Criseyde (Ithaca and London, 1984).

Whiting, Bartlett J. *Chaucer's Use of Proverbs*, Harvard Studies in Comparative Literature, 11 (Cambridge, MA, 1934).

Williams, H. F. "The French Valentine," *Modern Language Notes*, 67 (1952), 292–95.

Wilson, Edward. "*Sir Gawain and the Green Knight* and the Stanley Family of Stanley, Storeton, and Hooton," *Review of English Studies*, n.s. 30 (1979), 308–16.

Wimsatt, James I. "The French Lyric Element in *Troilus and Criseyde*," *Yearbook of English Studies*, 15 (1985), 18–32.

211

Witt, Ronald. "Boncompagno and the Defense of Rhetoric," *The Journal of Medieval and Renaissance Studies,* 16 (1986), 1–31.

Wolter, Paul. *William Fulwood, "The Enimie of Idlenesse" : Der älteste englische Briefsteller* (Potsdam, 1907).

Wright, Herbert. *Boccaccio in England from Chaucer to Tennyson* (London, 1957).

Yenal, Edith. *Charles d'Orléans: A Bibliography of Primary and Secondary Sources* (New York, 1984).

Young, John, and P. Henderson Aitken. *A Catalogue of the Manuscripts in the Library of the Hunterian Museum of the University of Glasgow* (Glasgow, 1908).

Ziolkowski, Jan. "Avatars of Ugliness in Medieval Literature," *Modern Language Review,* 79 (1984), 1–20.

Index

Lewis, C. S., 52n, 66n
Liber et dictamen ad dilectam sibi, 26n
Livre d'Enanchet, 142n
"Loo he that ys all holly yourȝ soo free," 137n
Lorris, Guillaume de, *Roman de la Rose*, 9, 123
Love, game of. *See* "Game of love"
Love document, 24–26, 90–91, 93–106, 108, 116–17, 118. *See also* Supplication
Love letter: *ars dictaminis* and, 2, 25, 26, 31; embedded in larger narrative, 28; genuine vs. artificial, 1–2, 30, 43; messenger or go-between as carrier of, 20, 54–60, 62–66, 104, 132, 138, 142; New Year's Day as occasion for sending, 92n, 133, 134n; Saint Valentine's Day as occasion for sending, 4–6, 45, 133; social function of, 55–56, 61, 64–65; woman's, 2–6, 12. *See also* Verse love epistle
"Lover and the Advocate of Venus," 90n
"Lutel wot hit any mon," 26–28
Lydgate, John, 16, 117, 124–25, 137n; "Allas for thought & inward peyne," 118n; "Balade in Commendation of Our Lady," 145; *Churl and the Bird*, 157n; *Court of Sapience*, 137n, 145; "An Epistle to Sibille," 93n, 98n; "Fresshe lusty beaute Ioyned with gentylesse," 124-25; "Goodly Balade," 124n; "Lover's New Year's Gift," 134n; "Lydgate's Letter to Gloucester," 93; "Princess of iouþe, and flour of gentiless," 124; *Temple of Glass*, 124, 132–33n, 152n; "To My Soverain Lady," 124n
Lyly, John, 90n, 150n

McAlpine, Monica, 80n
Macaulay, G. C., 43n, 51n, 95; (ed.), 38n
MacCracken, Henry N., 88, 89n, 124; (ed.), 12n, 93n, 109n, 114n, 116n, 134n
Machaut, Guillaume de, 35–36
McKerrow, R. B., 161n
McKinnell, John, 57n, 58n, 59n, 65n, 68n, 71n, 80n
McLeod, Enid, 89n
Manuscripts: Aberystwyth, National Library of Wales, Porkington 10, 128, 133n, 146n, 147; Cambridge, Gonville and Caius College 54/31, 29–32, Trinity College, R.3.19, 128, 129, 137n, 144–45, 146n, 147, 151n, University Library, Ff.1.6, 128, 133n, 136n, 146n, 152, 156,

Gg.4.27, 46n, 137n, 156; Edinburgh, National Library of Scotland, Advocates 1.1.6, 87, 92n, 127, 128, 129, 136, 137n, 144n, 146, 149, 150n, 151, 154, 156n, 160, 168; Glasgow, University Library, Hunterian 230, 128, 137n, 147n, 152n; London, British Library, Additional 17492, 87, 128, 131–32, 134, 136n, 147n, 148, 149–50, 156n, 160, Arundel 26, 109n, Cotton Vespasian D.9, 128, 146n, 151n, Harley 541, 128, 146n, 152-53, Harley 682, 87–90, 94, 99–113, 114, 116, 118–19, 120, 121, 123–25, 128, 166, Harley 2253, 26–28, Harley 2399, 92n, Harley 3362, 46n, Harley 3810, 128, 146n, Harley 3988, 28n, 32–35, 147, Harley 4011, 128, 147n, Harley 7578, 128, 146n, 150n, 151n, Royal 6B.ix, 128, 144, 146n, 152n, Royal 17B.xlvii, 11, 70n, Sloane 1212, 92n, 137n, Lambeth Palace 306, 128, 129, 133n, 136n, 137, 146n, 150n; Oxford, Bodleian Library, Arch. Selden B.24, 128, 147n, Douce 95, 46n, 128, 129, 137n, 146–47, 146n, 154, Douce 326, 128, 142–43, 146n, 151n, Douce 381, 152n, Fairfax 16, 87–89, 94, 107, 114–24, 128, 129n, 137, 139, 166–67, Lat. misc. c.66, 128, 135, 147n, 154, Rawlinson C.813, 5, 16, 87, 92n, 128, 129n, 134n, 135, 136, 137–38, 141n, 147-48, 150n, 151n, 152n, 153n, 154, 155, 156n, 157, 159n, 160, Rawlinson poet. 36, 46n, 128, 129, 139–41, 146n, 151n, 156; Paris, Bibliothèque Nationale, F. fr. 25458, 114n, Nouv. acq. fr. 7517, 19
Margolin, Uri, 6n
Marie de France, 35n
Maroill, Arnaut de, 72n
Married love, 33, 36, 42–43
Mead (ed.), William E., 138n
Meech, Sanford B., 51n, 52n, 57n, 58n, 66, 80n
Merke, Thomas, 26; *Formula moderni et usitati dictaminis*, 40n
Meyer, Paul, 29, 30, 31; (ed.), 34n
Minnis, A. J., 7n; and A. B. Scott, and David Wallace, 7n
Mitchell, Jerome, 97n, 141n
"Moder of norture, best beloved of al," 145, 151n
Monfrin (ed.), J., 25n
Moore, Arthur K., 14–15, 51n, 93, 108n
Muir (ed.), Kenneth, 132n, 136n, 148n; and

216

octave, 36-37, 105, 106, 110, 114, 136, 137, 144, 146–51, 154n, 167; quatrain, 147-49, 154, 161, 167; rime royal, 36, 89, 92n, 95, 104–6, 110, 114, 123, 137, 141, 142, 146–52, 155, 167

Verse love epistle: acronyms in, 150; *ars dictaminis* and, 32, 35, 46, 47, 57–58, 71–72; Blessed Virgin addressed in, 15, 141–45, 151; as *cento*, 137; Chaucer's shorter poems and, 44–45; "classic" form of, 49, 89–90, 110, 114, 116, 123, 139, 142, 146–49, 155, 160, 167; dating and attributing, problems of, 16, 87, 114n, 127; decline of, 159–62, 167–68; defining, problems of, 28, 32, 44–45, 109, 168; definition of, 6–16; departure or return of loved one as occasion for, 133–34; embedded in larger narrative, 19–24, 49, 52–53, 113, 130, 152, 166; epistolary form in, 14, 31, 34, 38–41, 46–47, 68–77, 80–84, 110–11, 113, 116, 120–22, 132, 136, 141n, 149–55, 160, 165, 166, 167; epistolary function in, 2–3, 41–42, 90, 107–10, 111n, 113, 134–36, 160, 166–68; *épître amoureuse*, 158; evolution of, 16, 165–67; to family member, 134, 150; farewell poem and, 153–54; form and function of, 6, 8; *formes fixes* and, 35, 45, 49, 89–90, 93–94, 167; formulaic language in, 14, 20, 38, 120, 123, 136, 139–40, 142; genre awareness, 5–6, 14, 18, 52–53, 114, 119, 134–45; genre terminology in, 13, 18, 20, 37–38, 41, 108, 114–18, 120, 135–36, 142, 165–67; gift, 132–34; greeting as formal dominant in, 152; greeting formulas in, 120, 136n (see also *Quottot; Salus; Salutatio*); greeting only, 152–53; greeting shifted from beginning in, 27–28, 40–41, 150–52; imported verse forms and, 160, 168; intertextuality in, 5, 129, 136–38, 167; Latin, 2, 17–19, 27n; leave-taking formulas in, 150 (see also *Conclusio*); love document and, 91, 93–94, 103, 105; love-talking and, 59–60, 131, 134n; macaronic, 45–48, 90, 147, 156; manuscript context of, 14, 29–30, 32-33, 51n, 88–89, 92, 94, 99, 104–7, 114–15, 124n, 127–29, 135–36, 148n; medieval letters and, 165; other varieties of love poetry and, 15–16, 165, 167; parody of, 138–41, 156, 167; popularity of, 6, 44, 127, 129, 132, 165; prologues in, 151–52; religious adaptation of, 141–45, 156, 167; response accompanying, 45–48, 78–79, 83–84, 139–41; social function of, 85, 130–34; supplication and, 37–38; themes of, 14–15, 20–21, 27, 41–45, 47, 96, 109–11, 113, 115–16, 122, 132, 140–43, 155–59, 166, 167 (*see also* Complaint; Physicality; Praise; Secrecy; Sending; Separation; Writing); verse compliment and, 150n; woman's, 43, 92n, 139–41, 156–59, 161. *See also* Ballade; Complaint; Letter; Love letter; *Salut d'amour; Salutz*

Viëtor, Karl, 7n

Vinsauf, Geoffrey of, 40n

Vising, Johan, 33

Walker, Ian C., 52n

Wallace, David, 52n

Walther, Hans, 27n

Waltz, Matthias, 8n

"Welcome be ye, my souereine," 133n, 136n, 156

Wetherbee, Winthrop, 50n

"Whatt tyme as Parys, son of Kyng Priame," 5n, 135, 137n, 138, 151–52, 159n

"When þe nyhtegale singes þe wodes waxen grene," 28

Whiting, Bartlett J., 57n

"Who hath more cawse for to complayne," 136n, 148n

Williams, H. F., 142n

Wilson, Edward, 114n

Wimsatt, James I., 52n

Windeatt, B. A., 52n, 66n

"With greate humylyte I submytt me to your gentylnes," 136n

"With woofull harte plungede yn dystresse," 154

Witt, Ronald, 9n

Wolter, Paul, 162n

"Worshepfulle brother and euer yn mynde," 92n

Wright, Herbert, 59

Wright, Thomas, and J. O. Halliwell (eds.), 92n

Writing of letter as theme, 14, 15, 21, 41, 62–63, 109, 119, 141n, 156

"W^t ryth al my herte now y yow grete," 152n

Wyatt, Sir Thomas, 161

Yenal, Edith, 88n

Ziolkowski, Jan, 140–41n